T0224598

Computer Supported Cooperative Work

Springer
London
Berlin
Heidelberg
New York
Hong Kong
Milan
Paris
Tokyo

Also in this series

Gerold Riempp
Wide Area Workflow Management
3-540-76243-4

Fay Sudweeks and Celia T. Romm (Eds)
Doing Business on the Internet
1-85233-030-9

Elayne Coakes, Dianne Willis and Raymond Lloyd-Jones (Eds)
The New SocioTech
1-85233-040-6

Elizabeth F. Churchill, David N. Snowdon and Alan J. Munro (Eds)
Collaborative Virtual Environments
1-85233-244-1

Christine Steeples and Chris Jones (Eds)
Networked Learning
1-85233-471-1

Barry Brown, Nicola Green and Richard Harper (Eds)
Wireless World
1-85233-477-0

Reza Hazemi and Stephen Hailes (Eds)
The Digital University
1-85233-478-9

Elayne Coakes, Dianne Willis and Steve Clark (Eds)
Knowledge Management in the SocioTechnical World
1-85233-441-X

Ralph Schroeder (Ed.)
The Social Life of Avatars
1-85233-461-4

J.H. Erik Andriessen
Working with Groupware
1-85233-603-X

Christopher Lueg and Danyel Fisher
From Usenet to CoWebs
1-85233-532-7

Kristina Höök, Alan J. Munro and David Benyon (Eds)
Designing Information Spaces
Technologies in Industry
1-85233-661-7

Bjørn Erik Munkvold
Implementing Collaboration
Technologies in Industry
1-85233-418-5

A list of out of print titles is available at the end of the book

Paul A. Kirschner, Simon J. Buckingham Shum
and Chad S. Carr (Eds)

Visualizing Argumentation

**Software Tools for Collaborative
and Educational Sense-Making**

Springer

Paul A. Kirschner, BA, MEd, PhD
Professor of Educational Technology, Open University of the Netherlands,
Educational Technology Expertise Center, PO Box 2960, 6401 DL Heerlen,
The Netherlands

Simon J. Buckingham Shum, BSc, MSc, PhD
Senior Lecturer in Knowledge Media, Knowledge Media Institute, The Open
University, Milton Keynes, MK7 6AA, UK

Chad S. Carr, BA, MA, PhD
Curriculum Development Manager, Retail Stores Training, Sears Roebuck and Co,
3333 Beverly Road, E2-213B, Hoffman Estates, Illinois, IL 60179, USA

Series Editors
Dan Diaper, PhD, MBCS
Professor of Systems Science & Engineering, School of Design, Engineering & Computing,
Bournemouth University, Talbot Campus, Fern Barrow, Poole, Dorset BH12 5BB, UK
Colston Sanger
Shottersley Research Limited, Little Shottersley, Farnham Lane
Haslemere, Surrey GU27 1HA, UK

British Library Cataloguing in Publication Data
Visualizing argumentation : software tools for
    Collaborative and educational sense-making editors. -
    (Computer supported cooperative work)
    1.computer-assisted instruction 2.Groupwork in education
    3.Reasoning 4.Visualization
    I.Kirschner, Paul A. II.Shum, Simon J. Buckingham III.Carr,
    Chad S.
    371.3'34
    ISBN 1852336641
Library of Congress Cataloging-in-Publication Data
A catalog record for this book is available from the Library of Congress.

CSCW ISSN 1431-1496

ISBN 1-85233-664-1 Springer-Verlag London Berlin Heidelberg
a member of BertelsmannSpringer Science+Business Media GmbH
http://www.springer.co.uk

Typesetting: Camera ready by Femke Kirschner
Printed and bound at the Athenæum Press Ltd., Gateshead, Tyne and Wear
34/3830-543210 Printed on acid-free paper SPIN 10882640

We dedicate this book to our partners,
Catherine, Jackie and Amy,
who continue to teach us about constructive
argumentation and lifelong learning!

Preface

The difficult part in an argument is not to defend one's opinion but rather to know it.

Andre Maurois (1885-1967) French biographer, novelist, essayist

He who knows only his side of the case, knows little of that.

John Stuart Mill (1806-1873) British philosopher, economist

Why a book on *Computer-Supported Argument Visualization?* A search on a major online bookstore reveals numerous titles matching the individual words *argumentation*, *visualization* and *computer-supported cooperative work*, but none on *visualizing argumentation* or *computer-supported argumentation*. However, a query on an internet search engine reveals over 1000 hits almost all of which describe relevant documents and projects, testifying to significant activity in this area—but still, not a single book. However, beyond plugging a hole in the book market, a less pecuniary motivation for this volume derives from observing the world around us.

Seeking quality communication and mutual understanding are hardly novel goals, but in our fragmented, pluralistic, but globally connected world, they have never been more important, nor harder to establish and sustain. Borrowing a biblical metaphor, there is a veritable Tower of Babylon in our intellectual, social, and political world. Although we don't believe that there is a Rosetta stone (gift of tongues?) that will translate all of the different tongues into one, we do believe that there are tools which can help us to establish common ground between diverse stakeholders, understand positions on issues, surface assumptions and criteria, and collectively construct consensus on whatever grounds can be found.

From this rather lofty stuff, let us focus the scope of discussion, and note some of the other tectonic forces in play. In educational theory, we see a paradigm shift from cognitivist ideas and approaches to teaching towards constructivist, competency-based ideas and approaches in order to help students cope with fast technological and societal changes. These approaches stress independent learning in rich information environments, authentic learning tasks, and of particular relevance here, the negotiation of meaning by understanding multiple perspectives. How are perspectives to be reified, contrasted, critiqued, integrated? Argument visualization tools are one candidate.

In operations research, cognitive science and business analysis, it is recognised that for many real world problems, agreeing on what the real problem is requires extensive discussion, as does agreeing on what might constitute a solution. Simulations, spreadsheets, and other modelling approaches can typically be deployed only after the problem has been sufficiently defined, bounded and constrained by assumptions, in other words, after much of the most intellectually demanding work has been done. This should ring bells for managers, engineers, lawyers, scientists, political and environmental strategists, conceptual designers, architects, urban planners, intelligence analysts, and so forth. Computer-Supported Argument Visualization (CSAV) tools are designed to assist in collating, and then making sense of, information and possible narratives that weave threads of coherence.

Making sense of multi-perspective problems and disparate information sources is of course just the first step. We need to make sense, in order to act and shape the future. Anticipating the future is as important as ever, and perhaps, getting harder. As Ogilvy (2002) has argued, we may be better employed in trying to construct, rather than predict, the future, by inventing and mentally inhabiting multiple possible futures that we would like to see. The growing use of scenarios to help groups identify hidden values, visions, constraints and contingencies switches the spotlight squarely on dialogue, sense-making, competing narratives, assumptions – all of which lie at the heart of argument visualization.

Ross Todd, describing the late twentieth century as the Age of Information where the external organisation, transformation and communication of information is emphasised, sees the twenty-first century as the Age of the Mind. "This transformation, commonly acknowledged as the "information society", is global in its reach, yet intimate and constant in its impact. An examination of its short history suggests that two phases of the transformation are evident. These two phases are seen in the notion of the "information society" as a global phenomena, and as responses within organisations and systems. Lawrence Heilprin identified these stages as the "age of information" and the "age of the mind" (Heilprin, 1989, p. 364). The "age of the mind" refers to the shift in focus from the production and availability of information and its associated technology, to concerns about how people utilise that information, the barriers and challenges they face in accessing and interacting with information, what they do with the information, and how it enables them to get on with their lives. For learning organisations, this means addressing the question of how information technology and the richness of the electronic information environment can be integrated in the learning process meaningfully. The focus must be on people as active information processors and on how information empowers and enables people, rather than on the information per se. Karl Weick's work on organisational sense-making also resonates with this, hence our conception of argument visualization tools as sense-making tools.

Whatever we make of the all-embracing umbrella of "knowledge management", we do find at least one robust concept that opens up and provides useful coverage: the community of practice. The dynamics of good communities of practice that enable skilled performance, situated learning, coordinated activity, and the elegant dissemination of know-how and expertise need to be better understood and nurtured.

One of the key lessons emerging from such work is that people need spaces – temporal, physical, cognitive, emotional, formal and informal – to simply talk and share ideas with colleagues. Within organisations, the locus of much knowledge production is the dialogue, the discussion, the argument: people expressing ideas, negotiating meaning, arguing viewpoints, pursuing agendas, and seeking – or avoiding – common ground. However, as we suspect most of our readers can verify, much of the energy poured into talking is often wasted, poorly channelled, never treated as a knowledge resource. Some chapters in this book (van Gelder; Conklin; Selvin) describe how argument visualization can help tackle the problem of dysfunctional communication.

What we have started doing is in fact tracing the roots and rationale behind different argument visualization approaches, a process that continues throughout this book in much greater depth. Suffice to say at this stage that given the pervasive need for task-oriented discourse, from "knowledge work", to academic learning, to political and organizational negotiation, there are intriguing possibilities for reifying in visual form structural aspects of that discourse to enable more effective, collective reflection.

Aims of this Book

This book – written by researchers and practitioners, for researchers and practitioners – presents the current state of the art of the new field of *Computer-Supported Argument Visualization*. Readers will find conceptual foundations, and application case studies in both organizational and educational arenas, as well as ideas for future research, and practical techniques to extend one's individual and collective sense-making ability.

The American Heritage® Dictionary of the English Language: Fourth Edition defines an argument to be:

1 a.	A discussion in which disagreement is expressed.
2 a.	A course of reasoning aimed at demonstrating truth or falsehood: *presented a careful argument for extraterrestrial life.*
2 b.	A fact or statement put forth as proof or evidence; a reason.
2 c.	A set of statements in which one follows logically as a conclusion from the others.

The etymology lies in the Latin *argmentum*, from *arguere* which means to make clear. And this is what it's all about. How do we make clear – at least so far as one is willing and able – what we think, what we mean, what we believe and need, so that we can work together to define and solve the problems that confront us? The above definitions frame *argumentation* not only as discourse for persuasion, logical proof, and evidence-based belief, but more generally, discussion in which disagreements and reasoning are presented. The precise form that argument visualization takes depends on the demands of the particular field, user community, and context of use. As the forthcoming chapters make clear, different business and academic contexts lead to very different goals, representations, and modes of working. Think of the differences between the argumentation one finds in a legal courtroom, a school classroom, a scientific workshop, a party political conference, and a corporate boardroom. Especially in organisational deliberation, disagreements and reasoning are rarely a matter of formal logic, and as already highlighted above, some chapters in this book are particularly concerned with capturing, and reifying for inspection, the whole range of constraints that impinge on everyday sense-making and debate.

Overview of the Book

The book has two sections. The first section deals with historical and conceptual foundations to the topic of visualizing argumentation. The second section illustrates the breadth of application that CSAV is finding, describing applications in education, organisational sense-making, and scholarly discourse

In Chapter 1, *The Roots of Computer Supported Argument Visualization*, Simon Buckingham Shum sets this book in historical context, tracing the twin roots of argument visualization and computer-supported argumentation that have converged to create CSAV in its current form. The earliest work he was able to find on visually mapping arguments dates back to 1913 in the work of John Henry Wigmore on mapping evidential argumentation in legal cases, whilst historians of technology will note with interest that Vannevar Bush and Douglas Engelbart, whose work laid the foundations for hypertext and interactive personal computing, both pinpointed scholarly argumentation as key applications of the nascent technologies they envisaged, and in Engelbart's case, actually built.

In Chapter 2, *A Cognitive Framework for Cooperative Problem Solving with Argument Visualization*, Jan van Bruggen, Henny Boshuizen and Paul Kirschner introduce research on problem solving cognition, and its relationship to CSAV tools and applications. They present a framework that identifies particular roles that CSAV tools can play as cognitive aids in cooperative problem solving, and then use this to make sense of the research literature on argumentation tools in learning.

Although these are the only two chapters in our *Foundations* section, we refer readers also to a different kind of framework proposed by Selvin in the first part of Chapter 7. This describes general principles and tool requirements to support collective sense-making applications of CSAV, with particular emphasis on the role of a facilitator, and applications to business teams.

Turning to specific applications of CSAV, and continuing the thread on learning started by van Bruggen, et al., we have three contributions on the affordances of argument visualization notations and tools for different kinds of learning.

In Chapter 3, *Designing Argumentation Tools for Collaborative Learning*, Gellof Kanselaar, Gijsbert Erkens, Jerry Andriessen, Maaike Prangsma, Arja Veerman and Jos Jaspers review their previous work investigating the educational affordances of different computer-supported argumentation tools, before reporting a study evaluating their TC3 software tool to support students in critical analysis and argumentative writing. Through detailed analysis of student protocols and use of a variety of tools to support writing, they present a rich and nuanced account which emphasises that the role played by argument maps in this task depended on other factors such as the task assigned to student, their preparation, and the instructions given.

In Chapter 4, *Using Computer Supported Argument Visualization to Teach Legal Argumentation,* Chad Carr focuses on law, which of all fields, arguably places greatest demands on its students to develop argumentation expertise. Carr reports research that analyses the role of the QuestMap CSAV tool in supporting the collaborative learning of legal argumentation skills, compared to a control group of students using conventional resources. Like Kanselaar, et al.'s work (Chapter 3), he concludes that in learning contexts, the diagrammatic representation may not always play the role expected. He shares insights gained while conducting a sixteen-week study at a leading ABA accredited law school.

In Chapter 5, *Enhancing Deliberation Through Computer Supported Argument Visualization,* Tim van Gelder focuses on CSAV to support deliberation about the plausibility of a position in an argument. He starts by considering the differences between maps and conventional prose for communicating arguments. He then reports research that demonstrated significant improvements in students' acquisition of critical thinking skills when they used a CSAV tool called Reason!Able. The chapter then switches focus to illustrate the same approach in a very different context, an industrial dispute about working conditions. Van Gelder describes the process and facilitation skills involved in helping staff understand the structure of their arguments and reach consensus on the way forward.

This second case study leads us into the second set of CSAV applications: facilitated CSAV for teams in business and other organisational contexts, trying to make collective sense of complex problems. Collaborative sense-making is of course "learning" in a broader sense, so we cannot draw too hard a distinction from the first set of chapters focusing on education. However, van Gelder's case study and the following two chapters are different in that CSAV must now demonstrate its value in supporting sense-making and decision-making in real workplaces, with all the constraints and complexity that they introduce that are not normally factors when CSAV is used by students on courses.

In Chapter 6, *Dialog Mapping: Reflections on an Industrial Strength Case Study,* Jeff Conklin describes how one of the most influential argumentation schemes dating back to the 1970s, Kunz and Rittel's Issue-Based Information System (IBIS), has been developed into a facilitated CSAV technique called Dialog Mapping. Dialog Mapping (like van Gelder's industrial case study) introduces the facilitator as a key player who adds value through expertise in argument mapping and group process. Conklin then presents what is probably the longest-term case study available of CSAV adoption in an organization, reflecting on the lessons that can be distilled from a company that has used the QuestMap tool continuously for the last decade to support synchronous and asynchronous work.

Conklin's work is developed further in Chapter 7, *Fostering Collective Intelligence: Helping Groups Use Visualized Argumentation,* in which Albert Selvin details the principles behind facilitating CSAV in real time, in business contexts, and the functional requirements on tools to support this. These are derived from his work on the Compendium approach, which extends Conklin's Dialog Mapping approach both conceptually (overlaying formal modelling on IBIS), and technically (bringing CSAV into the age of the web and open standards). Selvin then presents three examples of Compendium in use, to illustrate how the principles and tool functionalities he has proposed play out in different contexts.

The scene shifts once more for the final two chapters, where we move into the world of scientific argumentation, or more broadly, scholarly argumentation (including technical, medical, and humanities).

In Chapter 8, *Infrastructure for Navigating Interdisciplinary Debates*, Robert Horn describes his work on crafting maps of "great debates" in science, in order to clarify the key claims and arguments in play. Using examples such as the Turing Debate on machine intelligence, genetically modified food, and the mind-body problem in consciousness research, Horn describes the information design challenges that they have faced in order to reify the structure of complex debates clearly both in visual terms, and intellectually, at an appropriate level of detail. Another aspect of interest in this work is the question of large scale mapping on different media. The early work was done using large paper posters to manage the size of the maps. More recent work has started to work in web interfaces, which impose new constraints, as well as opening new possibilities for managing complexity.

In this latter respect, Chapter 9 picks up the baton to explore a CSAV scenario for scholarly publishing and argumentation. In *Visualizing Internetworked Argumentation*, Simon Buckingham Shum, Victoria Uren, Gangmin Li, John Domingue and Enrico Motta describe ongoing work to investigate how research results could be published and debated as claims and arguments over the internet, to augment conventional text publications. They describe the development of an ontology for scholarly discourse, which provides researchers with a language in which to summarise the key contributions of a research paper, and its connections to the literature. They then describe how CSAV tools can support both the construction of argumentation maps, and various forms of analysis of the argument network as it grows in order to navigate, detect and track structures of interest.

It is fitting that the book is concluded by Doug Engelbart, who figures as one of the main sources of inspiration for CSAV (reviewed in Chapter 1). In his *Afterword*, Engelbart reflects on the progress made since he first envisaged interactive software tools to augment human intellectual work in the 1950s and 60s. His historic 1962 report used interactive argument construction and analysis as a prime scenario to illustrate the potential of such tools. Engelbart outlines his continuing mission to build infrastructures to assist communities to improve the way they work, in order to better tackle the complex, urgent problems facing humanity. He concludes that computer-supported collaborative argumentation is a key element in this infastructure, and poses a number of questions that define an agenda for the future convergence of *Computer-Supported Argument Visualization* with his goal of "augmenting human intellect."

Book Website

The book's companion website – **www.VisualizingArgumentation.info** – provides links to online resources and references cited in chapters, full colour images, forums for discussion with authors and the wider community, and alerts to relevant events and resources. We trust that you find the combination of this volume and its website a valuable springboard for future work.

Paul Kirschner
Simon Buckingham Shum
Chad Carr   *August, 2002*

References

Heilprin, L. (1989). Foundations of information science reexamined. *Annual Review of Information Science and Technology, 24,* 343–372.

Katzenbach, J. R., & Smith, D. K. (1993). *The wisdom of teams: Creating the high-performance organization.* Boston: Harvard Business School Press.

Ogilvy, J. A. (2002). *Creating better futures: Scenario planning as a tool for a better tomorrow.* Oxford University Press.

Quinn, J. B., Andersen, P., & Finkelstein, S. (1996). Managing professional intell*ect: Making the most of the best. *Harvard Business Review,* March -April, 71-80.

Todd, R. and McNicholas, C. (1997). Electronic information and learning organisations. *Proceedings of the Eighth Australasian Information Online & On Disc Conference and Exhibition,* (pp. 363-373). Retrieved on August 30, 2002 from http://www.csu.edu.au/special/online97/proceedings/on1206.htm

Weick, K. E. (1996). *Sensemaking in organizations.* Newbury Park, CA: Sage.

A Word of Thanks

As first editor and "father" of this book, I'd like to thank a few people, without whom this book would not exist. First I'd like to thank my co-editor Chad who saw something in a crazy idea at the end of a pre-conference workshop at CSCL'99 in Stanford. The result was an approved book proposal at Springer. Then there's my other co-editor Simon who organized the notorious workshop and posed the "impertinent" question as to whether he might co-edit "our book". If he hadn't been so impertinent, this book would almost surely have ended up as an unfulfilled promise. I would also like to thank the Open University of the Netherlands, and especially the Educational Technology Expertise Center, which have been an endless source of inspiration and have always provided me a front row seat in the constantly evolving world of education. Then there's my daughter Femke who has spent much of the last two months doing the lay-out for this book in her usual calm, decided, careful and precise way. She has been dealing with authors on three continents, co-editors on two, the publisher and me in a more than professional way. I couldn't be more proud. And Jan van Bruggen, my co-author in one of the chapters and co-researcher at the university who is constantly manning the fort when I'm not around, up to and including the courier service of the final camera ready copy. And last, but definitely not least there's my better half Catherine who fills in all of the gaps that my work creates.

Paul Kirschner

As co-editor, I'd like to thank Paul for having the energy to get this off the ground and Simon, who came on board, provided us with tremendous guidance and support to bring this to fruition. I would like to offer a special thank you to Wim Jochems, Jeroen van Merrienboer and The Open University of the Netherlands Educational Technology Expertise Center, who graciously provided me with an opportunity to work with Paul and allow this idea to ferment. Finally, I would like to thank my wife, Amy, for being so open and supportive of my work.

Chad Carr

Finally, my thanks to Paul and Chad for letting me on board after they'd done the initial hard graft of launching the book project! I am also grateful to the UK Open University for having the vision to create the Knowledge Media Institute, which has provided a superb intellectual and technical environment for my work over the last 7 years. Last but not least, my love and thanks also to my wife Jackie for understanding when I needed to play absent husband (and dad) on the home straight of finishing the book.

Simon Buckingham Shum

Contents

The Authors

Jerry Andriessen (1956)

Is Associate Professor at Utrecht University. His basic areas of research are argumentative writing, computer-supported collaborative learning and telelearning. In 1991, he received his Ph.D. from Utrecht University on collaborative writing. He was visiting professor at the University of Poitiers in 1996. He co-edited an international book on argumentative text production (1999), and is currently editing a book on arguing to learn in electronic environments. He currently coordinates a Ph.D. project on electronic collaborative writing, in addition a project funded by the Dutch National science foundation (NWO) on the role of the interface in electronic communication, and two projects financed by the European Union (5th framework) involving the construction of an Internet-based intelligent tool to Support Collaborative Argumentation-based Learning (SCALE and DUNES). *Department of Educational Sciences, Utrecht University, Heidelberglaan 2, 3584 CS Utrecht, The Netherlands. Email: j.andriessen@fss.uu.nl*

Henny P. A. Boshuizen (1950)

Is Professor of Education and Educational Technology at the Open University of the Netherlands, Educational Technology Expertise Center (OTEC), where she is responsible for the educational technology study programmes. She is the former director of the master degree program on Health Professions Education (MHPE), University of Maastricht. Her field of expertise is learning and expertise development in professional domains, including medicine, law, education, accountancy and business administration. Furthermore, she has done research on effects of activating educational strategies, such as problem-based learning. She studied psychology at the University of Amsterdam where she received her M.Sc. degree in 1979; her Ph.D. thesis dealt with development of expertise in medicine, University of Maastricht, 1989. *Educational Technology Expertise Center, Open University of the Netherlands, PO Box 2960, 6401 DL Heerlen, the Netherlands. Email: els.boshuizen@ou.nl*

Jan M. van Bruggen (1953)

Is an educational technologist at the Educational Technology Expertise Centre at the Open University of the Netherlands. His research interests are in the areas of computer supported collaborative learning using external representations of argumentation and computer supported essay rating. *Educational Technology Expertise Center, Open University of the Netherlands, PO Box 2960, 6401 DL Heerlen, the Netherlands. Email: jan.vanbruggen@ou.nl*

Simon Buckingham Shum (1967)

Is a Senior Lecturer at the Knowledge Media Institute, Open University, UK. His research focuses on technologies to assist collective sensemaking, and covers applications such as collaborative learning, group memory capture, and scholarly publishing and discourse. He received his B.Sc. in Psychology at the University of York (1984), an M.Sc. in Ergonomics from University College London (1988), and a Ph.D. from the University of York (1991). His dissertation analysed the cognitive affordances of graphical argumentation schemes in the context of software design rationale capture. *Knowledge Media Institute, Open University, Milton Keynes, MK7 6AA, UK. Email: sbs@acm.org*

Chad S. Carr (1971)

Is Curriculum Development Manager for Sears, Roebuck and Co. He has engaged in research at Arthur Andersen, Northern Illinois University (as Assistant Professor), Educational Technology Expertise Center (OTEC) at the Open University of the Netherlands (as Research Fellow) and Pennsylvania State University (as Research Assistant). His research has focused on using networked computer applications to support argumentation in Legal Education. He received his B.A. in Biology from West Virginia University (1993), M.A. in Secondary Education from West Virginia University (1995) and Ph.D. in Instructional Systems from The Pennsylvania State University (2000). *Sears, Roebuck and Co., 3333 Beverly Road, Hoffman Estates, IL 60179. Email: ccarr3@sears.com*

Jeff Conklin (1951)

Is Director of CogNexus Institute, an independent consulting and research firm in Edgewater, Maryland, USA, and an adjunct professor in the School of Public Policy at George Mason University, Virginia, USA. He created the "Dialog Mapping" technique, which he employs with his consulting clients, and which he teaches in tutorials and workshops. His research focuses on collaborative tools for groups working on ill-structured problems. He received a B.A. from Antioch College in Yellow Springs, Ohio, and a M.Sc. and Ph.D. from the University of Massachusetts. His dissertation was on the role of visual salience in the natural and automatic generation of natural language descriptions of pictures. *CogNexus Institute, 304 Arbutus Drive, Edgewater, Maryland 21037 USA. Email: jeff@cognexus.org*

John Domingue (1961)

Is the Deputy Director of the Knowledge Media Institute, Open University, UK. His research covers the intersection of knowledge and user interface technologies. In particular his work focuses on how formal knowledge models can be collaboratively created and shared on the web, and how these models can be used to create semantic web services. He has applied his work in a wide range of domains including medical guidelines, engineering, and online shopping. He received his B.Sc. in Computer Science at the University of Warwick (1983) and a Ph.D. from the Open University (1987). His dissertation was on how automatic program debugging tools could support novice programmers. *Knowledge Media Institute, Open University, Milton Keynes, MK7 6AA, UK. Email: J.B.Domingue@open.ac.uk*

Douglas C. Engelbart (1925)

Is Director of the Bootstrap Institute and a Board Member of the Bootstrap Alliance, both USA. His primary focus is on launching a scalable model for the "Facilitated Evolution" of Collective IQ within and among a wide variety of organizations and their improvement communities. Early application of such improvements is aimed specifically at improving the improvement capabilities of improvement communities and of their component organizations, – the base of an explicitly cultivated "bootstrapping" strategy. His driving goal is to boost society's collective capability for coping with its complex, urgent problems. He received his B.S. in EE from Oregon State University (1948), and his Ph.D. from the University of California, Berkeley (1956). *Bootstrap Alliance, 6505 Kaiser Drive, Fremont, CA 94555 USA. Email: dengelbart@yahoo.com*

Gijsbert Erkens (1949)

Is Associate Professor at the Department of Educational Sciences at Utrecht University (the Netherlands) since 1984. He received his M.Sc. in Developmental Psychology at the University of Amsterdam, and a Ph.D. in Social Sciences from Utrecht University (1997). His dissertation was on computer-supported cooperative problem solving in education. He is now involved in research on computer-assisted collaboration, dialogue in learning, and argumentative writing. He is project leader of the COSAR and PRO-ICT research projects. *Department of Educational Sciences, Utrecht University, Heidelberglaan 2, 3584 CS Utrecht, The Netherlands. Email: g.erkens@fss.uu.nl*

Gangmin Li (1964)

Is a Research Fellow at the Knowledge Media Institute, Open University, UK. His research focuses on agent technologies to assist organisational knowledge management. He received his B.Sc. in Software Engineering at the Northwest Polytechnic University, China (1983), an M.Sc. in Computing from University of York (1995), and a Ph.D.

from the Open University (1998). His dissertation proposed a novel multi-agent cooperation method called "Shifting Matrix Management" for multiple autonomous agents to achieve a common social benefit. *Knowledge Media Institute, Open University, Milton Keynes, MK7 6AA, UK. Email: G.Li@open.ac.uk*

Tim van Gelder (1962)

Is Associate Professor (Principal Fellow) in the Department of Philosophy, University of Melbourne, Australia, and director of the Australian Thinking Skills Institute (Austhink). He received a B.A. in Philosophy at the University of Melbourne (1984), and a Ph.D. in Philosophy from the University of Pittsburgh (1989). His dissertation was on forms of representation and how knowledge is encoded in the mind and brain. After working for a number of years in the philosophical foundations of cognitive science, his interests have turned in an applied direction, particularly reasoning skill acquisition and intelligence augmentation. *Department of Philosophy, University of Melbourne, Australia and Austhink. Email: tgelder@ariel.ucs.unimelb.edu.au*

Robert E. Horn (1933)

Is a visiting scholar at the Program on People, Computers, and Design of the Center for the Study of Language and Information at Stanford University and Distinguished Consulting Faculty member of the Saybrook Graduate School and Research Center. In 2000 he received the Diana Lifetime Achievement Award from the Association of Computing Machinery SIGDOC for his work on the Information Mapping method and visual language. He has taught graduate courses at Columbia, Harvard and Sheffield universities. His most recently published book is Visual Language: Global Communication for the 21st Century (www.macrovu.com). He is a fellow of the World Academy of Art and Science. He is a Woodrow Wilson Fellow and a recipient of the Outstanding Research Award from the National Society for Performance and Instruction (NSPI). *Center for the Study of Language and Information, Stanford University, USA and Saybrook Graduate School, USA. Email: hornbob@earthlink.net*

Jos Jaspers (1956)

Is Assistant Professor at the Department of Educational Sciences at Utrecht University (the Netherlands) since 1991. He received his M.Sc. in Psychology in 1991 from Utrecht University. He now teaches courses on information technology in education and is involved in research on computer-supported collaborative writing. He wrote the TC3 groupware for the COSAR project and is currently working on the more exhaustive program VCRI for the PRO-ICT research project. *Department of Educational Sciences, Utrecht University, Heidelberglaan 2, 3584 CS Utrecht, The Netherlands. Email: j.jaspers@fss.uu.nl*

Gellof Kanselaar (1942)

Is Full Professor in educational psychology and ICT in education at Utrecht University since 1988. He received his Ph.D. in experimental psychology at Utrecht University in 1983. He is director of the institute for educational research (ICO-ISOR) at the University of Utrecht. He co-ordinates several research projects on the use of computers in education and on Computer supported Collaborative Learning, funded by the Dutch National Science Foundation (NWO). He has also served as president of the Dutch Educational Research Association and member of the Board of the Institute for Educational Research in the Netherlands. He was member of the scientific committee of the European CSCL-conference in Maastricht in 2001. *Department of Educational Sciences, Utrecht University, Heidelberglaan 2, 3584 CS Utrecht, The Netherlands. Email: g.kanselaar@fss.uu.nl*

Paul A. Kirschner (1951)

Is Professor of Educational Technology at the Educational Technology Expertise Center (OTEC) at the Open University of the Netherlands and Professor of Contact and Distance Education at the Faculty of General Sciences/Knowledge Engineering at Maastricht University. He has held the IBM-Learning Chair (International Chair in Computer Science) on the University of Gent, Belgium and is a member of the Educational Council of the Netherlands, the advisory board for the Dutch Minister of Education. He received his B.A. in Psychology and Education at the State University of New York at Stony Brook (1973), a M.A. in Educational Psychology at the University of Amsterdam (1978) and a Ph.D. from the Open University of the Netherlands (1991). His dissertation was on the use of practicals in higher science education for the achievement of complex cognitive skills. *Educational Technology Expertise Center, Open University of the Netherlands, PO Box 2960, 6401 DL Heerlen, the Netherlands. Email: paul.kirschner@ou.nl*

Enrico Motta (1961)

Is the Director of the Knowledge Media Institute, Open University, UK. Dr Motta has a Degree in Computer Science from the University of Pisa, Italy, and a Ph.D. in Artificial Intelligence from the Open University. His main interest is in knowledge technologies and his current research focuses on the specification of reusable knowledge-based components (ontologies and problem solving methods), and the application of these technologies to support the creation and configuration of semantic web services, and to facilitate knowledge capture, sharing and publishing in organisations. He has authored a book entitled "Reusable Components for Knowledge Modelling" (IOS Press). *Knowledge Media Institute, Open University, Milton Keynes, MK7 6AA, UK. Email: E.Motta@open.ac.uk*

Maaike Prangsma (1974)

Is a Junior Researcher in the Department of Educational Sciences at Utrecht University (the Netherlands) since 2000. She received her M.A. in English and Linguistics at the University of Groningen (1999). Her Master's thesis was on Second Language Acquisition. She is project manager for the COSAR and PRO-ICT research projects. *Department of Educational Sciences, Utrecht University, Heidelberglaan 2, 3584 CS Utrecht, The Netherlands. Email: m.prangsma@fss.uu.nl*

Albert M. Selvin (1959)

Is a Senior Manager in the Information Technology Group at Verizon Communications, USA, where he leads web design, software development and business process redesign teams. His research interests are helping groups understand and act from multiple perspectives in problem situations, which has touched on computer-supported collaborative work, knowledge management, hypertext, and collaborative sensemaking. He is lead architect of the Compendium approach and toolset and in that role has facilitated over 500 sessions for industry, academic, and public groups. He received his B.A. in Film/Video Studies at the University of Michigan (1982), and an M.A. in Communication Arts from the University of Wisconsin (1984). *Verizon Communications, White Plains USA. Email: albert.m.selvin@verizon.com*

Victoria Uren (1967)

Is a Research Fellow at the Knowledge Media Institute, Open University, UK. Her research explores ontological and graph theoretic aspects of argumentation maps, and their application as practical discovery tools in digital information systems. She received a B.Sc. in Chemistry at University College Swansea (1988), an M.Sc. in Information Studies from the University of Sheffield (1990), and a Ph.D. from the University of Portsmouth (2001). Her dissertation concerned statistical learning of classes in textual information systems. *Knowledge Media Institute, Open University, Milton Keynes, MK7 6AA, UK. Email: V.S.Uren@open.ac.uk*

Arja Veerman (1969)

Is presently a researcher for TNO Human Factors Research Institute, department of Training and Instruction. She received her Ph.D. in 2000 from Utrecht University. Her Ph.D. research focused on academic students who engaged in authentic, ill-structured and complex learning activities in electronic, networked-based environments. The role of argumentation was studied in relationship to collaborative learning-in-process. Contextual features, such as the role of the tutor, task and instruction, effects of structured interaction at the user interface and interface design, were related to the outcomes. Her focus in the coming years will be on telelearning, web-based training and the application of agent technology in "I"-CSCL systems (Intelligent CSCL). *Department of Training and instruction, TNO-Human Factors, Kampweg 5, 3769 ZG Soesterberg, The Netherlands. Email:* arja@xs4all.nl

Part I
Foundations

1

The Roots of Computer Supported Argument Visualization

Simon Buckingham Shum

Knowledge Media Institute, Open University, UK

"root" [n.1]

I. 1. a.   That part of a plant or tree which is normally below the earth's surface; in Botany, the descending axis of a plant, tree, or shoot, developed from the radicle, and serving to attach the plant to and convey nourishment from the soil...

8. a.   A person or family forming the source of a lineage, kindred, or line of descendants.

9. a.   That upon or by which a person or thing is established or supported; the basis upon which anything rests. In 19th cent. use common in the phr. *to have (its) root(s)* in (something).

10. a.   The bottom or real basis, the inner or essential part, of anything; *the root of the matter.*

14. c.   A unique node or vertex of a graph from which every other node can be reached. Also *root node.*

Oxford English Dictionary Online [dictionary.oed.com]

1.1   Excavating the Roots to CSAV

This chapter considers some of the "roots" to Computer-Supported Argument Visualization (CSAV). The definitions above point to historical ancestors and conceptual foundations, and this chapter seeks to identify the most influential work to whom CSAV owes an intellectual debt. Specifically, we will consider individuals who invented paper-based precursors of argument maps, and/or who envisioned the possibilities that computers opened up. In mapping CSAV's intellectual terrain, I may well omit important branches to its roots that I have not encountered, but hope that this chapter will serve to stimulate the forging of further connections to other traditions.

    CSAV is located at the intersection of an eclectic mix of disciplines. We must minimally include philosophy and rhetoric as background disciplines to argumentation

3

in general, with traditions going back to the dialogues of the Greek philosophers. It is beyond the scope of this book to review this huge literature in any more detail than to provide a few key pointers to Speech Act theory (Searle, 1969), and argumentation theory (e.g. Perelman and Olbrechts-Tyteca, 1969; van Eemeren et al., 1983; Walton, 1996). Law is, arguably, the most argument-intensive profession of all, with greater resources than other professions to devote to analysing the structure of arguments, and extensive research into computer-support for teaching argumentation skills (e.g. Aleven and Ashley, 1994; Marshall, 1989; Bench-Capon, et al., 1998).

The human-centred technology research fields such as computer-supported co-operative work (CSCW), computer-mediated communication (CMC), and computer-supported collaborative learning (CSCL) have developed their own flavours of CSAV, in order to support the coordination of distributed organisational activity (Malone et al., 1987), the structuring of contributions to group support systems (Turoff et al., 1999), and the creation of conversations in which learning takes place (Andriessen et al., in press). The chapters in this book demonstrate how widely CSAV is attracting interest and finding applications.

1.2   Mapping the History of Argument Visualization

There are numerous ways to organise this review, but for simplicity, it steps through chronological history, uncovering roots of different sorts along the way. In some cases, it is known that one individual drew on another's work, while in others we are left to wonder what might have happened had the two met or read each other.

1.2.1   Charting Evidence in Legal Cases

In 1913, John Henry Wigmore proposed a *Chart Method* for analysing the mass of evidence presented in a legal case, in order to help the analyst reach a conclusion:

> Our object then, specifically, is in essence: *To perform the logical (or psychological) process of a conscious juxtaposition of detailed ideas for the purpose of producing rationally a single final idea. Hence, to the extent that the mind is unable to juxtapose consciously a larger number of ideas, each coherent group of detailed constituent ideas must be reduced in consciousness to a single idea; until the mind can consciously juxtapose them with due attention to each, so as to produce its single final idea.* (Wigmore, 1913, 2nd Edition 1931, p.109)

He sets out the "necessary conditions" for such an "apparatus", following what we would now recognise as requirements analysis and schema modelling for a visualization tool. For a given case, one must be able to express different types of evidence, relations between facts, represent and on demand see all the data, subsume subtrees, and distinguish between facts as alleged and facts as believed or disbelieved.

As a tool to comprehend a potentially large dataset:

> It must, finally, be compendious in *bulk*, but *not too complicated* in the variety of symbols. These limitations are set by the practical facts of legal work. Nevertheless, men's aptitudes for the use of such schemes vary greatly. Experience alone can tell us whether a particular scheme is usable by the generality of able students and practitioners who need or care to attack the problem. (p.110)

Wigmore was also clear that:

> ...the scheme need *not* show us what our belief *ought* to be. It can hope to show only what our belief actually is, and *how* we have actually reached it. (p.110)

This echoes the difference of most CSAV tools from other classes of computer-supported argumentation that seek to evaluate argument or recommend conclusions based on a formal model of decision processes, or the meaning or relative weight of argument elements. Wigmore's scheme is a cognitive tool for reflection:

> Hence, though we may not be able to demonstrate that we *ought* to reach that belief or disbelief, we have at least the satisfaction of having taken every precaution to reach it rationally. Our moral duty was to approximate, so far as capable, our belief to the fact. We have performed that duty, to the limits of our present rational capacity. And the scheme or method, if it has enlarged that capacity, will have achieved something worthwhile. (p.111)

The final line encapsulates the motivation behind much CSAV work: to augment our intellectual ability in argument analysis and construction. The theme of "intellectual augmentation" resonates, of course, with the work of Engelbart, introduced shortly. Wigmore's Evidence Charts (Figure 1.1), showing how connections between *Testamonial Assertions and Circumstances* may lead to credible *Propositions*, continue to be used today in some law schools (see also Carr's work on legal argumentation mapping with hypertext technology: Chapter 4).

1.2.2 Trails of Ideas in the Memex

Having started with the "AV" roots to CSAV, we now start to uncover some "CS" roots. The contribution of Vannevar Bush to the invention of hypertext as a way to easily connect fragments of information has been documented exhaustively (for a retrospective from within the hypertext community, see Brown/MIT, 1995). In his 1945 article *As We May Think*, Bush (1945) envisioned a near future system based on microfilm records that could support the construction of trails of ideas for personal information management, and for sharing with others.

> Consider a future device for individual use, which is a sort of mechanized private file and library. It needs a name, and, to coin one at random, "memex" will do. A memex is a device in which an individual stores all his books,

records, and communications, and which is mechanized so that it may be consulted with exceeding speed and flexibility. It is an enlarged intimate supplement to his memory. (Section 6)

> **§ 33. Same: an Example Charted.** We shall thus have charted the results of our reasoning upon the evidence affecting any single probandum. But this probandum will usually now in its turn (*ante,* § 8) become an evidentiary fact, towards another probandum in a catenate inference. The process of charting and valuation has then to be renewed for this new probandum; and so on until all the evidence has been charted, and the ultimate probanda in issue under the pleadings have been reached.
>
> The following portion of a chart will illustrate (taken from the case of *Com.* v. *Umilian, post,* § 38):
>
>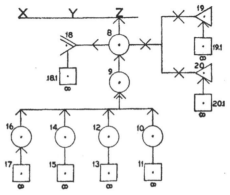
>
> Z is one of the ultimate probanda under the pleadings, viz. that the accused killed the deceased. Circle 8 is one of the evidentiary facts, viz., a revengeful murderous emotion. The arrowhead on the line from 8 to Z signifies provisional force given to the inference.

Figure 1.1: John Henry Wigmore's *Chart Method* for analyzing the evidence presented in a legal case, showing how different kinds of evidence (signaled by different node shapes, e.g. for *Testamonial Assertions and Circumstances*) are assembled to support or challenge (signaled by different arrow types) various *Propositions* (X, Y, Z, e.g. John Smith murdered Anne Baker). Each numbered node has an explanatory entry summarizing the evidence (e.g. John Smith knew that Anne Baker lived at Flat 42). (Reproduced with permission, Wigmore, H.J.A. 1931, p. 56: The Principles of Judicial Proof as Given by Logic, Psychology and General Experience and Illustrated in Judicial Trials. Boston: Little Brown, 2nd Edition).

In describing the "trail blazing" user interface, Bush envisages a rudimentary spatial display for connecting the two 'nodes':

> When the user is building a trail, he names it, inserts the name in his code book, and taps it out on his keyboard. Before him are the two items to be

joined, projected onto adjacent viewing positions. At the bottom of each there are a number of blank code spaces, and a pointer is set to indicate one of these on each item. The user taps a single key, and the items are permanently joined. In each code space appears the code word. Out of view, but also in the code space, is inserted a set of dots for photocell viewing; and on each item these dots by their positions designate the index number of the other item.

Thereafter, at any time, when one of these items is in view, the other can be instantly recalled merely by tapping a button below the corresponding code space. Moreover, when numerous items have been thus joined together to form a trail, they can be reviewed in turn, rapidly or slowly, by deflecting a lever like that used for turning the pages of a book. It is exactly as though the physical items had been gathered together from widely separated sources and bound together to form a new book. It is more than this, for any item can be joined into numerous trails. (Section 7)

It is natural for us to want to re-read Bush's article through 'CSAV lenses', for any clues that he explicitly envisioned argumentation as an application of associative linking, perhaps even a particularly important application. Alert to the risks of reading too deeply into a work to bolster one's prejudice, it is interesting, nonetheless, to find that in discussing the application of machine logic to supporting intellectual work, Bush states:

A new symbolism, probably positional, must apparently precede the reduction of mathematical transformations to machine processes. Then, on beyond the strict logic of the mathematician, lies the application of logic in everyday affairs. *We may some day click off arguments on a machine with the same assurance that we now enter sales on a cash register.* But the machine of logic will not look like a cash register, even of the streamlined model. (Section 5, emphasis added)

It is unclear what the intriguing "new symbolism, probably positional" refers to. It has connotations in today's human-computer interaction paradigm of a visual language of some sort. However, his use of the term positional in other places in the article suggests that he may have had a lower level machine processing logic in mind, such as punch card/photocell processing. His focus on argumentation is, however, unambiguous, and consistent with his focus on scholarship as a primary beneficiary of the Memex. Moreover, Bush proceeds to give examples to convince his reader why such a machine might have practical use. He begins with an historian collecting and organising disparate materials into a trail:

The owner of the memex, let us say, is interested in the origin and properties of the bow and arrow. Specifically he is studying why the short Turkish bow was apparently superior to the English long bow in the skirmishes of the Crusades. He has dozens of possibly pertinent books and articles in his memex. First he runs through an encyclopedia, finds an interesting but sketchy article, leaves it projected. Next, in a history, he finds another pertinent item, and ties the two together. Thus he goes, building a trail of many items. Occasionally he inserts a comment of his own, either linking it into the main trail or joining it by a side trail to a particular item. When it becomes evident that the elastic properties of available materials had a great deal to do with the bow, he branches off on a side trail which takes him through textbooks on elasticity and tables of physical constants. He inserts a page of longhand analysis of his own. Thus he builds a trail of his interest through the maze of materials available to him. (Section 7)

Obviously, we can imagine that the "semantics" of the comment that accompanies a trail might clarify the nature of the unclassified steps along the trail ("...is evidence for...", "...is inconsistent with...", "...tackles the same problem as..."), but Bush does not elaborate. The "twist in the tale" of this scenario from a CSAV perspective is that the trail is used later as evidence to substantiate an historical argument:

And his trails do not fade. Several years later, his talk with a friend turns to the queer ways in which a people resist innovations, even of vital interest. He has an example, in the fact that the outraged Europeans still failed to adopt the Turkish bow. In fact he has a trail on it. A touch brings up the code book. Tapping a few keys projects the head of the trail. A lever runs through it at will, stopping at interesting items, going off on side excursions. It is an interesting trail, pertinent to the discussion. So he sets a reproducer in action, photographs the whole trail out, and passes it to his friend for insertion in his own memex, there to be linked into the more general trail. (Section 7)

With respect to visualization, given the inherently spatial metaphor underpinning the Memex, it is perhaps surprising that Bush does not discuss diagrammatic overviews of trails; trails are constructed, viewed and navigated serially, albeit very rapidly if desired. His contribution to CSAV is nonetheless enormous, having envisaged the hypertextual linking that underpins navigation in many CSAV tools, all in the context of a specifically scholarly application to the organisation of information into coherent trails. It was left to some of his readers to take the project the next step, in particular, Doug Engelbart, reviewed shortly.

1.2.3   Mapping the Structure of Practical Arguments

The second AV root we review is *The Uses of Argument* by Stephen Toulmin (1958), originally written as a challenge to the dominance in philosophy of formal, Aristotelian logic. Toulmin's aim was to develop a view of logic which was grounded in the study of reasoning practice. Taking argumentation as the most common form of practical everyday reasoning, he posed the question, "what, then, is involved in establishing conclusions by the production of arguments?" His analysis of the logical structure of arguments led to a graphical format for laying out the structure of arguments, a representational approach reflected in much subsequent argumentation work.

The notation consists of five components and four relationships (Figure 1.2). According to the analysis, whether or not it is made explicit, all arguments logically comprise a fact or observation (a *Datum*), which via a logical step (a *Warrant*), allows one to make a consequent assertion (a *Claim*). The Warrant can be supported by a

Backing if necessary (why the assumed Warrant is valid), and the Claim qualified with a *Rebuttal* (specifying exceptions to the rule).

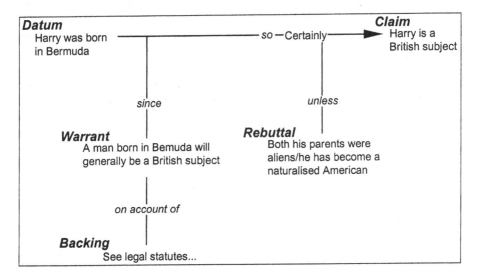

Figure 1.2: An example of Toulmin's graphical argument structure (Reproduced with permission from Toulmin, S., 1958, p.105, *The Uses of Argument*. Cambridge University Press).

Toulmin's scheme, through its use of a semiformal graphical representation, is perhaps the most often cited source (and a common demonstration example) in CSAV, and has found wide application in many other argument-based computer systems (Toulmin: ICAIL; Toulmin: Research Index, 2002).

1.2.4 Augmenting Human Intellect

In his seminal 1962 project report from the Stanford Research Institute, *Augmenting Human Intellect: A Conceptual Framework*, Douglas Engelbart (1962) laid out a framework for enabling people to augment their intellectual faculties by manipulating externalised "concept structures". In a subsequent article (Engelbart, 1963), he stated as follows:

> A concept structure (...) is something that can be designed or modified, and a basic hypothesis of our study is that better concept structures can be developed—structures that when mapped into a human's mental structure will significantly improve his capability to comprehend and to find solutions within his complex-problem solving situations. (Engelbart (1963), reprinted in Greif (1988, p. 54))

This vision of designing better computer-supported symbol manipulation tools marks a milestone on the trail this chapter is following. Engelbart, having been inspired by Bush's article, had available to him the exciting new world of mainframe, timeshare digital computers, albeit unreliable, and with appalling user interfaces. As has been now widely documented and recognised (Bootstrap; MouseSite), his team implemented the first working demonstrations of the power of a personal workstation with a refreshable cathode ray tube display, direct manipulation of graphics and text with a mouse and chord keyboard, hypertext linking, editable visualizations, shared displays and video conferencing. Much of the hardware and software of the modern personal computer was first built and integrated in the NLS system, decades before others understood its significance.

In his 1962 report, Engelbart presents extended scenarios of how a near-future tool could work. In the following extracts, we see probably the first articulation of what we would recognise as CSAV, detailing how a tool would support argument construction and analysis. The scenarios place the reader in the imaginary position of receiving a demonstration of the system from "Joe", who is speaking:

> "Most of the structuring forms I'll show you stem from the simple capability of being able to establish arbitrary linkages between different substructures, and of directing the computer subsequently to display a set of linked substructures with any relative positioning we might designate among the different substructures. You can designate as many different kinds of links as you wish, so that you can specify different display or manipulative treatment for the different types." (Engelbart, 1962, p. 85)
>
> "[...] let me label the nodes so that you can develop more association between the nodes and the statements in the argument. I can do this several ways. For one thing, I can tell the computer to number the statements in the order in which you originally had them listed, and have the labelling done automatically." This took him a total of five strokes on the keyset, and suddenly each node was made into a circle with a number in it. The statements that were on the second screen now each had its respective serial number sitting next to it in the left margin. "This helps you remember what the different nodes on the network display contain. We have also evolved some handy techniques for constructing abbreviation labels that help your memory quite a bit." (p. 88)
>
> "Also, we can display extra fine-structure and labelling detail within the network in the specific local area we happen to be concentrating upon. This finer detail is washed out as we move to another spot with our close attention, and the coarser remaining structure is compressed, so that there is room for our new spot to be blown up. It is a lot like using zones of variable magnification as you scan the structure—higher magnification where you are inspecting detail, lower magnification in the surrounding field so that your feel for the whole structure and where you are in it can stay with you." (p. 89)

Engelbart's highly interactive systems pointed the way forward for computers as personal, intellectual aids, capable of updating flexible symbolic displays as fast as one could issue the command, making possible a new coupling between one's thinking, and what was reflected back from the display. This computing paradigm lies at the heart of CSAV. Not far from Stanford Research Institute where Engelbart was building his systems, was Xerox Palo Alto Research Center, whose work we will review shortly.

1.2.5   Concept Mapping

A parallel stream of work developing in the worlds of education and critical thinking, goes under names such as Concept Mapping and MindMapping™. The earliest work on these is represented by individuals such as Joseph Novak and Tony Buzan. From the first studies in 1972, Novak has pursued a programme of work on concept mapping as a tool for high school and university students to construct, reflect on and discuss their conceptions of a domain with peers and tutors (Novak, 1976; 1998; Novak and Gowin, 1984). His work, grounded in a constructivist epistemology, has sparked significant research into the pedagogical properties of concept maps, student's ability (or lack thereof) to construct such diagrams, and their utility (e.g. in contrast to traditional essays) as a means of communicating, and assessing, learning. On a related theme, but to a different audience, Buzan has written extensively as a popular writer on improving thinking skills, from his 1974 BBC series and book *Use Your Head* (Buzan, 1974) to educational and organisational consultancy on the use of MindMapping™ (MindMap.com) for analysis and decision making.

Both of these strands emphasise the "visual" as a fundamental, but untapped, dimension for refining and communicating one's thoughts (cf. Horn, 1998, for a detailed analysis of visual communication). From an historical perspective, it is unclear how early on these two roots fused. (This author has not yet tracked down examples from before the 1990s of concept mapping researchers overlaying argumentation schemas to classify nodes and links.) Certainly, relatively recent work on concept mapping in educational technology has introduced the vocabulary of argumentation (e.g. as an aid to teaching scientific reasoning). Together with other educational technology research (Andriessen et al., in press; Baker, 1999; Veerman et al., 1999), diagrammatic reasoning (Diagrammatic Reasoning, 2002; Glasgow et al., 1995) and psychology of programming (PPIG, 2002), theoretical and methodological foundations for the rigorous analysis of diagrammatic representations are being laid, on which the CSAV research community should build. This brings to earth vaguer writings on 'tapping the hidden potential of the visual dimension', which is (not surprisingly) often short on detail when it comes to explaining exactly how visual representations support (or obstruct) individual (or collective) cognition in different contexts.

1.2.6   The Argumentative Approach to Wicked Problems

In the early 1970s, design theorist Horst Rittel characterised a class of problem that he termed "wicked", in contrast to "tame" problems. Tame problems are not necessarily trivial problems, but by virtue of the maturity of certain fields, can be tackled with more confidence. Tame problems are understood sufficiently that they can be analysed using established methods, and it is clear when a solution has been reached. Tame problems may even be amenable to automated analysis, such as computer configuration design or medical diagnosis by expert system. In contrast, wicked problems display a number of distinctive properties that violate the assumptions that must be made to use tame problem solving methods.

Wicked problems:
- cannot be easily defined so that all stakeholders agree on the problem to solve;
- require complex judgements about the level of abstraction at which to define the problem;
- have no clear stopping rules;
- have better or worse solutions, not right and wrong ones;
- have no objective measure of success;
- require iteration – every attempt to build a solution changes the problem;
- often have strong moral, political or professional dimensions, particularly for failure.

Rittel and Webber, made two testable claims of direct relevance to this review: first, that many design problems are "wicked," in contrast to "tame" or "benign" problems which can be modelled computationally, and secondly, that an "argumentative process" was the most effective way to tackle such problems.

> "Wicked and incorrigible [problems]...defy efforts to delineate their boundaries and to identify their causes, and thus to expose their problematic nature." (Rittel and Webber, 1973).

Such problems lack a single, agreed-upon formulation or well-developed plans of action, are unique, and have no well-defined stopping rule, because there are only "better" or "worse" (rather than right or wrong) solutions. Closure is often forced by pragmatic constraints (e.g. managerial or political) rather than "rational scientific" principles. Such problems could not be solved by formal models or methodologies, classed by Rittel as the "first-generation" design methodologies. Instead, an *argumentative* approach to such problems was proposed (a second-generation design method). The essence of this perspective is that an open-ended, dialectic process of collaboratively defining and debating issues is a powerful way of discovering the structure of wicked problems:

> First generation methods seem to start once all the truly difficult questions have been dealt with already (...) The second generation deals with difficulties underlying what was taken as input for the methods of the first generation.
>
> [Second generation] methods are characterised by a number of traits, one of them being that the design process is not considered to be a sequence of activities that are pretty well defined and that are carried through one after the other, like "understand the problem, collect information, analyse information, synthesise, decide," and so on...
>
> My recommendation [for the future of design methodologies] would be to emphasise investigations into the understanding of designing as an argumentative process ... how to understand designing as a counterplay of raising issues and dealing with them, which in turn raises new issues, and so on...
>
> [Argumentative design] means that the statements are systematically challenged in order to expose them to the viewpoints of the different sides,

and the structure of the process becomes one of alternating steps on the micro-level; that means the generation of solution specifications towards end statements, and subjecting them to discussion of their pros and cons. (Rittel, 1972)

This perspective motivated the development of Issue Based Information Systems (IBIS) as a medium to encourage the open deliberation of issues. The three key IBIS entities were *Issues, Positions and Arguments*, which could be linked by relationships such as *supports, objects-to, replaces, temporal-successor-of, more-general-than*, and their converses. Visualised as a graph, an IBIS grows into a network as more Issues are posted and debated (Figure 1.3).

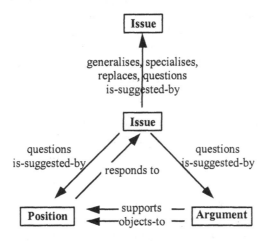

Figure 1.3: The basic IBIS structural unit of Issues, Positions and Arguments, developed in the 1970s by Horst Rittel to support his argumentative approach to wicked problem solving.

To summarise, Rittel's work established a bridge between design and argumentation. The argumentative approach to design elevated the importance of the *process* of understanding a problem from its minor status as a preliminary step to using first-generation design methods, to the central activity in tackling wicked design problems. Rittel and Webber, hypothesised that a particularly powerful way to tackle such problems is by an "argumentative approach," proposing IBIS as an argument mapping notation. In Chapter 6, Conklin reports on the use of an IBIS-based approach called *Dialog Mapping*.

1.2.7 Argument Mapping Meets Hypertext

Engelbart's work set in process research efforts in numerous locations. One of the most influential of these was based at the Xerox Palo Alto Research Center (PARC), where the interest in the early 1980s in human-computer interaction (which led to the modern graphical user interface) made the important move from word processing, to "idea processing". The availability (at least in computing research labs) of graphical user interfaces and large screens led to a very active decade in the building of prototype hypertext systems (summarised and reviewed in detail by Conklin, 1987), and the formation of what is now the hypertext research community (e.g. ACM SIGWEB). One of the most influential systems of this era was NoteCards (Halasz et al., 1987), a tool for idea processing that drew on the 3x5 inch filing card as its metaphor, each hypertext node being a "card".

"Idea processing" in general then took a specific direction towards argument mapping. In *The Next Knowledge Medium*, Stefik (1986, also at PARC) proposed collaborative argumentation tools as one example of "knowledge media." Such tools, "for arguing the merits, assumptions, and evaluation criteria for competing proposals" could provide "an essential medium in the process of meetings." "The languages provided by the tools encourage an important degree of precision and explicitness for manipulating and experimenting with knowledge", coupled with "augment[ing] human social processes." Van Lehn (1985) published a technical report documenting his experiences with NoteCards, concluding that using the system to map the argumentation in his thesis had exposed hidden flaws.

Brown (1986) further developed the theme:

> Current communications tools and methods force the crafting of complex arguments into linear form for presentation, so that the web-like connections among ideas is hidden from view, making it difficult to see alternate interpretations and points of view. (...) As a result many of the underlying ideas, arguments and assumptions either remain implicit or are lost altogether. But consider the possibility of crafting new information tools to capture not just conclusions and the view of matters that supports them, but to allow the explicit representation of underlying assumptions and argument structures. (p. 484)

It was noted in particular that work was needed on developing notations with an appropriate vocabulary for the task domain:

> To accomplish these goals, we need a taxonomy of epistemological links for relating ideas, as well as link-related filters. That is, we must now think about giving users access to and utilisation of not just undifferentiated links, but links with appropriate kinds of labels. (p. 485)

In a subsequent project on computational support for meetings, Stefik et al., (1987) envisioned a tool called *Argnoter*:

> [Design] is essentially a dialectic between goals and possibilities... in collaborative design tasks, this interaction and tension between goals and alternatives must play itself out in the communications among collaborators. [...] A major theme of Argnoter's design is that alternatives be made explicit: Proposals themselves are explicit, as are assumptions and evaluation criteria. (p. 38)

> A major working hypothesis behind the design of Argnoter is that making
> the structure of arguments explicit facilitates consensus by reducing
> uncommunicated differences. (p. 40)

The motivation behind Argnoter was clearly that of a "group CSAV" tool – a way to represent design arguments explicitly, but with the group process adding another dimension. It was hypothesised that the process of striving to agree on rankings and assumptions in Argnoter would help designers recognise where their differences lay. However, the actual system was not implemented.

Meanwhile, Rittel's work was serving as a major source of inspiration for researchers investigating software design as a participatory, dialectic process (Sjöberg and Timpka, 1995), and as the representational basis for capturing design rationale (a record of the reasoning behind design arguments and decisions – Moran and Carroll, 1996). Probably the best known of these was at MCC research labs, where Conklin's gIBIS system (Conklin and Begeman, 1988) pioneered the application of graphical hypertext views for the reification of IBIS structures. Issues, Positions and Arguments became system-recognised node types in a hypertext, and Rittel's rhetorical moves (*responds to, expands on, challenges,* etc.) defined the typology of link types, with direct manipulation, aerial views, and graph layout algorithms assisting in the management of the large network structures (see Figure 1.4 for an example).

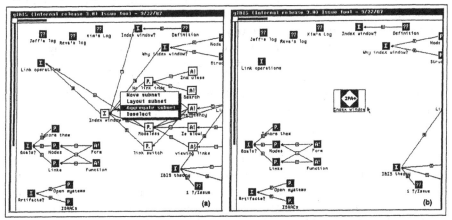

Figure 1.4: Screens from the *gIBIS* (graphical-IBIS) hypertext system to support design and policy deliberation. This example illustrates the support the tool provided for collapsing portions of a large IBIS map (*a*), into an aggregate node (*b*). Reprinted from Begeman and Conklin (1988), courtesy of BYTE <www.byte.com>

Also during the late1980s, Robert Horn was working at the intersection of hypertext and an approach to visual information design called Information Mapping. Horn (1989) published a book which included discussion of the application of hypertext to mapping argumentation, using Toulmin's scheme (see above) as an example.

A final strand of work to emerge in recent years is interest in hypertextual argumentation, that is, ways in which the non-linear aspects of argumentation may be better expressed as hypertext than prose. David Kolb (1994) used the Storyspace

(Eastgate Systems) hypertext writing tool to experiment with such forms, and envisioned how hypertext and visualization could develop in the future to support scholarly argumentation (Kolb, 1997). This thread has continued, with Carter (2000) considering other aspects of hypertextual argument, while Mancini and Buckingham Shum (2002) applied ideas from cognitive coherence relations research to propose how hypertext's disorienting impact can be controlled to support the construction and navigation of scholarly argument structures.

We return to some of these mid 1980's-mid 90's systems towards the end of this chapter, to reflect on their subsequent development.

1.2.8   CMC Meets CSAV

There has been a steady research stream flowing from the spread of Computer-Mediated Communication (CMC) technology, from the early Arpanet, to online communities such as the Well, to the current internet explosion. New research fields such as educational technology and cybersociology have analysed the exchanges between members of different kinds of communities (from students on a course conference, to voluntary members of online fora). It is not clear that CMC can be thought of as a root in terms of strongly influencing the emergence of CSAV in its current state. Rather, it is a parallel branch that has grown from a different research community, focused on asynchronous textual interactions (rather than visualizations).

Educational CMC research has naturally focused on the pedagogical benefits that may accrue from CMC (e.g. Mason and Kaye, 1989), primarily focused on analysing the nature of interactions, and on structuring the normally freeform interactions of email/text conferencing. One cluster of research is that of Dialogue Games, in which a knowledge-based system with a model of different dialogue "trajectories" influences the human-computer dialogue based on its trace of what has taken place so far (e.g. Pilkington et al., 1992; Ravenscroft, 2000; Sillince, 1997).

Another research cluster studies the quality of the argumentation in conventional CMC, and may also introduce a requirement (or user interface option) for an online participant to classify or connect argumentation-oriented contributions to a forum explicitly, such as *Hypothesis* or *Data*, or relational connectives such as *Supports* and *Challenges*. Scardamalia and Bereiter (e.g. Scardamalia et al., 1989) for instance, introduced these as student "scaffolds" in the CSILE (CSILE) and Knowledge Forum environments (Knowledge Forum). The earliest work is probably that of Turoff and Hilz, who comment on their early work from the 1970s on group support CMC systems such as EMISARI and TOPICS:

> Both systems had very specialized structures for group communications, very specific content type classifications and relationships related to the application domains (crisis management and unpredictable information exchange), specific human roles supported by software, and voting capabilities to be able to expose quickly and efficiently areas of agreement and disagreement. (Turoff et al., 1999, Section 1)

Although lacking any visual dimension, "content type classifications and relationships related to the application domains" are clearly an element in CSAV systems, and interestingly, Turoff (1970) describes an early implementation of the Delphi conferencing system which incorporates a meta-discussion structure based on the Hegelian Inquiry Process to scientific discourse. An explicit link to argumentation is made when they proceed to propose a future CMC system that could support varieties of "discourse template", one example being for "debating and argumentation", providing *Argument* contribution types, with *Pro* and *Con* links, plus a voting mechanism to resolve disagreements. Significantly, they conclude by introducing the idea of visualizing discourse grounded in the argumentation template:

> Right now one key missing element in asynchronous CMC systems is the appreciation of the evolution of the discussion that occurs in a face to face meeting. [...] What were the crucial arguments that caused agreement to occur? [...] The voting process is a logical approach to capturing the resulting group dynamics of the discussion and the type of tool to do this could be the following three dimensional visualization. Let us imagine something akin to a complex organic molecule that, on screen, can be rotated and "zoomed" to focus on different parts and their relationships. More importantly, the history of this structure can be played back through time. We are using the argumentation template for the example and there are two types of nodes or atoms (options and arguments); and three types of links or relationships (pro, con, and opposition). Any member of the group may add to the collaborative construction using these building modules.

Figure 1.5 reproduces the visualization they proposed.

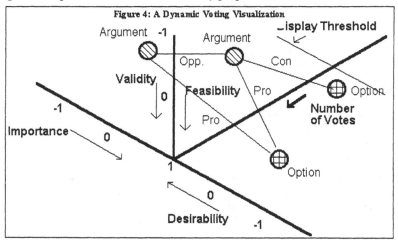

Figure 1.5: A visualization mockup for an argumentation-CMC system, proposed by Turoff et al., (1999). Reproduced with permission from Turoff, M., Hiltz, S. R., Bieber, M., Fjermestad, J., & Rana, A. (1999). Collaborative discourse structures in computer mediated group

communications. *Journal of Computer Mediated Communication*, 4(4). © 2001 IEEE
<www.ascusc.org/jcmc/vol4/issue4>

In the same year, Sillince and Saeedi (1999) published a paper analysing design issues for argumentation-augmented CMC, including the possibility of visualizations. Thus, in this branch of work we finally see the convergence of CMC and CSAV in proposals for future systems, albeit not until the late 1990s.[1] (An ongoing project to implement a CMC-CSAV system for scholarly research discourse is described in Chapter 9.)

1.3   From Prototypes to Sustained Work Practices?

To most of the individuals reviewed above, it was obvious that computer-supported argument visualization had many potential applications. However, the reality of making a new intellectual technology work for real people doing real work with a constellation of existing tools and constraints, often exposes many practical "details" that must be worked through, as the technology becomes sufficiently stable usable to deploy on everyday hardware and software.

Within the hypertext research community, for a decade from the early 1980s to early 1990s, argument mapping became something of an "experimental white rat", with many of the pioneering systems for idea processing and then collaborative hypertext choosing argumentation as one of their standard demonstration applications: consider Textnet (Trigg and Weiser, 1983), NoteCards (Halasz et al., 1987), gIBIS (Conklin and Begeman, 1988), rIBIS (Rein and Ellis, 1991), SEPIA (Streitz et al., 1989), AAA (Schuler and Smith, 1990), Colab (Tatar et al., 1991), and Aquanet (Marshall and Rogers, 1992). In addition to the gIBIS system introduced above, several other design rationale efforts (Fischer, et al., 1991; McCall, 1991) grounded their approaches in Rittel's concept of *argumentative design*. Others developed variations on gIBIS, varying the notation and its visual layout, determining how large and elaborate an argument could be expressed. Design Space Analysis (MacLean et al., 1991; 1993) changed IBIS's *Issues, Positions, Arguments* to the more design oriented *Questions, Options, Criteria*. The *Decision Representation Language* (Lee, 1991) extended gIBIS (e.g. with the *Goal* node type), allowing participants to explore *Alternatives, Claims* backing them, and to contest through *Questions* and counter-*Claims* the relationships between these constructs.[2]

However, after the initial flush of excitement at hypertext's representational possibilities, subsequent analyses of CSAV began to draw more sobering lessons. A number of critiques highlighted cognitive and social challenges for CSAV, and by extension, any approach that seeks to support intellectual work with semi-formal or formal representations. From a CSCW perspective, see Shipman and Marshall (1999),

---

[1] I of course welcome references to earlier examples that have been omitted in this review, with apologies in advance to those concerned.

[2] See Conklin (1987) for a review of hypertext systems in mid-1980s, and Buckingham Shum and Hammond (1994) for a more recent review, specifically from the perspective of argumentation-based design rationale.

from a design rationale perspective Buckingham Shum and Hammond (1994), on groupware see Grudin (1994), and on collaborative modelling (Selvin, 1999). Educational applications of CSAV have reported similar initial learning overheads for students in structuring their thoughts into network structures (Suthers and Weiner, 1995).

It has become apparent that CSAV's successes and failures result from a combination of one's expertise in the argument mapping approach, training in CSAV tools, user interface design, the kind of domain and problem being tackled, and the incentive to use CSAV. A focus on any one factor in isolation has proven to be shortsighted. What we have seen with CSAV – at least its history as proposed here – is typical of the maturation of many new intellectual technologies. After an initial (e.g. a decade's) flurry of prototype building in research labs, the complexities of making it work in the real world start to bite. Many move on to the next emerging technology, as is obviously important in technology research, but those who persevere may after a few years create stable versions/products that can be run reliably on what are by then everyday workplace computers. Crucially, in parallel, they slowly acquire the missing knowledge and craft skill that helps them embed and customise the raw tool in the workplace. In CSAV's case, learning ways to introduce it into the classroom or businesses often implicates integration with other technologies (e.g. standard office software; email and the web; specialist tools such as CAD), or organisational processes (e.g. national curricula; design methodologies).

Of all the factors that seem to influence uptake of argument mapping, one in particular is recurring (cf. van Gelder, Chapter 5, and Conklin, Chapter 6). The process of learning the representational notation inculcates a useful new ability to attend to the underlying structure of arguments and debates (whether spoken or written) in the terms of that particular notation. An important consequence of this, however, is that until one has had some practice, often prompted by some initial instruction, argument mapping initially feels like learning a new foreign language, and the temptation is to lapse back into more familiar languages (conversational patterns and modes of writing). The tools can be made user friendly, and the notations lightweight and informal, but the human element of the system must co-evolve as well. We are, in short, talking about a new *literacy* in being able to read and write in the new medium, and a new *fluency* in using these conversational tools in appropriate ways in different contexts.

1.4 Conclusion

Computer-Supported Argument Visualization has roots that this chapter has unearthed as far back as Wigmore's legal evidence charts in 1913. So, for almost a century, thinkers from many disciplines have envisaged and invented aids to assist in the mapping and analysis of arguments to tackle applied problems they were confronting. It is of particular note that "founding fathers" of today's interactive computing such as Bush and Engelbart envisaged argument construction and analysis as a key objective for the intellectual technologies they were conceiving.

As we enter the third millennium, the CSAV community is beginning to have available to it some reasonably usable, robust tools, and a growing body of knowledge about their uptake and application, as evidenced by this book. As the internet becomes the default mechanism for the dissemination of research knowledge, software applications and code, we can expect it to accelerate the evolution, deployment and evaluation of CSAV tools, and help connect the community behind them.

1.5 References

Aleven, V., & Ashley, K. D. (1994). An instructional environment for practising argumentation skills. *AAAI'94: Proceedings of Annual Conferrence American Assoc. Artificial Intelligence*, 485-492. Cambridge, Mass: MIT Press.

Andriessen, J., Baker, M., & Suthers, D. (Ed.). (in press). *Arguing to learn: Confronting cognitions in computer-supported collaborative learning environments*. Dordrecht: Kluwer Academic.

Baker, M.J. (1999). Argumentation and constructive interaction. In J. Andriessen & P. Coier (Eds.) *Foundations of Argumentative Text Processing*. Amsterdam: University of Amsterdam Press.

Begeman, M. and Conklin, J. (1988). The right tool for the right job. *BYTE*, Oct. 1988.

Bench-Capon, T. J. M., Leng, P. H., & Stanford, G. (1998). A computer supported environment for the teaching of legal argument. *The Journal of Information, Law and Technology, 3*. Retrieved on August 1, 2002 from http://elj.warwick.ac.uk/jilt/98-3/capon.html

Bootstrap Institute. Available from http://www.bootstrap.org

Brown, J. S. (1986). From cognitive ergonomics to social ergonomics and beyond. In D. Norman & S. Draper (Ed.), *User Centered System Design* (pp. 457-486). Hillsdale, NJ: Lawrence Erlbaum Associates.

Brown/MIT (1995). Brown/MIT Bush Symposium. Retrieved on August 1, 2002 from http://www.cs.brown.edu/memex/

Buckingham Shum, S., & Hammond, N. (1994). Argumentation-Based design rationale: What use at what cost? *International Journal of Human-Computer Studies, 40*(4), 603-652.

Bush, V. (1945). As we may think. *The Atlantic Monthly*. Retrieved on August 1, 2002 from http://www.theatlantic.com/unbound/flashbks/computer/bushf.htm

Buzan, T. (1974). *Use your head*. London: BBC.

Conklin, J. (1987). Hypertext: An introduction and survey. *IEEE Computer, 20*(9), 17-41.

Conklin, J., & Begeman, M. L. (1988). gIBIS: A hypertext tool for exploratory policy discussion. *ACM Transactions on Office Information Systems, 4*(6), 303-331.

CSILE: Computer Supported Intentional Learning Environment. Ontario Institute for Studies in Education, University of Toronto. Retrieved on August 1, 2002 from http://csile.oise.utoronto.ca/

Diagrammatic Reasoning (2002). Gateway to the diagrammatic reasoning website. Retrieved on August 1, 2002 from http://www.hcrc.ed.ac.uk/gal/Diagrams/

Eastgate Systems: *Storyspace*. Available from http://www.eastgate.com

Engelbart, D. C. (1962). *Augmenting human intellect: A conceptual framework* (SRI Project No. 3578, Summary Report AFOSR-3233). Stanford Research Institute. Retrieved on August 1, 2002 from http://sloan.stanford.edu/mousesite/EngelbartPapers/B5_F18_ConceptFramew orkInd.html

Engelbart, D. C. (1963). A conceptual framework for the augmentation of man's intellect. In P. Howerton & D. Weeks (Eds.), *Vistas in information handling* (pp. 1-29). Washington, DC: Spartan Books.

Fischer, G., Lemke, A. C., McCall, R., & Morch, A. I. (1991). Making Argumentation Serve Design. *Human-Computer Interaction, 6*(3&4), 393-419.

Glasgow, J., Narayanan, N. H., & Chandrasekaran, B. (Ed.). (1995). *Diagrammatic reasoning: Cognitive and computational perspectives*. Cambridge: MIT Press.

Greif, I (ed.), *Computer-Supported Cooperative Work: A Book of Readings*. Morgan Kaufman, San Mateo, California, 1988.

Grudin, J. (1994). Groupware and social dynamics: Eight challenges for developers. *Communications of the ACM, 37*(1), 92-105.

Halasz, F. G., Moran, T. P., & Trigg, R. H. (1987). NoteCards in a nutshell. *Proceedings of CHI and GI'87: Human Factors in Computing Systems and Graphic Interface*, 45-52. New York: ACM.

Horn, R. (1989). *Mapping hypertext: The analysis, organization, and display of knowledge for the next generation of on-line text and graphics*. Lexington, MA: Lexington Institute.

Horn, R. (1998). *Visual language: Global communication for the 21st century*. Bainbridge Island, WA: MacroVU, Inc.

Knowledge Forum. Ontario Institute for Studies in Education, University of Toronto. Retrieved on August 1, 2002 from http://www.learn.motion.com/lim/kf/KF0.html

Kolb, D. (1994). *Socrates in the Labyrinth: Hypertext, Argument, Philosophy (A Hypertext)*. Watertown: Eastgate Systems. http://www.eastgate.com

Kolb, D. (1997). Scholarly hypertext: Self-represented complexity. *Proceedings of the Eighth ACM Conference on Hypertext*, (Southampton), 29-37. Retrieved on August 1, 2002 from http://journals.ecs.soton.ac.uk/~lac/ht97/pdfs/kolb.pdf

Lee, J. (1991). Extending the Potts and Bruns model for recording design rationale. *Proceedings of the 13th International Conference on Software Engineering*, 114-125. New York: IEEE-ACM.

MacLean, A. Bellotti, V. and Buckingham Shum, S. (1993). Developing the design space with design space analysis. In P. F. Byerley, P. J. Barnard, and J. May (Eds.). *Computers, Communication and Usability: Design issues, research and methods for integrated services*. (North Holland Series in Telecommunication) pp.197-219. Amsterdam: Elsevier:.

MacLean, A., Young, R. M., Bellotti, V., & Moran, T. (1991). Questions, Options, and Criteria: Elements of design space analysis. *Human-Computer Interaction, 6*(3, 4), 201-250.

Malone, T. W., Grant, K. R., Lai, K.-Y., Rao, R., & Rosenblitt, D. (1987). Semistructured messages are surprisingly useful for computer-supported coordination. *ACM Transactions on Office Information Systems, 5*,(2), 115-131.

Marshall, C. C. (1989). Representing the structure of legal arguments. *Proceedings of the International Conference on AI and Law*, Vancouver, B.C., Canada.

Marshall, C. C., & Rogers, R. A. (1992). Two years before the mist: Experiences with aquanet. *Proceedings of the Fourth ACM Conference on Hypertext* (pp. 53-62)

Mason, R., & Kaye, A. (Ed.). (1989). *Mindweave: communication, computers and distance education.* Oxford: Pergamon Press. Retrieved on August 1, 2002 from http://www-icdl.open.ac.uk/literaturestore/mindweave/mindweave.html

McCall, R. J. (1991). PHI: A conceptual foundation for design hypermedia. *Design Studies, 12*(1), 30-41

MindMap.com - Tony Buzan. Available from http://www.mind-map.com/

Moran, T. P., & Carroll, J. M. (Ed.). (1996). *Design rationale: concepts, techniques, and use.* Hillsdale, NJ: Lawrence Erlbaum Associates.

MouseSite: Sloan School of Management, Stanford University, CA. Retrieved on August 1, 2002 from http://sloan.stanford.edu/mousesite/

Novak, J. D. (1976). Understanding the learning process and effectiveness of teaching methods in the Classroom, laboratory, and field. *Science Education, 60*(4), 493-512.

Novak, J. D. (1998). *Learning, creating, and using knowledge: Concept maps as facilitative tools in schools and corporations.* Mawah, NJ: Lawrence Erlbaum and Associates.

Novak, J. D., & Gowin, D. B. (1984). *Learning how to learn.* New York and Cambridge, UK: Cambridge University Press.

Perelman, C., & Olbrechts-Tyteca, L. (1969). *The new rhetoric: A Treatise on argumentation.* Notre Dame, IN.: Notre Dame University Press.

Pilkington, R. M., Hartley, J. R., Hintze, D., & Moore, D. J. (1992). Learning to argue and arguing to learn: An interface for computer-based dialogue games. *Journal of Artificial Intelligence in Education, 3*(3), 275-285.

PPIG (2002). Psychology of Programming Interest Group: Workshops. Retrieved on August 1, 2002 from http://www.ppig.org/workshops

Ravenscroft, A. (2000). Designing argumentation for conceptual development. *Computers and Education, 34*, 241-255.

Rein, G. L., & Ellis, C. A. (1991). rIBIS: A real-time group hypertext system. *International Journal of Man-Machine Studies, 24*(3), 349-367.

Rittel, H. W. J. (1972). Second generation design methods. *Interview in: Design Methods Group 5th Anniversary Report: DMG Occasional Paper, 1,* 5-10. Reprinted in: Developments in Design Methodology, N. Cross (Ed.), 1984, pp. 317-327.

Rittel, H. W. J., & Webber, M. M. (1973). Dilemmas in a general theory of planning. *Policy Sciences, 4*, 155-169.

Scardamalia, M., Bereiter, C., McLean, R. S., Swallow, J., & Woodruff, E. (1989). Computer supported intentional learning environments. *Journal of Educational Computing Research, 5*, 51-68.

Schuler, W., & Smith, J. (1990). Author's Argumentation Assistant (AAA): A hypertext-based authoring tool for argumentative texts. *Proceedings of ECHT'90: European*

Conference on Hypertext: Argumentation, Design & Knowledge Acquisition, 137-151. Cambridge, Eng.: Cambridge University Press.

Searle, J. (1969). *Speech Acts : An Essay in the Philosophy of Language*. Cambridge, Eng.: Cambridge University Press.

Selvin, A. (1999). Supporting collaborative analysis and design with hypertext functionality. *Journal of Digital Information, 1*(4). Retrieved on August 1, 2002 from http://jodi.ecs.soton.ac.uk/Articles/v01/i04/Selvin/

Shipman, F. M., & Marshall, C. C. (1999). Formality considered harmful: Experiences, emerging themes, and directions on the use of formal representations in Interactive systems. *Computer Supported Cooperative Work, 8*(4), 333-352. Retrieved on August 1, 2002 from http://bush.cs.tamu.edu:80/~shipman/cscw.pdf

SIGWEB Special Interest Group in Hypertext, Hypermedia and the Web. New York: ACM. Retrieved on August 1, 2002 from http://www.acm.org/sigweb/

Sillince, J. A. A. (1997). Intelligent argumentation systems: Requirements, models, research agenda and applications. In A. Kent (Ed.), *Encyclopaedia of Library and Information Science, 59(22)* (pp. 176-218). New York: Marcel Dekker.

Sillince, J. A. A., & Saeedi, M. H. (1999). Computer-Mediated communication: problems and potentials of argumentation support systems. *Decision Support Systems, 26*, 287-306. Retrieved on August 1, 2002 from http://staff.abs.aston.ac.uk/jsillince/ARTICLE8.htm

Sjöberg, C., & Timpka, T. (1995). Inside multidisciplinary design in medical informatics: Experiences from the use of an argumentative design method. *MEDINFO'95: Tri-annual World Conference in Medical Informatics*, Vancouver.

Stefik, M. (1986). The next knowledge medium. *AI Magazine, 7*(1), 34-46.

Stefik, M., Foster, G., Bobrow, D. G., Kahn, K., Lanning, S., and Suchman, L. (1987). *Communications of the ACM, 30*(1), 32-47

Streitz, N., Hanneman, J., & Thüring, M. (1989). From ideas and arguments to hyperdocuments: Travelling through activity spaces. *Proceedings of Hypertext'89*, 343-364. New York: ACM.

Suthers, D., & Weiner, A. (1995, October). *Groupware for developing critical discussion skills*. Paper presented at CSCL'95: Computer Supported Collaborative Learning, Bloomington, IN.

Tatar, D. G., Foster, G., & Bobrow, D. G. (1991). Design for conversation: Lessons from cognoter. *International Journal of Man-Machine Studies*, 34, 185-209. Reprinted from *Computer supported cooperative work and Groupware*, 55-80, by S. Greenberg, Ed., 1991, London: Academic Press.

Toulmin, S. (1958). *The uses of argument*. Cambridge, Eng.: Cambridge University Press.

Toulmin: ICAIL (2002). Results of a search on "Toulmin" in proceedings of International Conference on Artificial Intelligence and Law. ACM Digital Library. Retrieved on August 1 2002 from http://portal.acm.org/results.cfm?coll=ACM&dl=ACM&CFID=2680449&CFTOKEN=58630376

Toulmin: Research Index (2002). Results of a search on "Toulmin" in computer Science literature. Retrieved on August 1, 2002 from http://citeseer.nj.nec.com/cs?q=toulmin&cs=1

Trigg, R., & Weiser, M. (1983). TEXTNET: A network-based approach to text handling. *ACM Transactions on Office Information Systems, 4*(1).

Turoff, M. (1970). Delphi conferencing: computer based conferencing with anonymity. *Journal of Technological Forecasting and Social Change, 3*(2), 159-204.

Turoff, M., Hiltz, S. R., Bieber, M., Fjermestad, J., & Rana, A. (1999). Collaborative discourse structures in computer mediated group communications. *Journal of Computer Mediated Communication, 4*(4). Retrieved on August 1, 2002 from http://www.ascusc.org/jcmc/vol4/issue4/turoff.html

Van Eemeren, F., Grootendorst, R., Jackson, S., & Jacobs, S. (1983). *Reconstructing argumentative discourse.* Tuscaloosa and London: The University of Alabama Press.

VanLehn, K. (1985). *Theory reform caused by an argumentation tool* (Technical Report ISL-11). Xerox Palo Alto Research Center.

Veerman, A., Andriessen, J. E. B., & Kanselaar, G. (1999). Collaborative learning through computer-mediated argumentation. In C. Hoadly & J. Roschelle (Eds.), *Proceedings of the third conference on Computer Supported Collaborative Learning* (pp. 640-650). Palo Alto, California: Stanford University.

Walton, D. G. (1996). *Argumentation schemes for presumptive reasoning.* Mahwah, NJ: Lawrence Erlbaum Associates.

Wigmore, H. J. A. (1913). *The principles of judicial proof as given by logic, psychology, and General experience and illustrated in judicial trials.* Boston: Little Brown (2nd Edition, 1931. Reprint 2000, William S. Hein & Co., Inc.).

2 A Cognitive Framework for Cooperative Problem Solving with Argument Visualization

Jan M. van Bruggen, Henny P. A. Boshuizen and Paul A. Kirschner

Open University of the Netherlands, the Netherlands

2.1 Introduction

The chapters in this volume bear witness to the common belief of the authors that visualizing argumentation facilitates a number of processes that their users, professionals or learners, engage in. These processes, we surmise, can often be typified as cooperative[1] problem solving and there are many good reasons to assume that visualizing argumentation can facilitate this process. Unfortunately, there are other good reasons to assume that the reverse may occur as well. Argument visualization can quite effectively hinder problem solving. In this chapter we try to reach a better understanding of this "mixed blessing" of argument visualization and to formulate a number of recommendations on how to use it more profitably.

In order to do so, we first establish the relation between problem solving and argumentation. Most problems that we encounter in school books are fairly well structured; most problems that we encounter in "real life" are not. The solution of these so called *ill-structured problems* takes the form of an argument based on informal reasoning. Consider the problem of how to increase crop production in the Soviet

---

[1]   In this chapter we use the terms cooperative and collaborative interchangeably, that is we make no distinction between the situation where all problem solvers have the same task (collaborative setting) and the situation where there is a division of labor between the problem solvers (cooperative setting). In our multiple agent – multiple representation perspective we assume however that parts of the problem solving activities will be not be executed by all participants.

Union.[2] Although it is possible to generate a number of possible solutions to this problem, there are no solutions that will guarantee success and none of the proposed solutions can be tested and, based upon this testing, be revised. Therefore, it is not possible to prove that a solution will, or will not work. The problem solver can only present what (s)he considers to be good reasons and arguments to convince others that there are good reasons and arguments to accept the claim that the given solution is the best possible one. Unfortunately the criteria on which to evaluate these reasons may vary from person to person.

Based on analyses of (urban) planning and design methods and practices, and independent of the psychological research of those days, Horst Rittel – a mathematician and statistician who worked on developing socioeconomic prediction models and evaluating sociological field research – emphasized that the 'wicked' nature of problems in these domains requires an argumentative approach to problems solving. He saw the solution process as inherently argumentative, in which the problem solver continually raises questions and argues with him/herself and others over the advantages and disadvantages of alternative responses. What he called *wicked problems* look very similar to ill-structured problems, but Rittel added an important aspect to the problem context: there are many stakeholders whose views on the problem may vary (Rittel and Webber, 1973). In psychological terms, Rittel described a problem solving context where multiple actors, having different representations of the problem, are trying to solve the problem. This then brings us to the question how multiple agents, using multiple representations can collaborate to solve problems and how visualizing argumentation fits into this problem solving process.

There are several reasons to assume that collaborative problem solving will only work if the problem solvers succeed in coordinating their problem representations, their data, and the operators that they use. We describe general problem states through which solvers move back and forth until they reach a common solution and identify the different cognitive and communicative demands of each of the states. We argue that visualization of argumentation can facilitate problem solving in a number of ways. First, argumentation visualization is a means of explicating and sharing representations among the actors which may help them to build the partially shared representations that may be essential for collaborative problem solving (Alpay, Giboin, and Dieng, 1998). Second, it may help the problem solvers maintain focus, one of the success factors of collaborative problem solving. Finally, it may help problem solvers maintain

---

2   For those readers who are younger than the authors, the Soviet Union is the former northern Eurasian empire (1917/22–1991) stretching from the Baltic and Black seas to the Pacific Ocean and, in its final years, consisting of 15 Soviet Socialist Republics such as Armenia, Belarus, Estonia, Georgia, Kazakhstan, Latvia, Lithuania, Russia, Ukraine, and Uzbekistan. It had a centralized plan economy (5-year plans) that was known for its non-ability to meet the goals of the plans, especially with respect to agriculture.

consistency, accuracy and plausibility – three important aspects on which solutions are evaluated (Alpay, Giboin, and Dieng, 1998).

In this chapter we assume that the argumentation visualization is achieved through a computerized tool – hence the term Computer Supported Argument Visualization (CSAV). In describing CSAV we distinguish (see Suthers, 2001) representational *notation* (that defines the objects and relations that can be used), representational *tools* (the software that implements the notation) and the *artifacts* produced using the tool. Notation and tool not only define what can be expressed and how easy it is to express it, they also influence the interaction between the users and the support the system can offer to maintain focus, maintain consistency, increase plausibility and increase accuracy. We describe some characteristics of external representations that result from the notation and the tools and how they relate to the demands of the problem solving stages identified.

2.2 Problem Solving, Reasoning and Argumentation

CSAV is primarily used for the solution of ill-structured (Reitman, 1965; Newell and Simon, 1972; Selvin: chapter 7) as opposed to well-structured problems. *Well-structured problems* have (1) complete and unambiguous problem specifications; (2) clear criteria and procedures to evaluate whether a solution has been reached; (3) all of the knowledge necessary to solve the problem represented in one or more problem spaces with at least one problem space that can represent the initial state, the intermediate states and the goal state; and (4) an associated set of operators that can change a problem state into another state. Examples of these types of problems are the Tower of Hanoi, Tic-Tac-Toe, theorem proving, and traditional school book problems. The problem solving process for such well-structured problems often follows a progression through three distinct stages, namely *orientation*, where a problem representation is constructed, *solution*, where operators are applied to transform the problem state into a goal state, and *evaluation* where the solution and use of operators are evaluated.

Ill-structured problems, in contrast, (1) have an ambiguous and incomplete problem specification; (2) lack clear-cut criteria to evaluate whether a solution has been reached implying that there are no stopping rules; (3) make use of several potential information sources that may be used to represent problem spaces although it is unclear which ones should be used and how they should be integrated; and (4) have neither a complete enumeration of applicable operators nor a predetermined path from initial state to goal state. Examples of ill-structured problems are music composition, design tasks, planning tasks and management problems. When solving ill-structured problems, problem solvers do not progress in a linear way through the stages described, but rather work on partial solutions, return to refine their problem representation, jump to evaluation, revise criteria, et cetera. Visser (1990), for example, describes the actual activities of designers who themselves report their work as following a preconceived plan, as a data-driven opportunistic process.

To solve an ill-structured problem, problem solvers still have to represent the problem, define constraints, apply operators and evaluate proposed solutions, but since none of these are given, they first have to draw upon other knowledge sources to determine relevant or beneficial representations, constraints, operators and criteria (problem structuring) and then justify both to themselves and to others the decisions made. It is exactly for this reason that solving ill-structured problems is an argumentative process requiring informal and not logical or mathematical reasoning (alone). This informal reasoning requires the application of an argumentation structure consisting, minimally, of a claim with support (e.g., evidential reasoning). Evaluation of the arguments cannot be in terms of whether the argument is right or wrong, but requires the evaluator to make use of other criteria such as perceived plausibility (acceptability) of the claim, perceived support that the reason offers the claim, and the quality of the argumentation judged by taking counter-arguments into account. Here, as well as in the statement of problem constraints, individuals may differ in the evaluation of relevancy or importance (Voss, Wiley, and Sandak, 1999).

In a series of investigations Voss and his colleagues (Voss, Greene, Post, and Penner, 1983; Voss, 1991; Voss, Blais, Means, and Greene, 1986) applied a combination of Newell and Simon's information processing model (1972) and informal reasoning to problems in such diverse fields as social sciences, medicine, mathematics and foreign policy. Voss et al (1983) analyzed the protocols of experts trying to find a way to increase crop production in the Soviet Union. The problem solving process was decomposed into a *problem representation stage* where the subjects formulated the nature of the problem and a *problem solution phase*, where they solved the problem. In their analyses, Voss et al. distinguished between a *problem solving structure* with associated problem solving operators and a *reasoning structure* with a set of (informal) reasoning operators. Examples of problem solving operators are "state constraint", "state subproblem", "state solution", "evaluate". Examples of reasoning operators are verbal actions: "state argument", "state assertion", "state fact", "state reason", "state outcome", "state conclusion" or "state qualifier" – and operators such as "compare/contrast", and "elaborate/clarify". Note, that the reasoning operators are domain specific. The analysis of the reasoning of a person who studied a juridical case used operators like "state claim for defense", "state fact favoring defendant", et cetera.

This line of research studied experts and novices who *individually* solved ill-structured problems. The analysis of their thinking-aloud protocols used one set of reasoning operators characteristic of the domain of expertise of the problem solvers. The model underlying this research can be described as a single agent, single representation model. As we will show, this model needs to be broadened to support situations in which there are more problem solvers who do not bring the same representations and operators to the problem: such a model implies having multiple agents with multiple representations.

Interesting enough, the idea of multiple agents with multiple representations was implicit in the seminal perspective on problem solving that was originated by Horst Rittel who coined the term *wicked problem*. The kind of problems that "planners deal with – societal problems – are inherently different from the problems that scientists and perhaps some classes of engineers deal with. Planning problems are inherently wicked" (Rittel and Webber, 1984 p. 135-136). Rittel and Webber formulated a number of characteristics of such wicked problems, namely that they have no definitive formulation – the information needed to understand the problem depends on one's idea for solving it, that possible solutions cannot be tested and revised – one obviously cannot "try out" a trajectory for a freeway and that they have no stopping rule – "the planner terminates work on a wicked problem, not for reasons inherent in the "logic" of the problem. He stops for considerations that are external to the problem: he runs out of time, or money, or patience". "Solutions to wicked problems are not true-or-false, but good or bad." (op. cit., pp. 136-139).

Wicked problems are composed of an interlocking set of issues and constraints, rather than a definitive statement of the problem itself. These problems are often not fully understood until a solution has been developed. There are many stakeholders who have expertise in different aspects of the problem to be solved, making effective problem solving more a social process than a cognitive one. Getting the right answer is less important than having the stakeholders accept the solution that emerges. The description of a wicked problem is not without implicit, often political, assumptions: Is the trajectory of a freeway a problem of creating a transport infrastructure, an economic problem, or an ecological problem? According to Rittel, wicked problems are inherently multi-disciplinary, involving stakeholders from different backgrounds, and there is no monopoly on expertise. He used the provocative term "symmetry of ignorance" to describe this state of affairs. Solving wicked problems thus involves different actors (stakeholders) that entertain different problem representations, and none of the stakeholders dominates the problem definition or structure. To deal with these issues, Rittel developed a methodology called Issue Based Information Systems that tried to ensure that all stakeholders could put forward their issues. Essential to the IBIS method is the absence of premature problem structuring: the argumentation structure consists of a number of topics (issues) and positions that the stakeholders hold with respect to these issues and there are no means in the method to, for instance, create problem decompositions. Note that IBIS contains none of the domain dependent operators that Voss used to describe the problem solving behavior of experts and novices. Several CSAV environments were inspired by Rittel's IBIS method, including gIBIS, QuestMap and Mifflin (see Chapter 1 by Buckingham Shum on the roots of CSAV).

Understanding the role of CSAV environments in the problem solving contexts that Rittel sketches forces us to rethink how informal reasoning and argumentation proceeds if more agents from different backgrounds enter the scene. Somehow their different views, knowledge and operators have to be coordinated. This is what we address in the subsequent sections.

2.2.1   Coordination Problems for Multiple Agents

The amount and kind of knowledge and skills that must be coordinated between agents are the sources of problems that make cooperation problematic. Superficially, it may seem that involving more people in problem solving increases the chance that someone has the knowledge to solve the problem. Unfortunately, incomplete understanding and misunderstanding between agents are the more likely outcome, especially if the agents have varying levels of expertise within a single domain or if they come from different backgrounds. In these cases the agents will have different *problem representations* manifesting itself in different data, formats and operators that they apply. Agents may also differ in the *criteria* they apply to evaluate solutions and the arguments that underpin claims.

Misunderstandings due to differences in representation are not easy to avoid, especially between experts who have spent thousands of hours mastering their fields and novices whom they may be working with. Discussions between experts and novices have been shown to be notoriously difficult (Bromme, Nückles, and Rambow, 1999). Specific issues cannot be explained at the required level of understanding to a novice, and when the expert tries to explain more, the novice is overwhelmed. This is not only due to the nature of the knowledge to be conveyed, but also because experts tend not to be able to "tune in" to the level of novice understanding. This is not only true when dealing with very different fields like law and microbiology where one person can be an expert in one field and know absolutely nothing about another. Boshuizen and Tabachneck-Schijf (1998) found that cooperation problems also occur when different experts have fields of expertise that partially overlap and partially differ in content, concerns and/or paradigm. They call this "distributed or multiple representations in multiple agents" and define it as the circumstance where multiple human or artificial agents have dissimilar representations about an object, person, interaction or situation. They describe how representations may vary along the dimensions of *data*, *format* and *operators*.

When people think differently about an object or have different perspectives on it, their representations vary along the *data* dimension. Data is what we call 'content' in everyday life. Since the content mastered by an expert is vast and highly integrated, it is virtually impossible for a novice to learn that which is relevant for solving a certain problem. This is compounded by the fact that even when two people have mastered the same concepts, they still might not understand each other. Different people can have different perceptions or have different prototypes of the same concept. This is painfully apparent in the differences exhibited between the understanding of concepts via "real physics" and "lay physics", a phenomenon often labeled *misconception*. Other differences stem from different domain-specific representations: stakeholders of a wicked problem often represent problems in different ways, thus a problem in the production of a lawn mower is a logistics problem for the planner, a design problem for the industrial designer, a personnel problem for the human resources manager and a financial problem for the accountant. Recognizing such differences at the conceptual level can often take more time, result in more surprises and be more of a nuisance than is the case when people entirely lack each other's concepts. Different contents of representations can also be the source of many misunderstandings, for example the scheduling of a meeting between an English and a Dutch delegation at "half ten", which in Dutch means 9:30.

A second dimension along which representations may vary is *format*, for example when one representation is propositional and the other visual (e.g., mathematical notation vs. Venn diagrams). Note that argument visualization is a means of forcing the use of the same format, or "surface representation" as Stenning (1998) calls it, on different people. Stenning points out that using the same surface representation may help to unravel differences in conceptual structures.

The third dimension reflects that representations may differ regarding the *operators* applied. Differences along this dimension may appear unexpectedly and may lead to conflicts because one person thinks that the other's reasons are "unfair". Boshuizen and Tabachneck-Schijf (1998) give an example of the use of different sets of operators: a legal approach toward solving a misunderstanding between people versus using more common-sense ideas about solving it.

Another source of misunderstanding stems from differences in the *criteria* that agents use to evaluate solutions and arguments. While a blueprint for a containment construction may convince engineers that the container is an acceptable solution to a environmental problem, it is not likely an environmentalist will accept this as a solution. Differences in criteria between agents can be so fundamental that they lead to the complete rejection of specific approaches to problem solving or to certain reasoning patterns. An example is an abortion rights activist who considers life to begin at birth and a member of the clergy who considers life to begin at conception, if not earlier.

Data, formats, and operators can form extended procedures or lines of reasoning (macro-operators) which are needed for problem solving. We define such macro-operators as sequences of operators learned during past (problem solving) experience which can be shared by domain area experts (i.e., mathematical procedures, juridical reasoning). Argumentation strategies for a specific line of reasoning reflect common values and goals for solving problems in a specific domain and the role of argumentation therein. Scientific researchers, for example, attempt to *achieve consensus* based upon the exchange of arguments that are open for critical debate while lawyers try to *win a conflict* by convincing a ruling authority that their claims should be honored. However, even within a discipline, striking differences can be found in argumentation. More formal reasoning styles, for example, are tightly linked to scientific paradigms and are often not accepted by scientists with a different background.

The second author for this chapter recalls a situation where two different macro-operators from two scientific domains led to utter misunderstanding. While at university, she participated in a seminar on psycholinguistics and text-processing for psychology and linguistics students. The two groups had a hard time learning the relevance of each others' argumentation structures. The psychologists could only be convinced by hard empirical evidence and wanted experiments to judge theoretical claims, while the linguists were masters in generating examples and counter-examples such as Chomsky's master sentence "Colorless green ideas sleep furiously". With these examples, they evaluated the claims of linguistic theories. It took several sessions and a mini-lecture by the professor before the two groups of students could begin to understand the reasons for the mutual misunderstandings. It took even longer to learn to appreciate that the example and counter-example argumentation worked very well for linguistic theories, but that empirical argumentation was more valid for text-processing and understanding.

What this suggests, is that there are serious coordination problems when dealing with multiple agent, multiple representation situations. In the next section we try to formulate the coordination needs as part of the broader cognitive and communicative demands of collaborative problem solving. Before detailing these demands, we define a number of important preconditions and make a distinction between three stages of problem solving through which problem solvers move back and forth.

2.3   Cognitive and Communicative Demands of Collaborative Problem Solving

2.3.1   Preconditions

Before specifying cognitive and communicative demands put on CSAV environments we spell out a number of more or less social preconditions underlying collaborative problem solving, i.e. certain minimal levels of *shared understanding, accountability* and *trust* that must exist before any collaborative problem solving may occur. For other cognitive and social factors affecting facilitated group problem solving we refer the reader to Al Selvin's contribution to this volume.

The first precondition is a minimum of *shared understanding*. Shared understanding is the state where two or more people have equivalent expectations about a situation, that is that their explanations of the situation and their predictions for how it might develop are the same. In the lawn mower example, the agents share the understanding that there is a problem which they have to solve together and which they can solve together, namely that a lawn mower needs to be manufactured. Before they can tackle the problem of how best to manufacture (and market) it, they must first develop a minimum shared understanding of how the problem can be represented and which operators and reasoning schemes are admissible for solving the problem (as in the example of the linguistic vs psychological explanation).

A second precondition is *accountability*. Accountability is the social mechanism underlying responsible behavior between people; e.g., that one team member does not plagiarize a fellow team member, take the credit for work done by another team member or work to the disadvantage of a fellow team member. This precondition does not imply that agents necessarily have the same goals. Even in situations of adversarial collaboration (Cohen, Cash, and Muller, 2000) parties adhere to standards for exchanging and sharing views and information.

A final, but also very important factor is *trust*. Trust is the perceived ability to rely on the character, ability, strength, or truth of someone or something and is the deciding factor in a social process that results in a decision by an individual to accept or reject a risk based on the expectation that another party will meet the performance requirements (Zolin, Fruchter, and Levitt, 2002).

2.3.2   Problem Solving States

Research on problem solving distinguishes three general states in problem solving (Newell and Simon, 1972) namely an *orientation state* to determine what the problem is, a *problem solving state* which entails the actual problem solving process, and an *evaluation state* which determines both whether the problem has been solved and whether the "right" problem has been solved. Note that each state needs information that is often lacking in ill-structured or wicked problems. In such problems, the problem description and constraints are ambiguous at best; the applicable operators are not given, and the criteria to evaluate solutions are absent. This straight-forward, linear process through the three stages is only possible when solving well-structured problems using well-known algorithms. When dealing with ill-structured problems, problem solvers move back and forth between orientation, problem solving and evaluation. Trying out a partial solution (or rather a mental model of it), for example, may help the problem solvers to better understand the problem and may lead to adding or refining constraints and criteria (Norman, 1998). Visser (1990) described the activities of software designers as belonging to a data-driven and opportunistic control strategy rather than as following a plan or routine as reported by the problem solvers themselves. Although Goel and Pirolli (1992) found a somewhat more linear progress through sub-states of the problem solving state, they describe the control strategy as "limited-commitment-mode control" which allows the designer to put work on an unfinished design module on hold at any time and redirect attention to other modules or tasks.

In an *orientation state*, participants structure the problem. In this state they clarify the problem description, the constraints and the criteria for solution and evaluation. Participants ask themselves whether the actual problem is the one stated (surface level) or whether the "real" problem lies deeper, hiding behind the problem as it appears to them. Participants also need to clarify, and often state themselves, the boundary conditions and constraints, the context(s) the problem is embedded and who the "owners" of and "stakeholders" in the problem are, and so forth. Using the results of intermediate and partial solutions, the problem solvers will review and revise their understanding of the problem, its constraints and the criteria to evaluate a solution. In the *solution state* participants plan how to solve the problem and then try to execute the solution in a more or less systematic way. As previously described, this is often a data-driven process with a loose control strategy that lets problem solvers move back and forth between partial solutions, problem structuring and evaluation. In the *evaluation state* both process and outcome will be checked, i.e. the participants not only check the correct application of the operators, but they also determine whether the "problem as intended" has been solved. Since there is no clear-cut criterion to evaluate solutions or the correct application of operators in ill-structured problems, the problem solvers have to define, review and revise their criteria.

The orientation and solving phases of the process seem the most crucial for collaborative problem solving because the representation of problems which are made in the orientation phase is closely linked to the type of acceptable argumentative reasoning that can be used in the solution phase. In multidisciplinary teams, differences of interpretation of what the problem is and of what the problem solving strategy should be may lead to great difficulties if the different viewpoints do not converge. This is the point – in our opinion – where argumentation is most important and where the design and use of CSAV plays the greatest role. Cognitive and communicative demands vary across the states of problem solving (Duffy, Dueber, and Hawley, 1998) and these variations have important consequences for the design of CSAV environments. In their first efforts to structure a problem, the problem solvers often have different or only partially overlapping representations of the problem and to work on at least a minimal shared understanding of the problem. The communication between the problem solvers is relatively unfocused and issue-based, leaving room for them to explore interpretations of the problem, the constraints, and so forth (Duffy et al., 1998).

Others question whether the use of argument visualization tools such as external representations in this stage will facilitate the problem solving process, and indeed the contributions to this volume show different opinions and practices. Van Gelder, on the one hand, avoids using argument visualization in the early stage of problem representation while Selvin, on the other, starts using visualizations immediately, which has the additional advantage of creating a record of the problem structuring activities. Whatever the preferences, if external representations are used at this stage, then their representation of the argumentation has to be non-committal, i.e. the representational notation must allow expression of different perspectives on the problem.

One might also question whether the notations used to express the solutions should also be non-committal. Voss and his fellow researchers (Voss and Post, 1988; Voss et al., 1999) hold that since problem solvers use domain-dependent operators and macro-operators when solving problems, the solution process carried out should not be hampered by representational notations that lack such expressive power; a view that encourages the use of domain-specific representational notations and discourages the design and use of generic tools. But there is a trade-off here. In a situation where a number of agents are involved and where we want to use external representations as a means of mediating the problem solving process, the representation has to be such that it can be, in Selvin's words, "put in the middle". This requires that the representation be sufficiently understandable to all actors, and thus not *too* domain-dependent.

A direction towards a resolution of this apparent contradiction can be found in work by Alpay, Giboin and Dieng (1998) who – in studying how interdisciplinary teams of engineers and psychologists used multiple representations to analyze traffic accidents – identified a number of characteristics and dimensions of these representations. One dimensions is a *permanent – temporary* axis, where permanent representations correspond to systems, procedures and models that the experts use on a regular basis in standard situations. A second dimension is a *shared – unshared* axis, where, for example, a simple functional model of the driver involved in an accident was shared by engineers and psychologists, while a richer version was only shared between the psychologists in the team. These two dimensions are extremely important, since permanent and shared representations seem to be the core of the representational coordination! If we are to design and develop powerful CSAV environments, we cannot neglect that along with the permanent, shared representations, CSAV environments should also allow for temporary, unshared representations. Another important coordination mechanism that they found relates to the distinction between *control representation* and *topic representation*. Control representations are representations that guide operations on topic representations such as models, phase decompositions, et cetera. Selvin (see Chapter 7) makes similar distinctions and formulates requirements such as *preservation* (i.e., maintain information as well as conceptual frameworks), *rigor* (i.e., support rigorous methods) and *repeatability* (i.e., afford easily reproducible methods) all of which hint at common structures and control representations. Note that Selvin's requirements not only stipulate the re-use of structures (e.g., tasks, Toulmin structures, stages), but also the definition and representation of emerging structures as well. He provides examples of support built into the tools such as using databases to maintain consistency and the continuity. He also formulates relevant requirements. His reframing requirement can be seen as a means to (re)build consistency and plausibility. We should, however, keep in mind that his description of operators and requirements have been generated on the basis of studies in a professional context, i.e. with experts and experts are known to have available more, accurate representations which they can switch between with great flexibility.

The style of communication during solution formulation is more *focused* and *topic*-based (see van Gelder: Chapter 5, Duffy et al., 1998, Goel and Pirolli, 1992). The capability to maintain focus is one of the major success factors in collaborative problem solving (Erkens, 1997; Kanselaar, Erkens and Jaspers, 2001; Barron, 2000). Maintaining focus and coherence is often problematic, especially in asynchronous discussions where discussions tend to get scattered and loose coherence (Herring, 1999).

Table 2.1: The demands of the problem solving states.

Problem solving states	Cognitive demands	Communicative demands
Orientation	Problem Representation Constraints Problem structuring Establish shared representations	Issue-based communication Brainstorm Build trust Establish common ground

Solving	Apply macro-operators to
	   produce solutions
	Use topic and control
	   representations
	Maintain coherence
	Maintain accuracy
	Maintain plausibility
		Topic-based discussion
		Maintain common ground
		Maintain focus
		Conflict detection and
		resolution
		Knowledge negotiation

Evaluation	Evaluate solutions Evaluate constraints Evaluate process	Negotiate criteria

Evaluating whether the problem as intended has been solved, whether the operators that have been used have also been applied correctly and whether the constraints have been met is a continuous process when solving ill-structured problems which will not only lead the participants back to the solution states but also to reconsidering the evaluation criteria as well. A strategy often applied in this oscillation between solution and evaluation is "*satisficing*" where the problem solvers repeatedly evaluate their (partial) solutions against the constraints, leading to continual refinement. Solutions often seem to emerge more or less effortlessly out of this process (Voss et al., 1999). An important set of criteria to evaluate the argumentative underpinnings of proposed solutions (Alpay, Giboin, and Dieng, 1998) are those characteristics which are used to achieve representation-management goals, namely, maintaining consistency, accuracy and plausibility of the representations (compare to Voss' criteria to evaluate solutions). Making argumentation explicit and easy to inspect is one of the stronger points of argument visualization.

Before we consider how CSAV environments might help to meet the cognitive and communicative demands of the three stages of the problem solving process we recap them in Table 2.1. In the following sections we will show how the cognitive and communicative demands of collaborative problem solving may be translated into requirements on CSAV environments. We focus on representational features of CSAV environments.

2.4 Representational and Communicative Features of CSAV Environments

2.4.1 CSAV Environments

Many present day CSAV environments contain features which support the demands formulated in the previous sections, although we know of no system that has features to support all of them. The systems themselves are of varying nature (from industrial strength to research prototype) and have to serve different users and different purposes (from product design in multi-nationals to touchy problems in local government and community to collaborative learning in schools). There are, for example, systems and methodologies like Compendium (Selvin et al, 2001) that are used to support problem solving in business and public administration settings. Such settings define a context where professionals – experts in their areas – solve problems and where a number of requirements formulated by Alpay, Giboin and Dieng (1998) apply. Selvin (see Chapter 7) describes how an experienced facilitator implementing a methodology and operating the accompanying software tools can support expert problem solving. He specifies several requirements that professional problem solving puts on CSAV.

In contrast to this synchronous, facilitated mode of operation to support problem solving by experts, there are argumentative Computer Supported Collaborative Learning (CSCL) systems are to be operated by students, novices or beginning experts, who *learn* how to solve problems using argumentative devices (see Kanselaar et al.: Chapter 3). Their activities are not facilitated but are – at most – moderated by a teacher. This puts a number of additional demands on the functions, the interface and the representations that are used. According to Kolodner and Guzdial (1996) CSCL interfaces are designed for learners, i.e. they emphasize *structure* for novices who need guidance to succeed and *flexibility* for students with diverse needs. CSCL systems also offer (multiple) representations that lend themselves to extrapolation and discussion. Finally, CSCL software can support different logistical functions in that they can be used synchronously or asynchronously for either local or remote collaboration. They further note that CSCL systems can fulfill a number of *roles*, namely: (1) promoting inquiry and sense-making; (2) facilitating knowledge building by providing a forum for collaboratively presenting arguments, raising learning issues, and reaching consensus on new knowledge; (3) keeping records and/or functioning as an external memory; (4) enabling communication with distant communities; (5) promoting reflection of alternative perspectives, solutions, and critiques; and (6) supporting teacher planning and implementation of collaborative activities. Except for the support of teacher planning, these seem to be roles that may apply to CSAV environments in general.

The introduction and widespread use of CSAV is expected to lead to beneficial changes in the communication between actors as several chapters in this volume discuss. Van Gelder's chapter is called "Enhancing deliberation through computer-supported argument visualization". He regards deliberation to be a collective activity and describes how the use of argument visualization changes the nature of the debate in discussions in such a way that consensus building is stimulated. Selvin, in discussing media and tools, states that "the medium should serve the purposes of enhancing (or creating) dialogue". Similar observations can be made in the literature on CSCL where the effects of the use of external representations of argument on the learning process are sought in changes that occur in the dialogue between students (Suthers, 1999, 2001; Veerman, 2000; Veerman, Andriessen and Kanselaar, 1999; Kanselaar: Chapter 3). The cognitive demands that collaborative problem solving in multidisciplinary teams put on CSAV can be described as a means to explicitly share and coordinate basic representations, operators, (multiple) problem representations, macro-operators and constraints. Cognitive demands are met by implementing system functionalities to create representations, for example tools to make argument maps and to share these representations by putting them in a joint workspace or discussion group. CSAV systems also have to support the communication between actors. The functionalities offered to support communication can be as basic as the exchange of text-based messages, or as advanced as directing participants to issues on which they have conflicting opinions and initiating conflict resolution.

2.4.2   Characteristics of Argument Representations

CSAV environments aim to support collaborative problem solving by making shared external representations of their argumentation available to the problem solvers. These external representations are construed using a limited set of objects and relations and adhering to certain rules on their use and combination. In accordance with Suthers (2001), we distinguish between *representational notations* for representing the objects and relations, *representational tools* that implement the notation, and *representational artifacts*, i.e. the products constructed with the tools.

The *representational notation* contains the primitives – the objects and relations that can be used in the representation of the argumentation and the rules that govern their use. Such a notation may define objects like claim, data, warrant, as well as the type of relation between these objects and associated features like strength of belief, hierarchy, or causality. Finally, the notation specifies which combinations of objects and relations are allowed. It can stipulate, for example, that data can be related to one or more hypotheses and that no relation is allowed between hypotheses. Before such a representational notation can be used it must be (and is) implemented in a piece of software, the *representational tool*. Several design decisions are then made to implement the notation such as the choice of symbols used to denote the objects and the relations and tools used to handle them. A decision, for example, needs to be made with respect to what would happen if the user (following the example used before) tried to relate two hypotheses? Would the system allow this, ignore it, or ask/force the user to remove the relation? Functionalities can be added to the tool (e.g., focusing and zooming) and future usage considerations are taken into account (e.g., if the tool will be used in a synchronous or asynchronous setting, whether users will work alone or make use of joint workspaces). Using the representational notation embedded in the representational tools, the users create the *representational artifacts*: the argument maps, Toulmin structures, evidential diagrams, et cetera.

Many of the demands formulated here and in Selvin's contribution to this volume pertain to the representational notation and how it is implemented. Relevant here is:

1   The *ontology* of a representation which defines what can be seen in the domain represented and how it will be seen. The ontology "refers to the <u>content</u>, to the objects and relations one uses to represent a domain, not so much to the symbols by which objects and relations are denoted" (De Jong et al., 1998, p.11). Selvin refers to this characteristic as the "depth of palette" and indicates that having a smaller set of objects and relations can be an advantage. The development of the Belvédère environment (Suthers, Weiner, Connelly, and Paolucci, 1995; Suthers, 1999) corroborates these observations. Earlier versions of the Belvédère environment were developed as a tool to represent the argumentation in scientific inquiry and had a rich set of objects and relations. Learners, however, were disturbed by the richness of the representation and were often lured into off-task discussion. Later versions of Belvédère have a smaller set of those objects and relations that learners can concentrate on. Alpay, Giboin and Dieng (1998) as well as Selvin (see Chapter 7) indicate that the ontology of CSAV environments needs more than primitive objects and relations. It also requires complex structures such as the components of a task or a Toulmin argument structure that can be used as frames to represent interrelated data or as process control structures. These authors also stress the importance of re-use of these structures, thus in Selvin's terms enabling rigor and repeatability.

2   Closely related to the ontology is the *perspective* or view. This term is multivalent, and can be related to views on systems from, for instance, a functional, a behavioral or a physical perspective (see De Jong et al, 1998 for examples). We have chosen to follow Stahl (2001) and use the term to describe the different conceptualizations of a problem. One stakeholder, for example, may have an environmental perspective on a problem, whereas another may conceptualize the nature of the problem as technological or economic. Differences between these perspectives correspond to differences between "conceptual representations" (Stenning, 1998), that is between the underlying conceptual systems as is the case in wave versus particle theories of the nature of light.

3   A third characteristic is *specificity*, defined by Stenning and Oberlander (1995, p. 98) as "the demand of a system of representation that information in some class be specified in any interpretable representation". The specificity of a representation may require disambiguation: we cannot, in a diagram, represent that an object is "next to" another object, it has to be represented at a particular locality. Thus, graphical representations limit abstraction and aid processibility of the information. We interpret the term, again following Suthers (2001), as the categorical choice that the representational notation forces us to make.

4   Another characteristic of external representation, and one which is strongly related to the representational notation, is the *precision* or accuracy with which the representation reflects the underlying model. In science and mathematics this is related to quantitative vs. qualitative models. In other domains it will reflect the nature of the objects (e.g., differentiating between a hypothesis and a prediction) and their relations (e.g., making various relation types available). Obviously the precision of a representation is limited by the ontology: A limited set of objects and relations does not allow detailed, precise statements in most domains. It is difficult to draw a line here for determining how specific a CSAV environment should be, although Alpay, Giboin and Dieng (1998) point to a number of interesting directions that can help.

5   The last characteristic of external representations is its *modality*, the form of expression used for displaying information such as text, animation, graphs, et cetera. The modality corresponds with the way the representational notation is implemented in the representational tools. Thus notational systems with the same set of underlying concepts and relations (the ontology) may be expressed as graphs, hypertexts or feature-comparison matrices. Suthers (1999, 2001) has drawn attention to the effects that these different notations may have on the learner discourse and ultimately on learning. As he points out, these effects may even be greater if learners operate in a joint workspace. Experimental versions of Belvédère now offer graphical, text (outline) and matrix views.

Each representational notation will offer a restricted view of a domain and will make it easier to express certain aspects of the domain as well as certain types of argument that can be expressed. Belvédère, for example, supports evidential relations between data and hypotheses. The user may indicate that data is consistent or inconsistent with a particular hypothesis, or that data undercuts the support of other data to a hypothesis. There is no way in which data can directly *refute* either other data or a hypothesis. One may criticize the Belvédère coach for not correctly handling refutation (Chryssafidou, 1999), but that misses the point. Direct refutation is outside of the scope of the underlying representational notation. Ultimately, the representational notation determines what the actors can argue about in the CSAV environment and enables or limits its functionality. As an example of the latter: there is no way that a system can detect conflicts between data in the representation or between the beliefs of actors if these are not represented.

2.4.3 Support of Problem Solving States

We have identified three states in problem solving and identified a number of demands for each state. Few environments support (and afford) different types of communication and different representations in the different problem solving states. ACT (Duffy et al., 1998) and CROCODILE (Miao, Holst, Holmer, Fleschutz, and Zentel, 2000b) are environments that support problem based learning according to a problem solving process scenario. Most environments do not model the problem solving process and offer only generic support.

For *orientation* we identified problem structuring as the most important cognitive demand. The communicative demands pertain to communication style (issue-based) and the creation of common ground. Some writers (like van Gelder: Chapter 5) tend not to use external representations in the first stage of problem solving, or to confine themselves to non-committal representations. The wicked problem perspective in a method like IBIS, for example, encourages the user to avoid early commitment to a particular view on a problem. The Reason!Able environment is an example of a notation that is not committed to a particular domain or perspective. This does not, however, mean that IBIS or Reason!Able are completely neutral. Although they allow representation of several types of views on the problem, they are not without bias against particular views. It is difficult, for example, to express mathematical or logical problem representations, or argumentation for that matter, using these representational notations (see Horn: Chapter 8). Even if different perspectives on a problem can be represented without bias against particular perspectives, it may prove difficult to translate this representational notation into a software implementation that supports specific perspectives as well as comparisons between the different perspectives into the solving stage (Stahl, 2001). As Selvin (see Chapter 7) points out, most applications evade the whole issue by offering a limited set of objects and relations. Other routes that can be taken – following Alpay, Giboin and Dieng – are the creation of minimal shared representations including control representations.

The cognitive demands for the solution state concentrate on the application of operators on the one hand and the demands on *representation management* on the other. The communicative demands pertain to style (topic-based), maintaining focus and common ground, and conflict detection and resolution. CSAV environments assist problem solvers by allowing the establishment and management of shared representations such as partial models. These shared representations can be part of the representational notation of a tool to support the process. Environments which allow the definition of these structures during the problem solving process and their incorporation in the representational notation are sparse. In this volume Mifflin seems to be the only tool capable of doing that; other CSAV environments are dependent on predefined representational notations. As to the content of the representations there is little research available. Research in design rationale (Buckingham Shum and Hammond, 1994) as well as CSCL environments (Suthers, 1999) suggests that a mismatch between the representational notation and the task can have detrimental effects on performance. How to create a good match is less clear.

More structured representations can play an important role in helping meet a second demand, namely the *maintenance of coherence* (and strongly related to this *maintenance of focus*). On a basic level, making argumentation visible will show users whether there is a coherent structure in the argumentation at all. Having this structure available offers problem solvers a clear reference for maintaining focus. Control representations such as models, structures, and phases guide *topic representations*, that is they indicate the topic on which the actors should focus. An interesting example of this are the meta-cognitive nodes in CSILE where learners can indicate the type of knowledge or support needed. Other measures to promote coherence found in the CMC-based CSILE/Knowledge Forum environment are the "rise-above notes" that abstract information from a number of subsumed notes and the "knowledge maps" that link one node in the environment to several others (Hewitt, Scardamalia, and Webb, 1997). Other approaches try to increase coherence and consistency by forcing structural relations in the dialogue moves. The Collaboratory Notebook (Edelson and O'Neill, 1994), for example, allows only particular types of response notes to an entry in the discussion (e.g., one cannot react to a hypothesis note with a hypothesis note).

Another demand relates to the *maintenance of plausibility*. Systems such as Reason!Able and Belvédère allow its users to express their strength of belief in the claims and their supporting argumentations. These systems leave it to the user to draw any conclusions with respect to the plausibility of the claim and argumentation structure as a whole. One of the few systems that uses these evaluations to recalculate the plausibility of claims and dependent claims, which may lead to lowering beliefs in claims, is SIBYL (Lee, 1990). Often, systems do not allow individual users to express their beliefs in the claims made, which leads us to consider demands regarding *conflict detection and resolution*, which for obvious reasons presuppose that the opinion of individual actors may be expressed. The CROCODILE environment mentioned previously is one of the few environments that supports the expressing of "degreement" and that actively seeks to detect conflict and initiate conflict resolution (Miao et al., 2000a).

The demands put forward for the evaluation phase boil down to supporting the evaluation of the *appropriateness* of the problem representation (i.e., was it the right problem that was defined/solved?), the state of the constraints (i.e., are all of the constraints satisfied?) and the quality of the process (i.e., were the applied procedures applied correctly?). CSAV environments allow users to express the argumentation underpinning the claim that "Solution X is a satisfactory solution". The evaluation of this claim is related to the representation management goals of maintaining consistency, accuracy and plausibility of the representations (Alpay, Giboin, and Dieng, 1998). As stated, these characteristics of representations are also used as criteria to evaluate proposed solutions.

2.4.4   Summary and Conclusions

The final question to be considered is why features of CSAV environments help (or hinder!) problem solvers to reach their goals. There is an important trade-off with respect to the use of argument visualization techniques. On the one hand there is a "hang" towards specificity and disambiguation. As stated in the introduction to this book, making sense of multi-perspective problems and disparate information sources is a first step towards making a problem coherent and solvable. We need to make sense in order to act. The more specific an argument visualization technique is, the more it allows the users to disambiguate the problem and all of its aspects, the easier it will be to determine what the different perspectives on the problem are and the easier it should be to make sense of it and solve it. On the other hand, the more specific an argument visualization technique is, the more difficult and time-consuming it is to learn to use, the more complex it is to use it and the more room that is left open for not arguing the problem itself, but rather of discussing/arguing about the technique. The evolution of Belvédère offers examples of this dilemma. Suthers (1995) notes that learners are forced by the representational system used in Belvédère to indicate which type of object they add (the specificity of the representation forces disambiguation). This often lead to epistemological discussions between learners that will not and cannot be represented in the evidence maps. Suthers points out that a weaker representational structure could evade the issue, but that this could also obscure the need to discuss these important points. In terms of specificity, a weaker representation would leave room for different (implicit) interpretations of the representation. In subsequent versions of Belvédère the number of objects and especially the number of different types of relations (precision of the representation) were reduced, partly because they were considered redundant, and partly because the detailed level at which relations could be represented seemed to interfere with the task – that is, it caused students to spend a lot of time dealing with non-goal tasks (Suthers, Toth, and Weiner, 1997). There is some evidence from other areas in which collaborative argumentation is used that the representational scheme employed may interfere with task performance. In their review of argumentation-based design rationale methods Buckingham Shum and Hammond (1994) mention studies where issue-based notations sidetracked designers from construction, or where QOC (Questions, Options, Criteria) with its emphasis on stating design alternatives interfered with top-down refinement of design.

A second, and related trade-off is that of the effect of argument visualization on cognitive load (Sweller, 1988; Chandler and Sweller, 1991).

Cognitive load theory holds that information varies on a continuum from low to high in element interactivity (Paas, Renkl, and Sweller, in press) which determines its *intrinsic cognitive load.*. Each element of low element interactivity material can be understood and learned individually without consideration of any other elements. Elements of high element interactivity material can be learned individually, but cannot be understood until all of the elements and their interactions are processed simultaneously. Compare, for example, learning the operations of the 12 function keys in a photo-editing-suite and learning to manipulate a photo with that suite. In intrinsic cognitive load the demands on working memory capacity imposed by element interactivity are intrinsic to the material being learned, and cannot be altered by instructional manipulations.

The manner in which information is presented to learners and the learning activities required of learners can also impose a cognitive load. Where that load is unnecessary and interferes with learning, it is referred to as an *extraneous* or *ineffective cognitive load.* Much instructional material imposes extraneous cognitive load because it was developed without functionally considering the structure of information or cognitive architecture of the learner.

The last form of cognitive load is *germane* or *effective cognitive load*. As is the case with extraneous cognitive load and unlike intrinsic cognitive load, germane cognitive load is influenced by instructional design. The manner in which information is presented to learners and the learning activities required of learners are factors relevant to levels of germane cognitive load. Whereas extraneous cognitive load interferes with learning, germane cognitive load enhances learning. Instead of working memory resources being used to engage in search for example, as occurs when dealing with extraneous cognitive load, germane cognitive load results in those resources being devoted to relevant processes such as schema acquisition and automation.

Intrinsic, extraneous and germane cognitive load are additive in that together, the total load cannot exceed the *working memory resources* available if learning is to occur. Thus, with a given intrinsic cognitive load, the extraneous cognitive load should be minimized and the germane cognitive load should be optimised by instructional design (Sweller, Van Merriënboer, and Paas, 1998). According to cognitive load theory the cognitive load in complex tasks, where the learner has to maintain several information items in working memory, may become so high that it will prevent knowledge formation.

Argument visualizations are external representations that can augment cognitive activity (Pea, 1993) and offer new views (Jonassen, Peck and Wilson, 1999). As pointed out by Duffy and Cunningham (1996) one impact of this view is that "off-loading" basic cognitive demands may permit the learner to attend to higher-level representations. Van Bruggen, Kirschner and Jochems (2002) discuss how research on Belvédère shows that a cognitive off-loading effect is not something that comes naturally with an external representation. On the contrary: characteristics of a representation seem to impose extraneous cognitive load and may lead to activities that do not foster deeper representation of the domain. The characteristics of the representations seem to add to the coordination problem in the environment. Recent research by Veerman (2000) corroborated the review of Veerman and Treasure-Jones (1999) by demonstrating how complex the interactions are between tasks, dialogues, the coordination platform offered by the software environment (e.g. a chat-facility), and the contents of the argument representations produced in the Belvédère environment. The costs of preparing and coordinating representations associated with argument visualization can – if they are too complex and specific – be considerable since the number of information elements has an effect on the load experienced. This is because: (1) learners have to coordinate multiple representations – in Belvédère, for instance, learners have to coordinate a research question with descriptions of relevant research made available in web pages; (2) learners have to extract the information (hypothesis, data) in the descriptions and; (3) map the extracted information onto the elements of an external representation (element type, relations with elements already in the evidence map), while (4) adhering to the syntax and semantics of the external representation. According to cognitive load theory the cognitive load in complex tasks, where the learner has to maintain several information items in working memory, may become so high that it will prevent the formation of schemata.

2.5 Acknowledgement

The authors would like to thank Ton de Jong from Twente University, the Netherlands for providing them with critical, though always helpful comments on an earlier version of this chapter.

2.6 References

Alpay, L., Giboin, A., & Dieng, R. (1998). Accidentology: an example of problem solving by multiple agents with multiple representations. In M. W. Van Someren, P. Reimann, H. P. A. Boshuizen, & T. de Jong (Eds.), *Learning with multiple representations* (pp. 152-174). Amsterdam: Pergamon.

Barron, B. (2000). Achieving coordination in collaborative problem-solving groups. *Journal of the Learning Sciences, 9,* 403-36.

Boshuizen, H. P. A., & Tabachneck-Schijf, H. J. M. (1998). Problem solving with multiple representations by multiple and single agents: an analysis of the issues involved. In M. W. Van Someren, P. Reimann, H. P. A. Boshuizen, & T. de Jong (Eds.), *Learning with multiple representations* (pp. 137-151). Amsterdam: Pergamon.

Bromme, R., Nückles, M., & Rambow, R. (1999). Adaptivity and anticipation in expert-laypeople communication. In S. E. Brennan, A. Giboin, & D. Traum (Eds.), *Psychological models of communication in collaborative systems. Papers from the 1999 fall symposion* (pp. 17-24). Menlo Park, CA: AAAI.

Buckingham Shum, S., & Hammond, N. (1994). Argumentation-based design rationale: what use at what cost? *International Journal of Man-Machine Studies, 40, 603-652.*

Chandler, P., & Sweller, J. (1991). Cognitive load theory and the format of instruction. *Cognition and instruction, 8,* 293-332.

Chryssafidou, E. (1999). Computer-supported formulation of argumentation: a dialectical approach. *Presentation at the symposium 'Belvedere: review and new applications',* Heerlen, 29-9-1999.

Cohen, A.L., Cash, D. & Muller, M.J. (2000). *Designing to support adversarial collaboration.* CSCW 2000, December 2-6, Philadelphia: PA.

De Jong, T., Ainsworth, S., Dobson, M., van der Hulst, A., Levonen, J., Reimann, P., Sime, J. -A., Van Someren, M. W., Spada, H., & Swaak, J. (1998). Acquiring knowledge in science and mathematics: the use of multiple representations in technology-based learning environments. In M. W. Van Someren, P. Reimann, H. P. A. Boshuizen, & T. de Jong (Eds.), *Learning with multiple representations* (pp. 9-40). Amsterdam: Pergamon.

Duffy, T. M., & Cunningham, D. J. (1996). Constructivism: implications for the design and delivery of instruction. In D. H. Jonassen (Ed.), *Handbook of research for educational communications and technology* (pp. 170-198). New York: Macmillan Library Reference USA.

Duffy, T. M., Dueber, B., & Hawley, C. (1998). *Critical thinking in a distributed environment: a pedagogical base for the design of conferencing systems* (CRLT Technical report No 5-98). Bloomington, IN: Indiana University, Center for Research on Learning and Technology.

Edelson, D., & O'Neill, D. K. (1994). The CoVis Collaboratory Notebook: computer support for scientific inquiry. *paper presented at the Annual Meeting of the American Educational Research Association*, New Orleans.

Erkens, G. (1997). Coöperatief probleemoplossen met computers in het onderwijs; het modelleren van coöperatieve dialogen voor de ontwikkeling van intelligente onderwijssystemen. Dissertatie Universiteit Utrecht. (UBU DOBI O-36-ERK). Universiteit Utrecht

Goel, V., & Pirolli, P. (1992). The structure of design problem spaces. *Cognitive Science, 16*, 395-429.

Herring, S. (1999) Interactional coherence in CMC. *Journal of Computer-Mediated Communication. 4*. Retrieved August 10, 2002, from http://jcmc.huji.ac.il/vol4/issue4/herring.htm.

Hewitt, J., Scardamalia, M., & Webb, J. (1997). Situative design issues for interactive learning environments: the problem of group coherence. *Paper presented at the Annual Meeting of the American Educational Association*, Chicago.

Jonassen, D. H., Peck, K. L., & Wilson, B. G. (1999). *Learning with technology: A constructivist perspective*. Upper Saddle River, NJ: Prentice Hall.

Kanselaar, G., Erkens, G., & Jaspers, J. (2001). Computer supported collaborative learning. *Teaching and Teacher Education, 17, 123-129*.

Kolodner, J., & Guzdial, M. (1996). Effects *with* and *of* CSCL: tracking learning in a new paradigm. In T. D. Koschmann (Ed.), *CSCL, theory and practice of an emerging paradigm* (pp. 307-320). Mahwah, N.J.: L. Erlbaum Associates.

Lee, J. (1990). SIBYL: A qualitative decision management system. In P. H. Winston & S. A. Shellard (Eds.), *Artificial Intelligence at MIT; expanding horizons* (pp. 105-133). Cambridge, MA: MIT Press.

Miao, Y., Holst, S., Haake, J. M., & Steinmetz, R. (2000a). PBL-protocols: Guiding and controlling problem based learning processes in virtual learning environments. *Proceedings of the Fourth International Conference of the Learning Sciences (ICLS2000), Ann Arbor, MI, June 14-17*.

Miao, Y., Holst, S., Holmer, T., Fleschutz, J., & Zentel, P. (2000b). An activity-oriented approach to visually structured knowledge representation for problem-based learning in virtual learning environments. *paper presented at Fourth International Conference on the Design of Cooperative Systems (COOP 2000)*, Sophia Antipolis, France, 23-5-2000.

Newell, A., & Simon, H. A. (1972). *Human problem solving*. Englewood Cliffs, NJ: Prentice-Hall.

Norman, D. (1998). *The invisible computer: Why good products can fail, the personal computer is so complex, and information appliances are the answer.* Cambridge, MA: The MIT Press.

Paas, F., Renkl, A., & Sweller, J. (in press). Cognitive Load Theory. *Educational Psychologist.*

Pea, R. D. (1993). Practices of distributed intelligence and designs for education. In G. Salomon (Ed.), *Distributed cognition: psychological and educational considerations* (pp. 47-87). Cambridge: Cambridge University Press.

Reitman, W. (1965). *Cognition and thought.* New York: Wiley.

Rittel, H. W. J., & Webber, M. M. (1973). Dilemmas in a general theory of planning. *Policy Sciences, 4,* 155-169.

Rittel, H. W. J., & Webber, M. M. (1984). Planning problems are wicked problems. In N. Cross (Ed.), *Developments in design methodology* (pp. 135-144). Chichester: John Wiley & Sons. (published earlier as part of 'Dilemmas in a general theory of planning', Policy Sciences,4, 1973, 155-169)

Selvin, A., Buckingham Shum, S., Sierhuis, M., Conklin, J., Zimmermann, B., Palus, C., Drath, W., Horth, D., Domingue, J., Motta, E., & Li, G. (2001). *Compendium: Making Meetings into Knowledge Events.* Knowledge Technologies 2001, March 4-7, Austin, TX. Retrieved August 10, 2002 from http://www.CompendiumInstitute.org/compendium/papers/Selvin-KT2001.pdf

Stahl, G. (2001) *WebGuide: Guiding collaborative learning on the web with perspectives.* Journal of Interactive Media in Education. Accessed: 06-08-2002.

Stenning, K. (1998). Representation and conceptualisation in educational communication. In M. W. van Someren, P. Reimann, H. P. A. Boshuizen, & T. de Jong (Eds.), *Learning with multiple representations* (pp. 320-333). Amsterdam: Pergamon.

Stenning, K., & Oberlander, J. (1995). A cognitive theory of graphical and linguistic reasoning: logic and implementation. *Cognitive Science, 19,* 97-140.

Suthers, D. (1995). Designing for internal vs external discourse in groupware for developing critical discussion skills. CHI' 95 research symposium, Denver.

Suthers, D. (2001). Towards a systematic study of representational guidance for collaborative learning discourse. *Journal of Universal Computer Sciences, 7,* 254-277.

Suthers, D. D. (1999). Effects of alternate representations of evidential relations on collaborative learning discourse. In C. Hoadley & J. Roschelle (Eds.), *Computer Support for Collaborative Learning; designing new media for a new millenium: collaborative technology for learning, education, and training.* CSCL 99, December 12-15, Palo Alto, CA (pp. 611-620). Palo Alto, CA: Stanford University.

Suthers, D., Toth, E., & Weiner, A. (1997). An integrated approach to implementing collaborative inquiry in the classroom. In R. Hall, N. Miyake, & N. Enyedy (Eds.), *Proceedings of CSCL '97: The Second International Conference on Computer Support for Collaborative Learning* (pp. 272-279). Toronto: University of Toronto Press.

Suthers, D., Weiner, A., Connelly, J., & Paolucci, M. (1995). Belvédère: Engaging students in critical discussion of science and public policy issues. *7th World conference on Artifical Intelligence in Education (AI-ED 95),* Washington.

Sweller, J. (1988). Cognitive load during problem solving: Effects on learning. *Cognitive Science, 12,* 257-285.

Sweller, J., van Merriënboer, J. J. G., & Paas, F. G. W. C. (1998). Cognitive architecture and instructional design. *Educational Psychology Review, 10*, 251-296.

Van Bruggen, J., Kirschner, P., & Jochems, W. (2002). External representation of argumentation in CSCL and the management of cognitive load. *Learning and Instruction, 12*(1), 121-138.

Veerman, A. (2000). Computer-supported collaborative learning through argumentation. PhD dissertation University of Utrecht.

Veerman, A., Andriessen, J., & Kanselaar, G. (1999). Co-constructing meaning through diagram-mediated electronic discussion. *Paper presented at the 8th conference for European Research on Learning and Instruction*, 24-28 August, 1999, Gothenburg, Sweden.

Veerman, A. L., & Treasure-Jones, T. (1999). Software for problem solving through collaborative argumentation. In J. Andriessen & P. Coirier (Eds.), *Foundations of argumentative text processing* (pp. 203-229). Amsterdam: University of Amsterdam Press.

Visser, W. (1990) More or less following a plan during design: opportunistic deviations in specification. *International Journal of Man-Machine Studies, 33*, 247-278.

Voss, J. F. (1991). Informal reasoning and international relations. In J. F. Voss & D. N. Perkins (Eds.), *Informal reasoning and education* (pp. 37-58). Hillsdale, NJ: Lawrence Erlbaum Associates, Inc.

Voss, J. F., Blais, J., Means, M. L., & Greene, T. R. (1986). Informal reasoning and subject matter knowledge in the solving of economics problems by naive and novice individuals. *Cognition & Instruction, 3, 269-302.*

Voss, J. F., Greene, T. R., Post, T. A., & Penner, C. (1983). Problem-solving skill in the social sciences. In G. H. Bower (Ed.), *The psychology of learning and motivation: Vol. 17. Advances in research and theory* (pp. 165-213). New York: Academic Press.

Voss, J. F., & Post, T. A. (1988). On the solving of ill-structured problems. In M. T. H. Chi, R. Glaser, & M. J. Farr (Eds.), *The nature of expertise* (pp. 261-285). Hillsdale, NJ: Lawrence Erlbaum Associates.

Voss, J. F., Wiley, J., & Sandak, R. (1999). Reasoning in the construction of argumentative texts. In J. Andriessen & P. Coirier (Eds.), *Foundations of argumentative text processing* (pp. 29-41). Amsterdam: University of Amsterdam Press.

Zolin, R., Fruchter, R., & Levitt, R. E. (2002). *Simulating the process of trust: using simulation to test and explore a social process.* Retrieved August 10, 2002 from http://www.cacos.ece.cmu.edu/conference2000/pdf/Roxanne-Zolin.pdf.

Part II

Applications

3 Designing Argumentation Tools for Collaborative Learning

Gellof Kanselaar, Gijsbert Erkens, Jerry Andriessen, Maaike Prangsma, Arja Veerman and Jos Jaspers

Department of Educational Sciences, Utrecht University, the Netherlands
TNO Human Factors, the Netherlands

3.1 Introduction

The focus of education has shifted towards working actively, constructively and collaboratively, as this is believed to enhance learning. The studies discussed here deals with the influence of different CMC (Computer Mediated Communication) tools on argumentation processes during collaboration. The purpose of our research is to investigate the effect of computer supported environments and its tools on the final product through differences in the participants' collaboration processes. In this chapter we will concentrate on students collaboratively taking part in argumentation via CMC systems. Computer environments that support collaborative writing can emphasize both the constructivist and collaborative aspects through its active and interactive nature.

3.2 Argumentation and Collaboration in CMC Systems

One of the main principles of constructivist learning theory is the negotiated construction of knowledge through dialogue. Such learning through negotiation can consist of testing understanding and ideas against each other as a mechanism for enriching, interweaving and expanding understanding of particular phenomena. Active engagement in collaborative argumentation during problem solving fits this principle by giving prominence to conflict and query as mechanisms for enriching, combining and expanding understanding of problems that have to be solved (Savery and Duffy, 1995). After all, as von Glaserfeld (1989) has noted, other people are the greatest source of alternative views to challenge our current views and hence to serve as the source of cognitive conflict that stimulates learning.

Knowledge is actively constructed, connected to the individual's cognitive repertoire and to a broader, often team-based and interdisciplinary context in which learning activities take place (Salomon, 1997). Constructivism seems to be influenced not only by a Piagetian perspective on individual cognitive development through socio-cognitive conflict, but also by the socio-cultural approach emphasising the process of interactive knowledge construction in which appropriation of meaning through negotiation plays a central role (Greeno, 1997). From a constructivist perspective, collaborative argumentation during problem solving can be regarded as an activity encouraging learning through mechanisms such as externalising knowledge and opinions, self-explanation, reflecting on each other's information and reconstructing knowledge through critical discussion (Kanselaar, de Jong, Andriessen, and Goodyear, 2000; Kanselaar, and Erkens, 1996).

We consider an argument to be a structured connection of claims, evidence and rebuttals. A minimal argument is a claim for which at least doubt or disbelief is expressed (van Eemeren, Grootendorst and Snoeck Henkemans, 1995). Such doubt or disbelief can be expressed by an individual (if working alone) or by a partner in an argumentative dialogue. In response to such doubts a complex structure may be produced potentially including features such as chaining of arguments, qualifications, contraindications, counter-arguments and rebuttals. Hence the argument is the product, the structure linking claims, the evidence or rebuttals. The process by which the argument is produced we refer to as argumentation.

Our interest lies in argumentation structures that are built by groups of students involved in collaborative problem solving and writing. During problem solving we expect students to make various claims about the domain and the potential solutions. It is possible that during the problem solving no doubt is expressed regarding claims and solutions and hence no argument emerges in the dialogue. However, such a situation seems unlikely and we believe would not produce the best solution to the problem. Certainly if the students have not produced reasons to support the claims and solutions during the problem solving process itself then we have no reason to believe that they will be able to produce such reasons at a later date. Therefore we believe that students should be encouraged to use argumentation processes to build argument structures during problem solving.

We will concentrate on students collaborating via computer mediated communication (CMC) systems. Communicative tools give access to collaborating partners through Computer Mediated Communication (CMC) facilities like chat and discussion forums, but also to other resources, such as external experts, or information sources on the Internet. In this respect, the program functions as a communication medium (Henri, 1995). The collaborative aspect is mainly realized by offering computerized tools that can be helpful for collaborating students in solving the task at hand (e.g., the CSILE program of Scardamalia, Bereiter and Lamon, 1994; the Belvédère program of Suthers, Weiner, Connelly and Paolucci, 1995). These tools are generally one of two types: task related or communicative. Task related tools support task performance and the problem solving process (Roschelle and Teasley, 1995; Salomon, 1993; Teasley andand Roschelle, 1993). Programs that integrate both tool types are generally known as groupware: they are designed to support collaborative group work by sharing tools and resources between group members, and by offering communication opportunities within the group and with the external world.

This chapter addresses how argumentation processes can be supported in electronic environments. We studied students actively engaged in collaborative argumentation in order to solve open-ended problems such as writing argumentative texts, constructing hypotheses or designing computer-based learning programs. These types of problems are characterised by the existence of justifiable beliefs and multiple acceptable viewpoints, as described by Baker (1992), Andriessen, Baker, and Suthers (in press). In working on problems together, students first have to establish a (partially) shared focus, which can be changed, maintained or refined during the problem solving process (Roschelle, 1992). The focus determines the concentration on thematic parts (sub-problems) of the problem to be solved. Subsequently, information relevant to the sub-problem must be generated and gathered from mental or material resources. The next phase is to critically check its strength (Is the information true?) and relevance (Is the information appropriate?) before integrating it in the problem-solving process (for instance by assimilating new information in a writing assignment). Finally, after discussing alternative solutions the strongest and most relevant one must be chosen (Erkens, 1997).

3.2.1 Interface Design for Argumentation

To provoke and support argumentation in CMC systems, interaction can be structured at the interface. Dependent on task characteristics, students can be provided with dialogue markers, sentence openers and turn taking control (Veerman and Andriessen, 1997; Veerman, 2000; Veerman, Andriessen, and Kanselaar, 2000). These options might improve shared understanding, focus maintenance or critical assessment of new information. Additional options for free text interaction could stimulate elaboration whereas careful use of turn-taking control and dialogue rules could guide the interaction without constraining it. In addition, graphic representation of arguments might support exploration of multiple perspectives and identification of misconceptions and gaps.

Veerman and Treasure-Jones (1999) studied how to *provoke* and *support* argumentation in electronic collaborative problem-solving situations, considering the cognitive processes of critical information checking, argument elaboration and the taking of multiple perspectives. In addition, maintenance of focus was discussed as an important factor in effective argumentation and collaborative problem solving. Five studies on different CMC systems were reviewed, which were all designed for educational tasks and in which argumentation was emphasised as a method for collaborative problem solving or an end goal for learning. The selected CMC systems demonstrated a range of approaches to structuring interaction at the user interface in order to support communication, and more specifically, argumentation (e.g. turn-taking control, menu-based dialogue buttons, and graphical argument structures). In discussing the success of the systems at provoking and supporting argumentation, characteristics of the task, instruction and structured interaction were considered. The review revealed that structuring interaction at the interface does not necessarily *provoke* argumentation. Rather, the initiation of argument seems to be related to task characteristics, such as the use of competitive task design. However, providing a combination of structured and unstructured interaction modes may *support* argumentative processes. In communication windows (chat boxes), combining free text entry with well designed argument moves or sentence openers can stimulate students to critically check information. In task windows constructing argumentative diagrams can improve the exploration of multiple perspective taking and argument elaboration. However, some task characteristics can also enhance such processes. Therefore, task features and structured interaction at the user-interface must be considered in close relationship to each other in order to support argumentation in CSCL situations. In addition, offering support for focus maintenance was proposed as an important factor.

3.2.2 Argumentation in NetMeeting, Belvédère and Allaire Forums

In line with this research, three experimental studies were subsequently organised that examined student groups' academic discussions mediated by the synchronous CMC systems NetMeeting and Belvédère, and the asynchronous system Allaire Forums (Veerman, 2000).

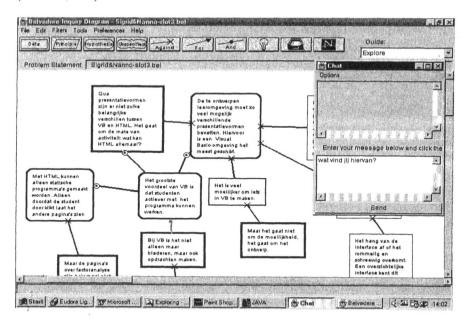

Figure 3.1: Screendump of the Belvédère system.

All discussions were analysed and compared on the factors of focusing, argumentation and the production of constructive activities, a measure that was used to define collaborative learning-in-process. In addition, various forms of pedagogical support were considered, provided by humans or the user-interface.

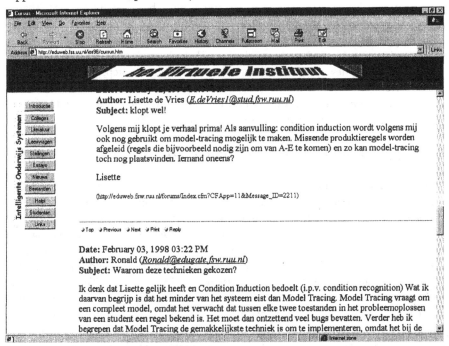

Figure 3.2: Screen dump of a discussion 'thread' in Allaire Forums.

The results can be summarised under the following three headings:

1 The results showed, first of all, that a study of collaborative learning from electronic discussions requires analyses of focus in relationship to argumentation. Constructive discussions were particularly focused on the meaning of concepts, and included focus shifts back and forth between the application of concepts, while information was critically checked.

2 Second, "indirect" forms of argumentation in particular were shown to be effective (i.e. checks, mainly by verification questions), in contrast to "direct" forms of argumentation (challenges, counter-argumentation). The more information was checked, the more constructive activities were produced. Absent effects of the "direct" forms of argumentation were explained by the use of the following paradox: to engage in critical debate, students should have well-established views on subjects and be able to mutually recognise opposed knowledge and attitudes (Baker, De Vries and Lund, 1999). However, a characteristic of the knowledge of students engaged in debates for collaborative learning purposes is that these views are not always well elaborated, since they are subject to the learning process.

3 Third, the discussions mainly contained additions, explanations and evaluations. Summaries or information transformations hardly occurred. This

was due to the cognitive effort required, but also to an incomplete, intuitive and personalised understanding of information under discussion (Kuhn, 1991). To transform information, there must be a certain level of (shared) understanding. In the studies considering task characteristics, students' preparation activities, prior knowledge and time available for discussion, obtaining (deeper) understanding may have been the highest goal achievable. Reaching new insights may have been just the next step, for instance, when students were sufficiently prepared and had established a mutual framework for interpreting each other's information in order to engage in critical, hefty discussions (Coirier, Andriessen and Chanquoy, 1999).

3.2.3 Synchronous and Asynchronous Discussions

Discussions mediated by the synchronous CMC systems NetMeeting and Belvédère and the asynchronous CMC system Allaire Forums, appeared to have different characteristics concerning focusing, argumentation and the production of constructive activities. Relatively speaking, the synchronous discussions in NetMeeting and Belvédère included more "direct" forms of argumentation (challenges, counter-argumentation), more focus shifts to non-task related issues, and they were less constructive than the asynchronous discussions in Allaire Forums. The asynchronous discussions were only "indirectly" argumentative (including information checks), they maintained a more conceptually oriented focus and contained more constructive activities. To maintain a conceptually oriented focus and to co-ordinate interactions appears to be particularly related to the asynchronous and synchronous modes of communication. In synchronous discussions students engage in a fast flow of communication. Real-time pressures them (psychologically) to read and respond to each other's contributions within seconds or at most minutes. Focus shifts to non-task related aspects or technical issues easily cause students to lose track of an argument or to lose the overview of the main issues under discussion. In asynchronous discussions students may take hours, days, weeks, and sometimes even longer to read, write and think about contributions that triggered their interest, instead of seconds or minutes. More time may afford re-reading and reflection, keeping track of the line of discussion and treating non-task related interactions or technical disturbances for what they are: temporary, peripheral interruptions.

3.2.4 Support in CMC Systems

In all three studies human or interface support primarily aimed at promoting argumentative processes. However, no effects were found from human "structure" coaches who supported the taking of multiple perspectives and counter-argumentation. "Reflective" support increased the number of check questions asked, which later turned out to be powerful in relationship to the production of constructive activities. Graphical support on the Belvédère interface triggered students to produce more counter-arguments, a "direct" form of argumentation. However, counter-argumentation was not related to effective student discussions. Then again, the

Belvédère discussions were relatively more often conceptually oriented and constructive than the NetMeeting discussions. Perhaps the separate window for argumentative diagram construction particularly facilitated focus maintenance, and subsequently stimulated the production of constructive activities. It may be possible, however, that a tool for regular concept mapping[1] might have been just as effective as the diagram construction tool (van Boxtel, 2000). It is not known (yet) to what extent the beneficiary effect is due to particular constructs of the Belvédère system.

To refer back to one of the earlier points mentioned, relatively speaking the asynchronous discussions in Allaire Forums were more often conceptually oriented and constructive than the synchronous Belvédère and NetMeeting discussions. The NetMeeting discussions were most often focused on finishing the task. However, in clustering the discussions on the factors of focusing, argumentation and constructive activities, some discussions in Allaire Forums were also found to be less effective; some Belvédère discussions were completely product-oriented and a few NetMeeting discussions were even found to be highly conceptually oriented and constructive. This indicates that in addition to features of the electronic systems and task characteristics, effective discussions also relate to individual group differences, such as task approaches, preparation activities or collaboration strategies, and to factors of the broader educational context.

3.3 The TC3 Environment

In addition to the studies described above with university students and well-known software applications, we will elaborate on a study in upper secondary schools with a new environment. In the COSAR project (Erkens, Prangsma, Jaspers, and Kanselaar, 2002) we developed the groupware program TC3 (Text Composer, Computer supported & Collaborative) with which the students carry out the main writing task. This environment is based on an earlier tool called CTP – Collaborative Text Production (Andriessen, Erkens, Overeem, and Jaspers, 1996), and it combines a shared text editor, a chat facility, and private access to a notepad and to information sources to encourage collaborative distance writing. The participants worked in pairs within TC3, each partner working at his/her own computer, and wherever possible partners were seated separately in different classrooms.

The main screen of the program displays several private and shared windows. The basic environment, shown in Figure 3.3, contains four main windows:
-    The upper half of the screen is private and the lower half is shared.
-    INFORMATION (upper right window): This private window contains tabs for the assignment, sources and TC3 operating instructions. Sources are divided evenly between the students. Each partner has 3 or 5 different sources

---

[1]   Concept mapping homepage:
    http://www.to.utwente.nl/user/ism/lanzing/cm_home.htm

plus one – fairly factual – common source. The content of the sources cannot be copied or pasted.

- NOTES (upper left window): A private notepad where the student can make non-shared notes.
- CHAT (lower left, 3 small windows): The student adds his/her chat message in the bottom box: every letter typed is immediately sent to the partner via the network, so that both boxes are WYSIWIS: What You See Is What I See. The middle box shows the incoming messages from the partner. The scrollable upper chat box contains the discussion history.
- SHARED TEXT (lower right window): A simple text editor (also WYSIWIS) in which the shared text is written while taking turns.

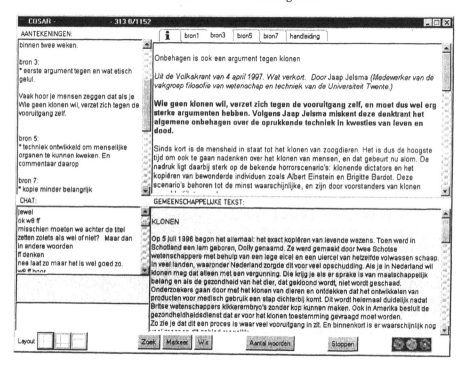

Figure 3.3: The layout of the interface of the TC3-basic environment.

Text from the private notes, chat, chat history and shared text can be exchanged through standard copy and paste functions. To allow the participants to adjust their focus between their private work and the collaboration, three layout buttons were added in the left-hand corner: the middle layout button enlarges the private windows, the rightmost button enlarges the shared windows, and the leftmost layout button restores the basic layout. The buttons search, mark and delete (*zoek*, *markeer* and *wis*) can be used to mark and unmark text in the source windows and to search through the marked texts. The number of words (*aantal woorden*) button allows the participants to count the number of words in the shared text editor at any given moment. The stop (*stoppen*) button will end the session. The traffic light button serves as the turn taking device necessary to take turns in writing in the shared text editor.

In addition, two planning modules were developed in the TC3 program for the experimental conditions: the Diagram and the Outline. The Diagram (see Figure 3.4) is a tool for generating, organizing and relating information units in a graphical knowledge structure comparable to Belvédère (Suthers, Weiner, Connelly, and Paolucci, 1995; Suthers, and Hundhausen, 2001). The tool was conceptualized to the students as a graphical summary of the information in the argumentative essay. Students were told that the information contained in the Diagram had to faithfully represent the information in the final version of their essay. We hoped that this requirement would help students to notice inconsistencies, gaps, and other imperfections in their texts, and encourage them to review and revise. In the Diagram, several types of text boxes can be used: information (Informatie), position (Standpunt), argument pro (Voorargument), support (Onderbouwing), argument contra (Tegenargument), refutation (Weerlegging), and conclusion (Conclusie). Two types of connectors were available to link the text boxes: arrows and lines. The Diagram can be used to visualize the argumentative structure of the position taken.

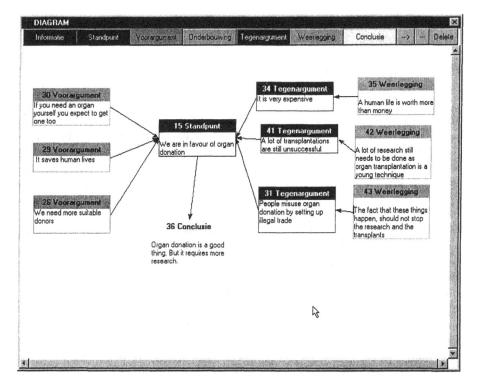

Figure 3.4: The Diagram Window in the TC3 program.

The Outline (see Figure 3.5) is a tool in the TC3 program for generating and organizing information units as an outline of consecutive subjects in the text. The

Outline tool was designed to support planning and organization of the linear structure of the texts. The tool was designed to allow students to construct an overview or hierarchical structure of the text to be written, to help in determining the order of content in the text. In addition, the Outline tool has the didactic function of making the user aware of characteristics of good textual structure, thus allowing the user to learn to write better texts. The Outline has a maximum of four automatically outline numbered levels. Both planning windows are WYSIWIS.

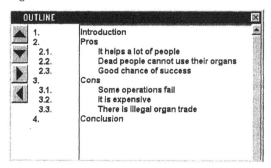

Figure 3.5: The Outline window in the TC3 program.

3.3.1   Hypotheses and Experimental Design

The effects of the organizer (Diagram) were expected to be related mostly to the consistency and completeness of the knowledge structure in the text (Veerman and Andriessen, 1997). The effects of the lineariser (Outline) were expected to be related mostly to the persuasiveness of the argumentation and the adequate use of language in the shape of connectives and anaphora (Chanquoy, 1996). We expected these effects to take place especially when both organization and linearization were supported, and explicit attention was being paid to translating the conceptual structure into the linear text. The main indicators of this would be increasing attention to the opposite position, and the use of counterarguments. A help facility, the Advisor, gave advice on how to use the Diagram and Outline tools.

In order to compare the effects of the planning tools on the process of collaborative argumentative writing a (quasi) experiment was set up varying the different combinations of planning tools. The effect of the tools on collaborative writing were investigated in the experimental conditions shown in Table 3.1.

The participants were 290 Dutch students aged 16 to 18 from six secondary schools. 145 randomly assigned pairs were asked to write an argumentative text of about 600 to 1000 words defending a position on cloning or organ donation. The shared text had to be based on information sources given within the groupware program.

All communication and activities during the collaboration were logged automatically in a chat and activity protocol. It is possible to replay a whole session with all the keyboard input, including typing errors, deletions, mouse clicks, etc. on the basis of the log file.

Table 3.1: Experimental design.

	Condition	Tools
C	Control	TC3 basic
D	Diagram	Basic + Organizer
DA	Diagram Advisor	Basic + Organizer + Advisor
DO	Diagram Outline	Basic + Organizer + Lineariser
DOA	Diagram Outline Advisor	Basic + Organizer + Lineariser + Advisor
O	Outline	Basic + Lineariser
OA	Outline Advisor	Basic + Lineariser + Advisor

3.3.2 Writing in a Shared Space

The main task in this study was a collaborative writing task. The assignment was to write an argumentative text on cloning or organ donation. For organ donation each partner had five private sources plus one common source, so there were eleven sources in total. The sources were taken from the Internet sites of Dutch newspapers. The assignment was to convince the Minister of Health, Welfare and Sport of the position they had taken. For cloning the partners each had three sources and one common source, so there were seven sources in total. In all groups, partners were seated in separate computer rooms, to encourage them to communicate only through TC3.

The assignment was completed in two to six sessions with an average total duration of 3.9 hours.

3.3.3 MEPA: a Tool for Multiple Episode Protocol Analysis

We use the program MEPA to analyze all the data the students produce in the TC3 environment. The purpose of MEPA[2] (Multiple Episode Protocol Analysis), a program for protocol analysis, is to offer a flexible environment for creating protocols from verbal and non-verbal observational data, and annotating, coding and analyzing these.

The program is multifunctional in the sense that it allows for development of both the coding and protocolling systems within the same program, as well as direct analysis and exploration of the coded verbal and non-verbal data using several built-in quantitative and qualitative methods of analysis. In its current version, MEPA can execute frequency and time-interval analyses; construct cross-tables with associative measures; perform lag-sequential analysis, interrater reliability, visual, word frequency and word context analyses; and carry out selecting, sorting and search processes. Also, some aids for inductive pattern recognition have been implemented. MEPA uses a multidimensional data structure, allowing protocol data to be coded on multiple

---

[2]   MEPA was developed as a general program for protocol analysis and is being used in several research projects at Utrecht University, as well as abroad. For further information, please contact G. Erkens (G.Erkens@fss.uu.nl).

dimensions or variables. To minimize the work associated with coding protocols and to maximize coding reliability, MEPA contains a module that can be used to program complex structured if-then rules for automatic coding. Figure 3.6 shows a screen dump of the MEPA program.

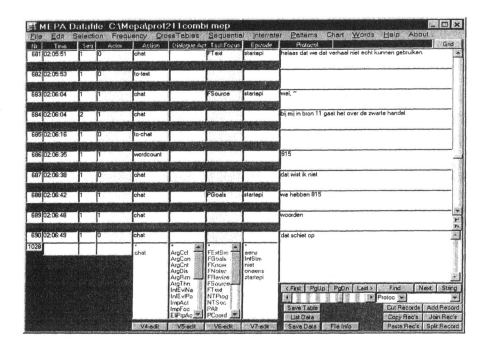

Figure 3.6: MEPA program for protocol analyses.

3.3.4 Analysis of the Argumentative Texts

Each of the 145 student pairs produced one text, and these were analyzed on several dimensions. As a preparation for the final assessment, the texts were imported into MEPA, with a single sentence – defined by a period – per line. The sentences with potentially multiple argumentative functions were split into smaller units using an automatic splitting filter, so that the constituents of sentences such as "Cloning is good, but it can also have side effects" could be properly coded as position and argument contra. The sentences were split automatically where necessary on the basis of argumentative and organizational markers, such as but, however, although, therefore, unless. Before coding, the experimenters manually divided the final texts into segments, largely based on the existing paragraph structure. The final argumentative texts were scored on five variables (see Table 3.2).

Table 3.2: Description of text quality measures.

Variable	Description
Textual structure	The formal structure of the text as defined by introduction, body, and conclusion.
Segment argumentation	The quality of the argumentation within the paragraphs.
Overall argumentation	The quality of the main line of argumentation in the text.
Audience focus	The presentation towards the reader and the level of formality of the text.
Mean text score	The mean of the four scores above.

3.3.5   Analyses of the Chats

The chat protocols were not analyzed at a propositional level like the argumentative texts, but rather at an episode level based on the task oriented collaboration process.

The chat protocols were manually divided into episodes of different Task act categories. Whenever the focus of the discussion changed within a particular type of Task act, a new episode was started as well. In addition, MEPA automatically coded a new episode whenever the partners had not used the chat window for more than 59 seconds.

3.4   Results

3.4.1   Structural Characteristics of the Chat Dialogue

This section[3] contains a description of the results for the structural characteristics of the dialogue in terms of communicative functions and dialogue patterns within the collaboration dialogues, and the relationship between these features and the final product, the argumentative text. Table 3.4 shows the distribution for the five communicative functions for the Control group and for each experimental condition.

The distribution for all groups together shows that Informatives occur most frequently (37.66%), followed by Responsives (24.06%). Argumentatives make out an encouraging 10% of the communicative functions, and Imperatives are the least frequent with 7.93%.

Compared to the other conditions, the Control group uses significantly fewer Argumentatives, especially in comparison to the Diagram, Diagram-Advisor and Outline conditions. Imperatives are more frequent in the Diagram-Outline-Advisor condition, but less frequent in the Diagram and Diagram-Advisor conditions. The

---

[3]   Thanks to Floor Scheltens who assisted in the analyses of the data.

Diagram-Outline-Advisor condition also used fewer Informatives, and the Outline-Advisor group used relatively few Responsives.

Table 3.3: Communicative functions and Dialogue acts in chat discussions.

Communicative function	Dialogue act	Specification	Explanation
Argumentatives	Reason		Ground
	Contra		Counterargument
Argumentative task focus	Conditional		Condition
	Then		Consequence
	Disjunctive		Disjunctive
	Conclusion		Conclusion
Responsives	Confirmation		Confirmation of information
	Deny		Refutation of information
Reaction, or response to an elicitative	Acceptation		Acceptation of information, without confirming or refuting the information
	Reply	Confirm	Affirmative response
		Deny	Negative response
		Accept	Accepting response
		Statement	Response including a statement
		Performative	Response containing an action performed by saying it
Informatives	Performative		Action performed by saying it
	Evaluation	Neutral	Neutral evaluation
Transfer of information		Positive	Positive evaluation
		Negative	Negative evaluation
	Statement		Statement
		Action	Announcement of actions
		Social	Social statement
		Nonsense	Nonsense statement
	Task		Task information
Elicitatives	Question	Verify	Yes/no question
		Set	Set question/ multiple choice
Questions or utterances requiring a response		Open	Open question
	Proposal	Action	Proposal for action
Imperatives		Action	Order for action
Commanding utterances		Focus	Order for attention

Table 3.4 shows the mean percentages of the main Dialogue acts. The distributions within the communicative functions (see Table 3.3 for specific categories) are very similar for all conditions, so we will only discuss the total sample here. Within the Argumentatives, the relatively most frequent Dialogue act is Contra: counterarguments (4%). This is a nice surprise, as relatively novice writers are usually thought to use counterarguments quite sparsely (Veerman, 2000). The verifying question is relatively most frequent in the Elicitatives (10%), followed by proposals (6%) and open questions (5%). Urging the partner to take action or fulfill a task is the more frequent Imperative with 5%, although asking for attention follows closely behind at 3%. Task information is exchanged relatively often (Statement Info 26%), while evaluative informatives are

used less frequently (4%). Finally, within Responsives the most frequent Dialogue acts are Confirmation (13%) and plain replies (Reply Statement 4%).

Table 3.4: Distribution of communicative function in the chat dialogues in percentages.

	Total	C	D	DA	DO	DOA	O	OA
	Mean	M	M	M	M	M	M	M
Argumentatives	9.80	8.98	10.74	10.51	9.72	9.03	10.70	9.04
Elicitatives	20.55	20.46	21.26	20.39	20.92	19.30	20.11	21.30
Imperatives	7.93	8.06	6.40	6.36	7.68	10.74	9.18	9.18
Informatives	37.66	38.65	36.04	38.28	37.93	33.94	36.50	40.22
Responsives	24.06	23.84	25.56	24.45	23.75	26.99	23.51	20.26
Total number of contributions	425.37	421.15	312.59	441.81	518.00	460.27	401.72	385.91
N (dyads)	145	39	17	26	23	11	18	11

Note: Standard deviations of the variables were between 1.82 and 6.11. See Table 3.3 for a description of the categories in the first column and Table 3.1 for a description of the conditions.

3.4.2 Transitions Between Dialogue Acts

Figure 3.7 and Figure 3.8 show the transition diagrams made by the MEPA program for the Control and the Diagram condition. We will discuss the other transition diagrams too, but they are not shown here. The transition diagrams result from lag-sequential analyses (Wampold and Margolin, 1982). In lag-sequential analysis the number of transitions of one event to the next (lag = 1) are tested for significance with regard to the expected number of transitions of that type based on the distribution of probability. In the diagrams, only the significant transitions are shown, with the width of the arrows indicating the level of significance. A large number of different transitions in the diagrams points towards unstructured dialogues: the fewer arrows, the more structured the dialogues were for that condition. A relatively high number of autocorrelations – indicated by the circular arrows – also indicates relatively unstructured dialogues. For readability reasons, a number of categories from Table 3.3 were merged in these analyses.

The Control group with only the TC3 basic environment, shown in Figure 3.7, differs from the experimental conditions with extra tools: this group shows a lot more different significant transitions between the Dialogue acts. The Control group displays relatively more different patterns than the experimental groups, and 8 out of 19 of its Dialogue acts show autocorrelations, which means that the dialogue is less structured in the Control group. Possibly, the planning tools in the experimental groups stimulate structuring of the dialogue.

All transition diagrams show one typical pattern in particular: the arrows from open questions (EliQstOpn) and verifying questions (EliQstVer) to statement replies (ResRplStm). Although the obvious answer to a verifying question would be a denying or accepting reply (ResDen or ResAcc) in all seven conditions verifying questions are relatively often answered with an elaborated statement.

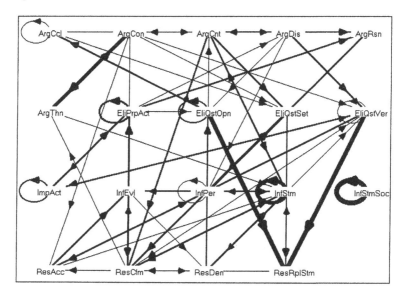

Figure 3.7: Transition diagram for the Control group.

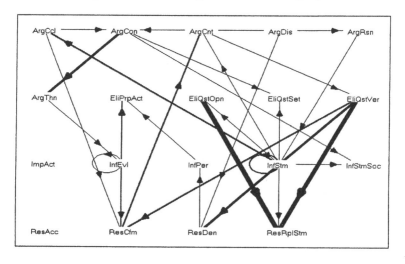

Figure 3.8: Transition diagram for the Diagram condition.

Another characteristic pattern is the strong presence of argumentative sequences throughout the conditions (see upper half in Figure 3.8). Only the Diagram-Advisor condition differs on this point, as it shows fewer transitions between argumentatives than any other condition. The Diagram-Advisor condition generally differs from the other experimental conditions in its transitions. There are more significant transitions and these transitions are different from the ones that occur in the other experimental groups. For example, argumentative conclusions (ArgCcl) are followed significantly by social statements (InfStmSoc), conditionals (ArgCon) are followed significantly by imperative actions (ImpAct), and there are relatively many transitions to accepting responsives like *mmm* or *oh* (ResAcc). Just like the Control group, the Diagram-Advisor condition contains a relatively large number of autocorrelations.

The transition between "if"-argumentatives (ArgCon) and "then"-argumentatives (ArgThn) is not significant for the Outline and Outline-Advisor conditions, whereas the transition *is* significant in the Control group and the conditions with the Diagram. Possibly, the diagram stimulates the use of if-then patterns, whereas the Outline suppresses these patterns.

3.4.3 Relation of Dialogue Structure and CMC-tools with Text Quality

Four out of five measures for dialogue structure in the chats show some significant correlations with the quality of the final text (Table 3.5). The Elicitatives correlate positively with most of the text scores, while the Informatives are predominantly negatively correlated. This suggests that asking questions and making proposals leads to a productive argumentative writing process, whereas exchanging neutral information brings about the opposite. This assumption is supported by the more detailed analyses of the subtypes of Dialogue acts: these show that the main contributors to the negative correlations for Informatives are the nonsense statements and the social talk. The Argumentatives and Imperatives each correlate positively with only one text quality measure. The Responsives do not correlate with text quality at all.

Table 3.5: Correlations between communicative functions and final text scores.

	Textual structure	Segment argumenta-tion	Overall argumenta-tion	Audience focus	Mean text score
Argumentatives	-.01	-.01	.13*	.05	.06
Elicitatives	.00	.17**	.12*	.21**	.18**
Imperatives	.14*	.01	.01	-.09	.02
Informatives	-.06	-.10	-.24**	-.13*	-.19**
Responsives	-.03	-.02	.10	.01	.02

Note: * p < .05; ** p < .01.

We also tested for the effects of dialogue structure in the chats and conditions with different tools on the quality of the final text. To check the possibility that condition and communicative function affect text quality independently of each other, we tested the model presented in Figure 3.9.

Table 3.6 shows the directions of the effects of condition and communicative function on text quality. In these regression analyses all communicative function measures and all conditions were entered in the regression with the quality measures as dependent variables. Independent of the dialogue activity (communicative function), the Diagram-Advisor condition negatively influences textual structure, whereas the Diagram-Outline-Advisor condition has a positive effect. Adding a third planning aid – the Outline – seems to enhance the structural quality of the final text (either directly or through some unidentified factor).

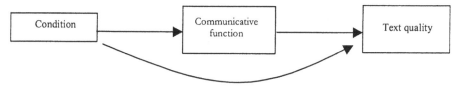

Figure 3.9: Effect of the conditions and of the dialogue structure of the chats on text quality.

Elicitatives have a positive effect on audience focus and on quality of the argumentation at the segment level. Informatives have a negative effect on the argumentative quality of the text as a whole. In addition, a lower percentage of Informatives in the chat goes together with higher overall text quality. Collaboration with an argumentatively and structurally good result requires little informing, but does require frequent argumentation, asking accurate questions, responding to the partner, and use of imperatives.

Table 3.6: Relation of communicative function and experimental condition with text quality.

	Textual structure	Segment argumentation	Overall argumentation	Audience focus	Mean score
Argumentative					
Elicitative		+		+	
Imperative					
Informative			-		-
Responsive					
D					
O					
DO					
DA	-	-			
OA					
DOA	+				

This model hypothesizes that the experimental condition affects text quality through the dialogue, but also directly, independent of the communicative function of the chat.

3.5   Discussion and Conclusion

Education can be viewed as an ongoing process of argumentation (Petraglia, 1997). It is the process of discovering and generating acceptable arguments and lines of reasoning underlying scientific assumptions and bodies of knowledge. In collaborative learning, students can negotiate different perspectives by externalising and articulating them, and learn from each other's insights and different understandings. Thus, through negotiation processes, including argumentation, they can reconstruct and co-construct knowledge in relationship to specific learning goals.

The present research suggests that the role of argumentation needs to be reconsidered. Across studies, "direct" forms of argumentation (challenges, counter-argumentation) did not relate well to the production of constructive activities, a measure to define learning-in-process. This may be explained by the paradox that students should have a well-established understanding of knowledge in order to take firm positions. However, their knowledge is under discussion and subject to the learning process itself. Therefore, offering support to students to challenge and counter each other's information may not be the most fruitful approach. However, information checking was shown to be important, which was regarded as an "indirect" form of argumentation. The more information was checked, the more constructive activities were produced. Students can be provoked to critically check each other's information through instruction and task design.

With regard to computerised learning environments, the research indicates that students particularly need facilitation by means of tools and explicit instruction in co-ordinating electronic and text-based communication, and in keeping track of the main issues while producing networked-based discussions. Technical disturbances and a loss of thematic focus easily occur, especially in synchronous CMC systems, and have a negative effect on collaborative learning processes. Additional tools to keep a (graphical) overview of the issues at hand can be helpful, such as the diagram construction tool provided by the Belvédère system and the TC3 program.

In research by Erkens (1997), focusing, checking and argumentation were revealed as essential factors in collaborative learning processes. In addition, parallel studies aimed at argumentation, epistemic interactions and grounding processes contributed to gaining more understanding of the mechanisms that can support collaborative learning through (electronic) dialogue. We presented some results of a couple of studies in this chapter to explore those relations more in depth.

We found that the Diagram, Outline and Diagram-Advisor conditions all have a positive affect on the number of Argumentatives. This suggests that the moderate availability of extra tools has a positive influence on the number of arguments in the chat, and also on some aspects of the quality of the argumentative text.

The transition patterns show that the experimental groups are more structured in their direct communication than the Control group. This suggests that the planning tools (Diagram, Outline, Advisor) stimulate a more structured dialogue. The same difference in the structure of dialogues can be observed when comparing high scoring and low scoring dyads. This leads us to conclude that the experimental condition (extra tools) has a direct effect on text quality, but also through the communicative function in the chat dialogues.

Some of the results in the last study (Erkens, Prangsma, Jaspers, and Kanselaar, 2002) are not simple to interpret.

The analyses of chat dialogues about the Diagrams suggest that for some participants this tool did not serve as a basis for discussion or a tool for idea generation, as it was intended, but rather functioned as a visual representation. The correspondence of arguments between Diagram and the final text reveals a discrepancy between the two: only about a third of the arguments are found both in the final text and the Diagram. Although the use of wholly original arguments seems to be slightly positively related to text quality, these are hardly used, and most of the arguments are taken directly from the given sources.

With respect to these results, the study of Veerman (2000) can be mentioned in which students used the Belvédère environment to chat electronically and to visualize their discussion about a computer-based design by the use of an argumentative diagram construction tool. It showed that the students only gained from the Belvédère environment, when they linked their chat discussions closely to their diagrams. A significant relationship was found between the amount of overlapping information between chats and diagrams, and the amount of constructive activities produced (Veerman, 2000). However, student groups varied in linking information between chats and diagrams. This appeared to depend heavily on student groups' task approaches and preparation activities.

We also found that using the private – hence non-collaborative – notes window (the upper left window in Figure 3.3) is detrimental to the quality of the collaborative product. This confirms our idea that collaboration is necessary on all subtasks, including planning, idea generation, coordination and information processing.

We also found that explicit argumentation on content, coordination, and metacognitive strategies is related positively to text quality, whereas argumentation on technical aspects of the task and on non-task related topics is related negatively to text quality. The relation between non-task chat and text quality is negative throughout the groups, although the relation is the most clear for the Control group.

When we compare the Diagram (Figure 3.4) with the Outline (Figure 3.5), the Outline tool was more successful. Availability and proper use of this planning tool have a positive effect on the dialogue structure, and on the coordination processes of focusing and argumentation, as well as on text quality. The Diagram often functions as a visual representation, and not as a basis for discussion or a tool for idea generation. When a diagram reflects the discussion itself, it can be a valuable starting point for writing the text, and of benefit to textual structure. Students don't have much experience with the use of Diagram tools. Perhaps a different approach to the task instruction – for example by giving the students time to practice using the complex Diagram tool – could encourage the students to use the tool as it was intended, and thus lead to different results.

Much is possible in electronic learning environments, but so far not enough is known about the relationships between collaborative learning, argumentation and educational technology. This research has shown that such relationships are neither simple nor very predictable. Hence, much more research is needed that examines the role of (interactive) mechanisms such as argumentation and focusing in relationship to features of CSCL situations.

3.6 Acknowledgements

The research reported in this chapter was made possible by grant from the Dutch Scientific Organization (NWO-project 575-33-008)

3.7 References

Andriessen, J., Baker, M., & Suthers, D. (in press). In J. Andriessen, M. Baker & D. Suthers (Eds.), *Arguing to learn: Confronting cognitions in computer-supported collaborative learning environments.*

Andriessen, J., Erkens. G., Overeem, E., & Jaspers, J. (1996, September). Using complex information in argumentation for collaborative text production. Paper presented at the UCIS '96 conference, Poitier, France.

Baker, M. (1992). Modeling negotiation in intelligent teaching dialogue. In R. Moyse & M. T. Elsom-Cook (Eds.), *Knowledge negotiation.* London: Academic Press Limited.

Baker, M., De Vries, E., & Lund, K. (1999). Designing computer-mediated epistemic interactions. In S. P. Lajoie & M. Vivet (Eds.), *Proceedings of the 9th International Conference on Artificial Intelligence in Education* (pp. 139-146). Amsterdam: IOS Press.

Boxtel, C. Van (2000). *Collaborative concept learning.* Unpublished PhD thesis, Utrecht University, Utrecht, The Netherlands.

Chanquoy, L. (1996, October). *Connectives and argumentative text: a developmental study.* Paper presented at the First International Workshop on Argumentative Text Processing, Barcelona, Spain.

Coirier, P., Andriessen, J. E. B., & Chanquoy, L. (1999). From planning to translating: The specificity of argumentative writing. In J. E. B. Andriessen & P. Coirier (Eds.), *Foundations of argumentative text processing* (pp. 1-29). Amsterdam: Amsterdam University Press.

Erkens, G. (1997). *Cooperatief probleemoplossen met computers in het onderwijs: Het modelleren van cooperatieve dialogen voor de ontwikkeling van intelligente onderwijssystemen* [Cooperative problem solving with computers in education: Modelling of cooperative dialogues for the design of intelligent educational systems]. Unpublished doctoral dissertation, Utrecht University, Utrecht, The Netherlands.

Erkens, G., Prangsma, M. E., Jaspers, J. G. M., & Kanselaar, G. (2002). *Computer supported collaborative and argumentative writing.* Utrecht : Utrecht University, ICO-ISOR Onderwijsresearch.

Glasersfeld, E. von (1989). Cognition, construction of knowledge and teaching. *Synthese, 80,* 121-140.

Greeno, J. G. (1997). Response: On claims that answer the wrong question. *Educational Researcher, 20,* 5-17.

Henri, F. (1995). Distance learning and computer mediated communication: Interactive, quasi-interactive or monologue? In C. O'Malley (Ed.), *Computer supported collaborative learning* (Vol. 128, pp. 145-165). Berlin: Springer.

Kanselaar, G., Jong, T. de, Andriessen, J. E. B., & Goodyear, P. (2000). New technologies. In P .R. J. Simons, J. L. van der Linden & T. Duffy (Eds.),. *New learning* (pp. 49 - 72). Dordrecht: Kluwer Academic Publishers.

Kanselaar, G., & Erkens, G. (1996). Interactivity in co-operative problem solving with computers. In S. Vosniadou, E. DeCorte, R. Glaser & H. Mandl (Eds.), *International perspectives on the design of technology-supported learning environments* (pp. 185-202). Mahwah, New Jersey: Lawrence Erlbaum.

Kuhn, D. (1991). *The skills of argument.* Cambridge: University Press.

Petraglia, J. (1997). *The rhetoric and technology of authenticity in education.* Mahwah, NJ: Lawrence Erlbaum.

Roschelle, J. (1992). Learning by collaborating: Convergent conceptual change. *The journal of the learning sciences, 2,* 235-276.

Roschelle, J., & Teasley, S. D. (1995). Construction of shared knowledge in collaborative problem solving. In C. O'Malley (Ed.*), Computer-supported collaborative learning* (pp. 69-97). New York: Springer Verlag.

Salomon, G. (1993). On the nature of pedagogic computer tools: The case of the writing partner. In S. P. Lajoie & S. J. Derry (Eds.), *Computers as cognitive tools* (pp. 289-317). Hillsdale, NJ: Lawrence Erlbaum.

Salomon, G. (1997, August 26-30). *Novel constructivist learning environments and novel technologies: Some issues to be concerned.* Invited key-note address presented at the EARLI conference, Athens.

Savery, J. R., & Duffy, T. M. (1995). Problem based learning: An instructional model and its constructivistic framework. *Educational Technology, 35,* 31-38.

Scardamalia, M., Bereiter, C., & Lamon, M. (1994). The CSILE project: Trying to bring the classroom into world 3. In K. McGilly (Ed.), *Classroom lessons: Integrating cognitive theory and classroom practice* (pp. 201-229). Cambridge, MA: MIT Press.

Suthers, D., Weiner, A., Connelly, J., & Paolucci, M. (1995, August). *Belvedere: Engaging students in critical discussion of science and public policy issues.* Paper presented at the AI-Ed 95, the 7th World Conference on Artificial Intelligence in Education, Washington, DC.

Suthers, D., & Hundhausen, C. (2001). Learning by constructing collaborative representations: An empirical comparison of three alternatives. In P. Dillenbourg, A. Eurelings & K. Hakkarainen (Eds.), *European perspectives on computer-supported collaborative learning: Proceedings of thé first european conference on computer-supported collaborative learning* (pp.577-584). Maastricht, the Netherlands, University of Maastricht.

Teasley, S. D., & Roschelle, J. (1993). Constructing a joint problem space: The computer as a tool for sharing knowledge. In S. P. Lajoie & S. J. Derry (Eds.), *Computers as cognitive tools* (pp. 229-257). Hillsdale, NJ: Lawrence Erlbaum.

Van Eemeren, F. H., Grootendorst, R., & Snoeck Henkemans, A. F. (1995). *Argumentatie.* Groningen: Woltersgroep, The Netherlands.

Veerman, A. L., & Treasure-Jones, T. (1999). Software for problem solving through collaborative argumentation. In P. Coirier & J. E. B. Andriessen (Eds.), *Foundations of argumentative text processing* (pp. 203-230). Amsterdam: Amsterdam University Press.

Veerman, A. L. (2000). *Computer-Supported collaborative learning through argumentation.* Doctoral dissertation. Enschede: Print Partners Ipskamp.

Veerman, A. L., & Andriessen, J.E.B. (1997, September, 4-6). *Academic learning & writing through the use of educational technology.* Presented at the conference on Learning & Teaching Argumentation, Middlesex University, London.

Veerman, A. L., Andriessen, J. E. B., & Kanselaar, G. (2000.) Enhancing learning through synchronous discussion. *Computers & Education, 34,* (2-3),1-22.

Wampold, B. E., & Margolin, G. (1982). Nonparametric strategies to test the independence of behavioral states in sequential data. *Psychological Bulletin, 92,* 755-765.

4 Using Computer Supported Argument Visualization to Teach Legal Argumentation

Chad S. Carr

Sears, Roebuck & Co.

I choose the word "argument" thoughtfully, for scientific demonstrations, even mathematical proofs, are fundamentally acts of persuasion. Scientific statements can never be certain: they can only be more or less credible.

Joseph Weizenbaum in Computer Power and Human Reason (1976)

4.1 Legal Reasoning and the Process of Argumentation

According to the American Bar Association (ABA), legal reasoning is one of the "fundamental lawyering skills"; listed among those skills the ABA task force deems most important (MacCrate, 1994). In response to this recent report, many law schools have introduced courses in "lawyering skills" to help support legal reasoning (in addition to other skills listed in the report) (Schrag, 1989). However, there is not much indication as to how this "fundamental lawyering skill" is, or should be, acquired inside the law classrooms or in the legal education literature (Blasi, 1995; MacCrate, 1994). Further, many law professors still believe that a law school education should focus on doctrine and theory, leaving the development of these fundamental skills up to the students (Maurer and Mischler, 1994).

Maurer and Mischler (1994) see students in traditional legal courses developing research, reasoning, and legal writing skills in isolation by drafting briefs and memoranda based on multiple fact patterns prepared by the course instructors. Though everyone agrees that legal reasoning is one of the most important skills learned in law school (Gordon, 1989), too many students graduate without the ability to research, reason, and write effectively (Woxland, 1989; Marke, 1989).

According to Perelman (1980), legal reasoning is "an argumentation aiming to persuade and convince those whom it addresses, that such a choice, decision or attitude is preferable to concurrent choices, decisions and attitudes." Argumentation is a process of making assertions or claims and providing support and justification for these claims using data, facts, and evidence (Toulmin, 1958). The origins of argumentation date back to Aristotle who believed that most arguments in the real world (i.e., informal) were practical in nature and took place outside of highly rigorous systems of logical (i.e., formal) and mathematical proof (Saunders, 1994). Thus, the goal of argumentation is to *persuade* or *convince* others that one's reasoning is more valid or appropriate.

Many lawyers lack a basic understanding of the structure and process of legal argumentation (MacCrate, 1994). Their limited understanding, which often leads to less than effective advocacy, stems from "the legal education's failure to make the structure and process of legal argument explicit and systematic" (Saunders, 1994).

4.2 How do we Support the Development of Argumentation Skills?

In order to make the structure and process of legal argument explicit, many advocate formally representing arguments using Toulmin's Model of Argument, as introduced in Chapter 1 (Leeman, 1987; Saunders, 1994). Toulmin's Model encourages students' argument development in three primary ways: (1) by equipping the student with language by which to examine personal commitment, (2) by introducing the role of probability in reasoning, and (3) by revealing the chain of argumentation (Toulmin, 1958). Toulmin's Model provides students with specific language for discussing what they have largely done without conscious examination. Students do not think of their own everyday arguments in terms of claims and warrants, data and qualifiers, yet such are present in those arguments (Toulmin, 1958). Further, Toulmin's model provides a mechanism for "slowing down" the reasoning process in order to better understand it (Leeman, 1987).

4.2.1 Stephen Toulmin's Model of Argument

Without systems of language symbols, it would be very difficult to reason or argue. These symbols (words) have meanings shared by the members of the group who are also participants in the social action. Argumentation entails the analysis, evaluation and formulation of arguments based on reasons (Toulmin, 1958). Toulmin's model provides the language symbols that support this process (see Figure 4.1).

Toulmin's model is procedural, not static or spatial (Toulmin Rieke, and Janik, 1984). Based on legal reasoning, the layout of his argument model focuses on the movement of accepted data through a warrant, to a claim. Toulmin recognizes three secondary elements that may be present (and sometimes implicit) in an argument: backing, qualifier, and rebuttal. According to Saunders (1994, p. 569):

> Backing is the authority for a warrant; it provides credibility for the warrant and may be introduced when the audience is unwilling to accept the warrant at face value. A qualifier indicates the degree of force or certainty that a claim

possesses; it converts the terms of the argument from absolute to probable. Finally, rebuttal represents certain conditions or exceptions under which the claim will fail; it anticipates objections that might be advanced against the argument to refute the claim.

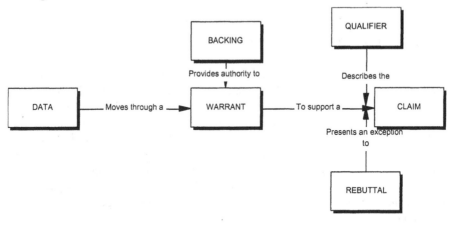

Figure 4.1: Toulmin's Model of Argument.

In the following example, an argument with regard to an employee termination case is represented using Toulmin's model of argument (see Figure 4.2). A man (referred to as 'E') has been dismissed from his position as a steel mill worker and met with his lawyer to discuss a possible lawsuit. The lawyer suggests that there could be grounds for a lawsuit regarding breach of his employment agreement. The lawyer will support this assertion with precedent, and recognizes that the employer may use a defence by proving that this man was an employee at will.

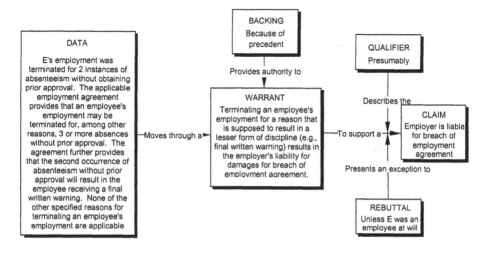

Figure 4.2: Example of legal argument using Toulmin's model.

As such, Toulmin's model of argument becomes the mechanism for structuring argumentation between law students. It aims to clarify reasoning by encouraging parties to make explicit important assumptions, distinctions, and relationships as they construct and rationalize ideas (Buckingham Shum, MacLean, Bellotti, and Hammond, 1997).

4.2.2   Representing Arguments Collaboratively

Decades of research into cognitive and social aspects of learning has developed a clear picture of the importance of learners active involvement in the expression, examination, and manipulation of their own knowledge (Chi, 1989; Perkins, et al. 1995; Scardamalia, et al. 1994). Recently these findings have been reflected in software technology for learning: systems are now providing learners with the means to construct and manipulate their own solutions while interacting with other learners (Suthers, 1999). This process is commonly referred to as Computer Supported Collaborative Learning (CSCL). This study examines the use of a computer-based representational tool, QuestMap™,[1] to support collaborative argumentation in legal education.

Though much research has been conducted with individuals using knowledge representation tools, surprisingly little has been conducted on collaborative use (Suthers, 1999). *Representational tools* for data manipulation and knowledge mapping range from basic office tools such as spreadsheets and outliners to "knowledge mapping" software (Jonassen and Carr, 1999). Such tools provide representational guidance that help learners see patterns, express abstractions in concrete form, and discover new relationships (Goldenberg, 1995). These representational tools can function as cognitive tools that lead learners into certain knowledge-building interactions (Jonassen and Reeves, 1996; Lajoie and Derry, 1993).

The current study assumes that representational tools will guide collaboration (at least) as well as individual learning interactions (since studies have proven that computer-assisted instruction is as effective in group learning as in individual learning (Johnson, 1985)). Specifically, as learner-constructed external representations created in QuestMap™ become part of the collaborator's shared context, it is expected that "the distinctions and relationships that are made salient by these representations may influence their interactions in ways that influence learning outcomes" (i.e., argumentation skills) (Suthers, 1999).

4.2.3   Computer Supported Argument Visualization

Computer supported argument visualization (CSAV) is the process of using technology to support argumentation as groups solve problems (Jonassen and Carr, 1999; Buckingham Shum, 1996). Law students are normally given problems to analyze throughout a course. The argumentation process typically takes place as follows:

---

[1]   QuestMap is a trademark of GDSS, Inc., Washington, DC, USA and is described in detail by Conklin in Chapter 6

1   Pose / define problem
2   Generate proposals
3   Create supporting arguments
4   Evaluate proposals / arguments
5   Make a decision (based on agreement or consensus)

To support this process, CSAV (specifically, QuestMap™, which is structurally parallel to Toulmin's model of argument) provides a framework to help organize, display, and record the argumentation process (see Figure 4.3).

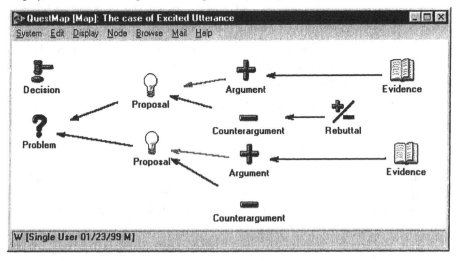

Figure 4.3: Sample CSAV structure including multiple components of Toulmin's Model of Argument, recorded using QuestMap™ from The Soft Bicycle Company.

In this structure, a *problem* is a statement of an unknown, or something that is unsettled, such as a controversy, an issue, etc. The problem is introduced by the professor in the form of a question (e.g., should this evidence be allowed in court?). A *proposal* is a recommendation for action in response to the problem (e.g., it should be admitted). Finally, an *argument* is comprised of evidence that supports a proposal (because of mandatory precedent). Thus, to elaborate on a **problem**, students submit **proposals** with supporting **arguments**. Additionally, students can create links (e.g., supports, contradicts, competes with, etc.) that indicate relationships between arguments. Students can then respond further with counter-arguments and rebuttals. In this example, there are two claims (labeled, "proposals" in accordance with legal terminology), several warrants, with backing (labeled, "arguments" and "counterarguments"), and grounds or data (labeled, "evidence"). This is a very rudimentary example; legal arguments can become extremely complex and elaborate.

4.2.4   Developing Argumentation Skills Collaboratively

Collaborative Learning has been defined as "the mutual engagement of participants in a coordinated effort to solve [a] problem together" (Roschelle and Behrend, 1995). According to Resnick (1991), "…directly experienced events are only part of the basis for [knowledge] construction. People also build their knowledge structures on the basis of what they are told by others. Our daily lives are filled with instances in which we influence each other's constructive processes by providing information, pointing things out to one another, asking questions, and arguing with and elaborating on each other's ideas." According to Jonassen and Carr (1999):

> social constructivists see learning more as conversation, relying on knowledge negotiation as an essential part of knowledge construction. Rather than internal and individual, cognition is socially shared.

As such, CSAV becomes a scaffolding through which students can socially construct knowledge and practice argumentation. Through CSAV, the incorporation of social discourse helps to:

> crystallize the issues and forces students to recognize the weaknesses of their case… and students have to face squarely the weaknesses of their case and create strategies for handling unfavorable law and facts. After this experience, students are not likely to ignore counter-arguments in their appellate briefs. (Maurer, and Mischler, 1994).

Counter-arguments necessarily require the student to engage in higher-order reasoning (to be able to reason about their prior reasoning) (Jonassen and Carr, 1999). Further, research on a variety of tasks and forms of reasoning suggests that peer interaction may not only engage existing competencies, but, over time, foster developmental progress (Dimant and Bearison, 1991; Kruger, 1992).

A study by Moshman and Geil (1998) provides clear evidence for the cognitive value of collaborative learning. Wason's (1968) four-card task was presented to 143 college students in its original, most difficult, version. To assess the role of collaboration in reasoning, 32 students worked on the task individually and the remaining 111 worked in 20 groups of five or six students each. Consistent with previous evidence, only 9% of students in the individual condition selected the correct response pattern. In contrast, the correct pattern was selected by 75% of the groups.

Why such a difference? A further review of the videotapes of the interactions suggested that the high level of reasoning was due to rational social processes such as requests for clarification and justification, critical evaluation, presentation of alternatives, and reflection on disagreements (Moshman and Geil, 1998).

CSAV supports all of these activities by providing an opportunity for students to develop reasoning skills in a social context – working with their peers and comparing their responses to the professor's.

By providing a mental model upon which to reason, CSAV supports the organization and representation of reasoning skills, enabling students to organize their oral and written argumentation process. Research suggests that what makes a good lawyer is not the quantity of detailed knowledge, but the quality of its organization (Blasi, 1995).

4.2.5   CSAV Support for Developing Legal Argumentation Skills

The remainder of this chapter describes a research study conducted to determine if CSAV could support the legal argumentation skills of law students. Law students were chosen because the field of law is an ill-structured domain (Blasi, 1995). An ill-structured knowledge domain is one in which the following two properties hold: (a) each case or example of knowledge application typically involves the simultaneous interactive involvement of multiple, wide-application conceptual structures (multiple schemas, perspectives, organizational principles, and so on), each of which is individually complex (i.e., the domain involves concept-and case-complexity); and (b) the pattern of conceptual incidence and interaction varies substantially across cases nominally of the same type (i.e., the domain involves across-case irregularity) (Spiro et al., 1992).

Second-year law students used CSAV to solve ill-structured problems relating to the use of evidence in the court of law. Expertise in problem-solving involves the ability to make the best individual or "local" decisions at the nodes of the network, *together* with a superior ability to consider the "global" effects of potential "local" decisions as their consequences are carried forward through time and in interconnection with other decisions. Blasi (1995) observed that not only do novices often seem too much distracted by the trees to see the forest; sometimes they are completely absorbed by a single leaf. Additionally, Voss and Means (1991) observed similar "piecemeal" behaviour among novice problem solvers in ill-structured domains, such as law. They concluded that CSAV supports a student's ability to "see the forest" by (1) providing for collaboration, (2) providing a visual representation of the "forest", (3) capturing the process of argumentation, (4) providing a means to search and index the contents of the process, and (5) storing the process for later review.

4.3   A Study of CSAV in Legal Education

This next section describes a study of the relationship between using CSAV and argumentation processes during five case-based learning activities involving the use of evidence in the court of law. The relationship between using CSAV and argumentation skills will be investigated by comparing the arguments created on a practice final exam between the experimental (CSAV) group with the control (traditional written assignment) group.

The primary research question in this study was: How does using CSAV, while groups of 3-4 second-year law students generate arguments throughout the semester, affect the quality and type of arguments generated on a practice final exam?

Our hypothesis was that groups using CSAV to construct arguments throughout the study will create higher quality arguments on a practice final exam than those who construct written arguments throughout the study. Quality of argumentation will be analyzed by two measures: (1) the number and types of arguments, counterarguments, rebuttals and evidence used according to Toulmin's Model of Argument (Toulmin, Rieke and Janik, 1984 – see Chapter 2), and (2) practice final exam scores as assessed by the professor.

In the current study, law students already communicate using a formalized "legal" language which includes citing evidence, rebuttals, counter arguments and so on. Though QuestMap™ was not specifically designed to incorporate such language representations, nodes can be easily relabelled with such legal terminology. Again, the intelligence of the software is not an issue in the current study because the intelligence resides in the course instructor. According to Suthers (1999), further research is being conducted to investigate the ways in which Belvedere can support scientific argumentation.

The purpose of this study was to investigate the effect of Computer supported argument visualization (CSAV) on the argumentation skills of second year law students in an evidence course. This effect was measured in three ways: (1) by describing the change in argument structures of the treatment group – submitted using QuestMap™ – over time, (2) by comparing the practice final exam scores of the treatment and control groups, and (3) by comparing the practice final exam responses of the treatment and control groups using Toulmin's argument coding scheme (Toulmin, Rieke, and Janik, 1984).

A quasi-experimental static-group comparison design (Gall, Borg, and Gall, 1996) was used to assess the effectiveness of the CSAV tool in developing argumentation skills in second-year law students over the course of one semester. This design is not as reliable as the post-test only control group design, but was necessary due to the nature of the population: students were allowed to select whether they participated in the treatment or control group in order to increase the number of participants. The treatment group completed assignments using the CSAV tool – QuestMap™ – in groups of 3 to 4, and the control group completed them as usual: students typically completed the assignments alone or in small "study" groups they form voluntarily and have no access to the QuestMap™ tool – only legal research databases and resources. The amount of collaboration in each study group (in both control and treatment groups) was assessed by an exit survey administered during the practice final exam to determine whether collaboration was a factor that contributed to any differences found between the treatment and control groups.

We now discuss the experimental design of the study, describe the procedure in detail, and discuss the methods used to assess the effectiveness of the study.

4.3.1   Experimental Design

Independent Variable
Use of QuestMap™ (CSAV tool): The independent variable was operationalized by allowing the treatment group to create arguments through the use of QuestMap™ to solve five problems throughout the semester in groups of 3 to 4 students, while the control group solved them without access to QuestMap™.

Dependent Variable

Quality of Argument: The dependent variable was measured by three indicators: (1) the number and types of argument structures present according to Toulmin's Model of Argument (Toulmin, Rieke, and Janik, 1984), (2) the performance on the practice final exam as assessed by the professor, and (3) by examining the richness (number of nodes created) of arguments saved in the QuestMap™ tool throughout the semester to describe progress.

Subjects

The subjects included 76 second-year law students: 36 volunteered to join the treatment group and 40 volunteered to join the control group. Students in each group attended one of two sections of "Evidence" taught by the same professor at an ABA/AALS approved law school. Of the 36 students in the treatment group, 28 attended section one while eight attended section two. The threats to validity presented by such a design are addressed later in this chapter.

The professor (in accordance with policies at the law school) cannot require students to participate in the treatment group, so, students were asked to volunteer their participation. According to Rosenthal and Rosnow (1975), volunteers tend to be better educated, have a higher social class, be more intelligent, be more unconventional, be female (for this type of study), be less authoritarian, be Jewish, and tend to be less conforming than those who do not volunteer. To help to account for any systematic biases between the treatment and control group, student gender, LSAT scores, Lawyering Skills scores, and class rank were compared between both groups.

Materials

The materials used for the course include: "Evidence Under the Rules" (3rd Edition) by Mueller and Kirkpatrick and "Federal Rules of Evidence" (1998 Edition). Further, all students were allowed to conduct online research using legal reference tools, such as WestLaw™. Both the control and the treatment group had access to the same materials. The treatment group was also allowed access to QuestMap™.

Five problems were generated by the professor and addressed current legal issues related to evidence. Students were then allowed to review cases, notes, rules, and examples to determine whether or not certain types of evidence should be admitted in a court of law. For example, see a sample problem involving wrongful death (Figure 4.4).

Throughout the semester, students were asked to submit responses to each problem including their arguments, expected counterarguments, and rebuttals. The control group handed those responses in on paper while the treatment group recorded their responses graphically using QuestMap™. The graphs were then automatically converted to outline form and printed out for submission (see Figure 4.5).

In addition to the normal legal resources, the treatment group also had access to QuestMap™. These students gathered once a week throughout the semester in the computer lab to construct their arguments using QuestMap™.

After each group exhausted their ability to create further arguments that related to the current case, they would stop and print out their arguments to turn in. Meanwhile, the students in the control group constructed arguments without access to QuestMap™ and turned their assignments in as well.

Sample Problem:

Case / Problem:

On an open stretch of two-lane highway in Nevada, Jay Gadsby, traveling eastbound in a red Z-Car with racing stripe, collided with Roy Reinhart, headed westbound in a pickup truck with gun rack. Both Jay and Roy were killed instantly. The road was straight, the noonday sun bright overhead, and afternoon thermal winds had not yet picked up – in short, driving conditions were optimal. Physical facts yield no clues as to the cause of the accident.

In her wrongful death action against Gadsby's estate, Roy's widow offers testimony by another eastbound driver – one Hill, who was first to come upon the accident – that 30 miles west of the point of the collision the red Z-Car had overtaken him going "at least 80 miles per hour." The defense objects, arguing that Hill's testimony is "irrelevant" when offered as proof of that Jay was speeding at the time of the accident, at least in the absence of further proof that Gadsby likely continued to travel at the rate observed for the 30 miles between the sighting and the point of impact.

Question:

Is the evidence relevant on the question of Gadsby's speed at the time of impact? Should the judge admit the evidence only if the proponent offers additional proof to satisfy the condition suggested by defendant?

Figure 4.4: Sample Evidence Problem.

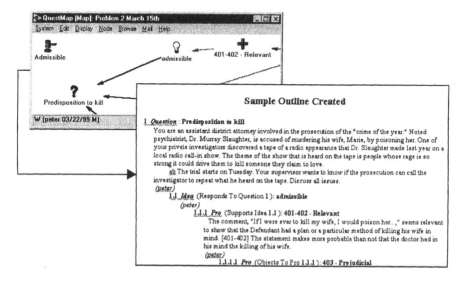

Figure 4.5: Sample QuestMap™ Map and corresponding Outline.

Finally, each week the professor would provide the "expert" opinion, by creating an answer to the current case that considered all relevant arguments. The researcher converted this narrative document into an argument map using QuestMap™. That map was then reviewed by the professor to ensure its accuracy of depicting his narrative version. Using this narrative document (control group), or the graphical document (treatment group) the students could compare their responses to determine the appropriateness of their answers.

4.3.2 Static-Group Comparison Design

The static-group comparison design consists of a treatment group and a control group. The control group participated in the course as usual, while the treatment group was allowed to use a special software application – QuestMap™. The static-group comparison design controls for all sources of invalidity except for attrition and pre-existing differences (Campbell, Stanley and Gage, 1966). In this study, three students dropped out of the treatment group after week one, but agreed to remain in the study by joining the control group. Pre-existing differences were assessed by comparing reported indicators, including LSAT, GPA, Class Rank, Lawyering Skills score, and Gender.

Procedure
The study consisted of 76 second-year law students recruited from two sections of "Legal Evidence" taught at an ABA/AALS approved law school. The members of the treatment group (who received access to the QuestMap™) were selected by their volunteering for an optional one-hour training session and fixed meeting time. The professor reserved the computer laboratory for one hour each week to provide students with access to QuestMap™. Students were made aware both by the course description and by the professor, that by volunteering for this one-hour per week session, they were volunteering to receive access to QuestMap™. Thirty-six volunteered for the treatment (CSAV) group, three dropped out after the first week, leaving 33 to finish the study. Purpose and measure procedures of the study were explained to all potential subjects; only those who voluntarily agreed to participate were included in the study. Subjects each signed an informed consent form prior to the study, and received a copy of the signed form. Thirty-three of those students volunteered to participate and remained in the treatment group throughout the study. All students who agreed to participate in the study also self-reported their Gender, Class Rank, GPA, section, LSAT score, Lawyering Skills score, and group membership (treatment vs. control) under conditions blind to the researcher and professor.

Students in the treatment group received one hour of training on the use of QuestMap™ during the first session. Students were given a user's guide that detailed the training module. In summary, students viewed a sample argument constructed by the professor, were introduced to the most common screens and features of QuestMap™, reviewed a sample problem, and began constructing arguments for and against the problem using legal resources.

Approximately every two weeks, all students were assigned a problem upon which to construct arguments throughout the semester (a total of five problems were assigned). Typically, students work on them in groups using legal references available from the course and the law library. The treatment group was assigned the same five problems and constructed arguments in groups of 3-4 students using those same resources and QuestMap™ during scheduled weekly sessions. The treatment group each logged in to their own computer, but worked in a shared "virtual" space (such that each person could view and modify its contents) and were seated beside one another to facilitate communication.

All students were instructed to generate coherent arguments, counter-arguments, rebuttals, and summary judgments for each of the problems. The arguments created by the control group were completed in narrative form. The arguments created by the treatment groups were captured in the QuestMap™ database, printed, and submitted. Problem two and Problem five completed by the treatment group were analyzed to described progress throughout the semester.

At the end of the semester, all students completed a practice final exam within one class period toward the end of the semester (due to privacy issues, the researcher was not given access to the final exams as exam questions are reused on occasion). On the practice final exam, students were given a problem (similar to the problems given throughout the semester) and were to construct all relevant arguments individually and without legal resources. Their responses were scored by the professor using a grading rubric and coded by the researcher according to Toulmin's model of argument (Toulmin, Rieke, and Janik, 1984). Each are discussed more fully in the next section.

Collection of Data

The entire group of subjects was asked to solicit their responses to a practice final exam for further analysis. They submitted them blindly, indicating only whether or not they were members of the treatment group in codes that were not apparent to the reviewers at the time of coding. Participants were specifically asked not to put their names on the practice finals and no code was used to personally identify the students in any way. The results were then analyzed using Toulmin's coding scheme (Toulmin, Rieke, and Janik, 1984). The primary researcher coded the final written exams. An additional rater reviewed a randomly selected subset of the practice final exam responses to ensure the reliability of the rating system. To determine inter-rater reliability, the number of agreements was divided by the number of total observations (Gall, Borg and Gall, 1996).

Coding Final Written Arguments

In order to further interpret the practice final exam responses, the exams were coded according to Toulmin's model of argument.

Statistical Analysis

The quantitative categorical data (codes resulting from the analysis of the problem answered on the practice final exam) yielded by this experimental design were analyzed using Chi-square tests to analyze all dichotomous variables and T-tests between all other codes.

Additionally, a simple T-test was performed to test for the amount of variation in the mean practice final exam scores between the treatment and control group as assessed by the professor.

A multiple regression analysis was calculated to compare group membership with each predictor: LSAT, Class rank, gender, section, and Lawyering Skills Score.

4.3.3   Results

The results of this study indicated that (1) there were no significant pre-existing differences between the control and treatment group, (2) arguments did not get more elaborate throughout the semester (M=17.5, SD=4.14 for problem two, M=17.9, SD=7.97 for problem five), (3) the treatment group did not have a significantly different score (t(73)=-1.505, p=.137) on the practice final than did the control group, and (4) the hierarchical cluster analysis of the practice final exams of the treatment group did not yield meaningful clusters of data. Exit surveys indicated that study groups in both the control and treatment groups spent between one to two hours studying together each week for this evidence course.

Analysis of Pre-Existing Differences between Groups
A linear regression was conducted using LSAT (LSAT), Gender (GENDER), Class Rank (CRANK), and Lawyering Skills Score (LAWSKILL) to predict group (COMP) (treatment versus control). All of these factors combined failed to significantly predict group membership (COMP) (t(68)=17.217, p=.305) (See Table 4.1). Thus, the researcher could detect no significant pre-existing differences between the treatment and control groups.

Change in QuestMap™ Arguments Over Time
The treatment group used QuestMap™ to construct arguments to five problems throughout the semester. Problem two and five were analyzed to determine whether arguments were becoming more elaborate throughout the semester. The average number of nodes (argument components according to Toulmin's model of argument) created by each study group was M=17.5, SD=4.14 for problem two, M=17.9, SD=7.97 for problem five. The mean rose only slightly throughout the semester and, in many groups, it actually went down. Unconfirmed observations of QuestMap™ use by law students suggests that little coaching was required to begin constructing arguments using the software efficiently.

Analysis of Practice Final Exam Scores
Practice final exams consisted of one question students in both groups were to respond to within one class period. Students wrote responses in class without access to any legal resources. The professor then composed an exemplary solution to the problem by including all relevant arguments related to the admissibility of the evidence presented.

After creating an exemplary response, the professor created an answer key with which to assess the student exams by outlining the relevant rules, arguments, and evidence.

The professor (in the presence of the researcher) then applied this rubric to each student response on the practice final exam using a "think aloud" protocol for one high-scoring student response and one low-scoring student response. The professor looked for specific keywords or phrases found in the student responses that were also present on the Practice Exam Answer Key. In some instances, the professor gave partial credit for providing a certain response (e.g., mentioning rule 803(2) but not 803(3) under IB5 above). Specific key words not found on the answer key were also helpful in identifying key phrases (e.g., Thus, Consequently, and Therefore usually prefaced IC or IIE).

After identifying all answers present in a student response, the total points were tallied to determine the student's final score. Each branch in the answer key was worth one point except for IB and IIC(which were worth two points). The highest possible score was 20.

Significance Testing

An independent-samples t test was conducted to evaluate the hypothesis that students using CSAV to construct arguments throughout the study would have higher scores on the practice final exam than those who didn't use CSAV throughout the study (as assessed by the professor). The test was insignificant, $t(73)=-1.505$, $p=.137$. The students who used CSAV ($M=5.15$, $SD=1.62$) did not score higher on the practice final exam than the students who did not use CSAV ($M=4.50$, $SD=2.03$). See Table 4.1 and Figure 4.4.

Thus, the practice final exam scores for the treatment group were not significantly higher than those of the control group as assessed by the professor.

Analysis of Practice Final Exams using Toulmin's Coding Scheme

In order to further interpret the practice final exam responses, the exams were coded according to Toulmin's model of argument (Toulmin, Rieke, and Janik, 1984). The professor outlined the most complete lines of reasoning according to Toulmin's model of argument.

The first map created, corresponds with the rudimentary model of argument (Toulmin, Rieke, and Janik, 1984) with the addition of one intermediate, or "minor" claim (Claim2). The map has been modified to correctly represent one line of reasoning present in the professor's response. In this case, there is a major claim (Claim1), supported by a minor claim (Claim2), in turn, supported by basic truths (Grounds). All components of the model were explicitly stated in the professor's response, including Rebuttals, Qualifiers, Warrants, and Backings.

In the second spatial map created from the remainder of the professor's response, the professor has not explicitly identified Qualifiers, Grounds, or a minor claim.

After creating the spatial maps, the practice final exam responses for each student were coded to determine the number of each type of argument components present. The inter-rater reliability coefficient between the researcher and the second rater was calculated to be 83 percent agreement (>70 percent is acceptable) (VanLeeuwen, 1997). The results are summarized in Table 4.1.

The results indicate the average number of codes present per student exam (e.g., 0.50 would mean that half of the students' exams contained that argument code). No students explicitly mentioned any grounds (G) for their arguments, relying entirely on rules (warrants) and backing.

In summary, the treatment group did not contain significantly more total argument components (5.21) than did the control group (4.91). The rest of the codes are remarkably similar except for the number of rebuttals in case I (R) and case II (IIR), and the total number of Warrants (W).

Table 4.1: Summary of Toulmin's Argument Codes in Practice Exam Per participant.

Code	Treatment	Control	Expert
Backings (B)	0.94	0.95	3.00
Claim1 (C1)	0.45	0.42	1.00
Claim2 (C2)	0.91	0.95	1.00
Grounds (G)	0.00	0.00	1.00
Qualifiers (Q)	0.03	0.00	1.00
Rebuttals (R)	1.45	1.19	2.00
Warrants (W)	0.58	0.33	4.00
IIBackings (IIB)	0.42	0.47	1.00
IIClaim1 (IIC1)	0.12	0.12	1.00
IIRebuttals (IIR)	0.27	0.47	1.00
IIWarrants (IIW)	0.03	0.02	1.00
Totals:	5.21	4.91	17.00

Practice Final Exam Scores

An independent-samples t test was conducted to evaluate the hypothesis that students using CSAV to construct arguments throughout the study would have higher scores on the practice final exam than those who didn't use CSAV throughout the study (as assessed by the professor). The test was insignificant, $t(73)=-1.505$, $p=.137$. The students who used CSAV ($M=5.15$, $SD=1.62$) did not score higher on the practice final exam than the students who did not use CSAV ($M=4.50$, $SD=2.03$).

The researcher expected a higher score in both groups, but, when approached, the professor indicated that this was common for two reasons: (1) the exam was given two weeks before finals (implying that the students may not have thoroughly prepared for this practice final), and (2) exam questions are intentionally difficult to prevent a ceiling effect in final grades. As for the former statement, this suggestion was supported by the unconfirmed data collected on the exit survey which asked students the average time spent preparing for this practice final. The responses ranged from none to less than one hour.

4.3.4   Conclusion from this Study

The primary objective of this study was to determine the effect of using CSAV on argumentation skills in second-year law students. To this end, the study has provided some insights into the use of a CSAV (i.e., QuestMap™) in a context not previously researched – the context of legal education – where argumentation is central and students possess robust knowledge of the legal domain and of argumentation, in general. Previous studies have focused on children (Suthers, 1999; Bell, 1997), software designers (Buckingham Shum and Hammond, 1994), and undergraduate students (Marttunen, 1992) who possessed either limited domain knowledge, argumentation skills, or both.

Law students are highly skilled in argument and argumentation is central to their success in law school and beyond (Blasi, 1995). Findings indicated that law students who used QuestMap™ did not score significantly higher on the final written exam than did the control group. Additionally, through direct and unconfirmed observations, students exhibited scarcely any cognitive overhead in adapting to the use of QuestMap™ to create arguments. It appears that CSAV may tend to provide students with more robust domain and argumentation knowledge more support for the process of argumentation than for the product of written arguments.

Level of Expertise
The results were not significant in favour of the treatment group (as hypothesized), which, when compared with similar research, could imply that further studies are needed to test whether or not CSAV might be effective in improving the quality of arguments constructed by law students. Specifically, research suggests that CSAV may be more effective in supporting the construction of arguments by students with limited domain or argumentation knowledge. For example, studies have shown that argumentation skills are linked with intelligence (Perkins, 1985), age (McCann, 1989) and the level of education (Voss, Blais, Means, and Greene, 1986; Kuhn, 1991). Consequently, one might expect a first-year first semester student to benefit more from CSAV than a second-year, second-semester student – who is older and possesses a higher level of domain familiarity (i.e. knowledge of the law) and argumentation skills.

In general, older children are better at writing argumentative text than are younger children (Golder and Coirier, 1994; Golder 1992). In a study of children aged 7-16, the youngest children did not express a position, slightly older children took a position without justifying it, still older children developed minimal arguments, later providing elaborated arguments, and counterargument occurred typically at about age 14 (Golder and Coirier, 1994). Golder (1992) also found that personal involvement (i.e. domain knowledge) with the topic is related to better argument generation. Zammuner (1991) had subjects write about their position on abortion and found that the construction of argumentative text was more elaborated for individuals favoring abortion. The result was attributed to the anti-abortion sociocultural atmosphere of Italy, where the study took place.

First semester law students in many law schools are now required to take a "lawyering skills" course to introduce them to the basic skills of legal research, reasoning, and writing. Since law is a new domain for first-year students, research suggests that they should be less able to argue than second-year students. For example, Penner and Voss (1983), presented social science problems to research chemists and found that their solutions were more like those of novices than experts. The chemists, although excellent problem solvers in their own discipline, lacked both the content knowledge and specific skills necessary to tackle a social science problem. Since first-year students come from such varied backgrounds, CSAV may have the potential to support first-year students argumentation skills more so than second-year students who have developed more robust legal understanding and argumentation skills.

Cognitive Overhead

Unlike design users who experienced much cognitive overhead in constraining their thinking to the symbols available in CSAV (Buckingham Shum, MacLean, Bellotti, and Hammond, 1997), law students began using the software as the proverbial duck did to water. Students were able to create complex, natural arguments after only one hour of training. This may have also served to inhibit the overall benefit that is usually inherent in using CSAV – it is supposed to constrain thinking (Bell, 1997; Suthers, 1999; Buckingham Shum, 1996). If law students already think in this manner normally, then CSAV software may not offer a relative advantage over dialogic argument experienced in the control group.

Since the students were already skilled at argument, CSAV may benefit the efficiency more than the effectiveness of argumentation. CSAV then becomes more of a performance support tool that represents knowledge and serves as a focus of discussion, than a tool that will force students to constrain their thinking.

Focus of Discourse Through CSAV

Suthers (1999) reports on an epiphany that parallels one that the researcher experienced throughout the observation of QuestMap™ use by law students:

> Belvédère 1.0 was initially used with students aged 12-15 working alone or in pairs in our lab, as well as by students working in small groups in a 10th grade classroom. During this time, we learned some important lessons about the role of external representations in collaborative learning.
>
> Belvédère was designed under the assumption that a visual representation language…can help students learn the nuances of scientific argumentation, provided that (a) the language is *capable of capturing all of these nuances*, and (b) *students express their arguments in the language*. However, we found that much relevant argumentation was "external," arguing *from* the representations rather than arguing *in* the representations.
>
> Faced with a decision concerning some manipulation of the representations, student would begin to discuss substantial issues until they reached tentative agreement concerning how to change the representation. In the process, statements and relations we would have liked students to represent went unexpressed.

Our initial frustration soon gave way to an understanding that this is an opportunity: proper design of manipulable representations can guide students into useful learning interactions. Thus, we downplayed the following potential roles of the representations: (1) as a medium *through* which communication takes place, (2) as a complete record of the argumentation process, and (3) as a medium for expressing formal models – in favour of their role in *stimulating and guiding collaborative learning discourse.* (Suthers, 1999, pp. 16)

In this study, QuestMap™ was used for legal education in much the same way. Students would begin constructing an argument, see another counter-argument appear, and then begin discussing the counter-argument with its creator outside the software. The software then becomes a support for the process of argumentation, rather than a representation of it.

4.4 Conclusion and Future Research

Since argumentation is central to legal education, it is important to continue to explore ways to support the effectiveness and efficiency with which law students create arguments. Benefits of using CSAV to support learning have been reported to include: (1) providing a mechanism for "slowing down" the reasoning process in order to better understand it (Leeman, 1987); (2) supporting collaborative learning, which has been shown to foster the development of reasoning skills (Dimant and Bearison, 1991; Kruger, 1992; Moshman and Geil, 1998), and (3) serves as a type of representation tool, which have been positively related to memory, problem solving, and inferential thinking (Jonassen and Reeves, 1996). The following pages outline in more detail the reported benefits of CSAV.

In this study, there were dozens of questions that divulged themselves throughout the research process. Future studies should consider the complex interactions between factors, including: domain and argumentation knowledge, training in CSAV tools, user interface design, and motivation to use CSAV. In similar studies, future research should help explicate the group argumentation processes in both the control group and the treatment group. Does CSAV change the interactions between group members or the process of constructing arguments? Video-taping both processes and analyzing transcripts would help identify key differences that may be taking place with and without CSAV present.

Analyzing Legal Argument
Toulmin's coding scheme has been proven effective in analyzing legal arguments. In a rhetorical analysis of 536 writing samples, Hausmann (1987) found that writing prompts appearing as part of the Law School Admission Test influences both composing processes and the written product based on Stephen Toulmin's model of argument. There were more grounds and warrants in texts from the decision problem than in those from the general response question. Further, the inter-rater reliability of

Toulmin's scheme was reported as 92%. "The Toulmin scheme is a promising way to characterize full texts," (Hausmann, 1987). The researcher concurs.

Research suggests that younger students who have less domain knowledge and argumentation knowledge tend to show more significant learning gains than those highly skilled in the content domain and argumentation. Further research should investigate the effect of integrating CSAV earlier in the legal education process. One option is to integrate CSAV into a lawyering skills course, which is commonly offered as an introductory course in legal education. First-year law students have a diverse array of backgrounds, often including, philosophy, history, religion, biology, and political science. Often, legal argument is a foreign domain to these students. Since CSAV has been shown to help provoke and guide collaborative learning discourse in novices (Suthers, 1999), CSAV may allow first-year students to focus on issues and arguments within the context of law.

Students may benefit from being assigned roles "for and against" certain issues. Similar to a plaintiff and defendant, students benefit from arguing for and against positions (Cerbin, 1988). In fact, many students assigned roles to their group members throughout the study, carrying out discussions with their adversaries as they progressed.

Visualizing Argumentation

Formalizing knowledge through visualized nodes and structures can create cognitive overhead for novices in the argumentation (Buckingham Shum, 1996). All notations possess a "Representational Bias" in that they provide users with an ontology through which to construct meaning (Suthers, 1999). Further, as argumentation takes place, instances of "Representational Drift" may occur as users or groups re-purpose argument notations according their own or collective ontologies. Research should help elucidate which visualization notations and techniques are appropriate in domains of knowledge or types of CSAV use.

Boosting the "CS" in CSAV

Many CSAV tools do not leverage the capabilities of the technology that supports them. Can machines provide procedural advice in terms of possible argumentation moves or strategies? Can machines log and analyze CSAV usage? Future research should help increase the intelligence of these CSAV tools to help support the argumentation process.

Integrating CSAV with Other Tools and Modes of Working

Myriad implementation issues have been discovered while implementing CSAV in academic and corporate contexts (Buckingham Shum and Hammond, 1994). A consortium of orgnisations has created the Compendium Institute to help determine ways in which CSAV systems can exchange information with spreadsheets, word processing programs, diagramming software, and other systems. The primary objective for this line of research is to incorporate CSAV as another software tool to help support knowledge construction, organization, and re-use.

Re-using CSAV

One of the most valuable potentials of CSAV is the ability to re-use knowledge (Conklin and Begeman, 1987). Legal argumentation is a classic domain where re-use is valued. Many arguments include "precedent" as the warrants for the claims (e.g., "because in a similar case, the ruling was..."). How can we increase the re-usability of CSAV structures? How can we reconstruct the context surrounding those structures (i.e. what was happening when they were created)? How can we reconstruct the sequence in which the argumentation structures were formed?

4.5 References

Bell, P. (1997). Using argument representations to make thinking visible for individuals and groups. Paper presented at the *Second International Conference on Computer Support for Collaborative Learning*, Toronto.

Blasi, G. L. (1995). What lawyers know: Lawyering expertise, cognitive science, and the functions of theory. *Journal of Legal Education, 45*(3), 313-97.

Buckingham Shum, S. (1996). Design argumentation as design rationale. *The Encyclopedia of Computer Science and Technology, 35*(20), 95-128.

Buckingham Shum, S., & Hammond, Nick. (1994). Argumentation-based design rationale: What use at what cost? *International Journal of Human-Computer Studies, 40*(4), 603-652.

Buckingham Shum, S. J., MacLean, A., Bellotti, V. M. E., & Hammond, N. V. (1997). Graphical argumentation and design cognition. *Human-Computer Interaction, 12*(3), 1997, 267-300.

Campbell, D. T., Stanley, J. C., & Gage, N. L. (1966). *Experimental and quasi-experimental designs for research*. Boston, MA: Houghton Mifflin Company.

Cerbin, B. (1988). The nature and development of informal reasoning skills in college students. (ED298805)

Chi, M. B., J. (1989). Learning from examples via self-explanations. In L. Resnick (Ed.), *Knowing, learning and instruction: Essays in honor of Robert Glaser* (pp. 251-282). Hillsdale, NJ: Lawrence Erlbaum Associates.

Conklin, J., & Begeman, M. L. (1987). gIBIS: A hypertext tool for team design deliberation. Paper presented at *Hypertext '87*, Chapel Hill, NC.

Dimant, R. J., & Bearison, D. J. (1991). Development of formal reasoning during successive peer interactions. *Developmental Psychology, 27*(2), 277-84.

Gall, M. D., Borg, W. R., & Gall, J. P. (1996). *Educational research: An introduction*. White Plains, NY: Longman Publishing Group.

Goldenberg, E. P. (1995). Multiple representations: A vehicle for understanding understanding. In J. S. D. Perkins, M. West, & M. Wiske (Ed.), *Software goes to school: teaching for understanding with new technologies* (pp. 155-171). New York: Oxford University Press.

Golder, C. (1992). Production of elaborated argumentative discourse: The role of cooperativeness. *European Journal of Psychology of Education, 7*(1), 51-59.

Golder, C., & Coirier, P. (1994). Argumentative text writing: Developmental trends. *Discourse Processes, 18*(2), 187-210.

Gordon, J. D. I. (1989). An integrated first-year legal writing program. *Journal of Legal Education, 39*, 609.

Hausmann, F.J. (1987). Die vokabularisierung des lehrbuchs: Präsentation und vermittlung von wortschatz in lehrwerken für den französischunterricht [The vokabularisierung of the text book: Presentation and mediation of vocabulary in educational materials for learning French]. *Die Neueren Sprachen* (85), 426-445.

Jonassen, D. H., & Carr, Chad S. (1999). Mindtools: Affording multiple knowledge representations for learning. In S. P. Lajoie (Ed.), *Computers as cognitive tools II: No more walls: Theory change, paradigm shifts and their influence on the use of computers for instructional purposes.* Mahwah, NJ: Lawrence Erlbaum Associates.

Jonassen, D. H. & Reeves., T. C. (1996). Learning with technology: Using computers as cognitive tools. In D. H. Jonassen (Ed.), *Handbook of research on educational communications and technology* (pp. 693-719). New York: Simon and Schuster.

Kruger, C. W. (1992). Software Reuse. *Computing Surveys, 24*(2), 131-183.

Kuhn, D. (1991). *The skills of argument.* Cambridge, MA : Cambridge University Press.

Lajoie, S., & Derry, S. J. (1993). *Computers as cognitive tools.* Hillsdale, N.J.: L. Erlbaum Associates.

Leeman, R. W. (1987). Taking perspectives: Teaching critical thinking in the argumentation course (ED292147).

MacCrate, R. (1994). Preparing lawyers to participate effectively in the legal process. *Journal of Legal Education, 44*(1), 89-95.

Marke, J. J. (1989). How legal research should be taught. *New York Law Journal, 202*(74), 4 77.

Marttunen, M. (1992). Commenting on written arguments as a part of argumentation skills--Comparison between students engaged in traditional vs on-line study. *Scandinavian Journal of Educational Research, 36*(4), 289-302.

Maurer, N. M., & Mischler, L. F. (1994). Introduction to lawyering: teaching first-year students to think like professionals. *Journal of Legal Education, 44*(1), 96-115.

McCann, T. M. (1989). Student argumentative writing knowledge and ability at three grade levels. *Research in the Teaching of English, 23*(1), 62-76.

Moshman, D., & Geil, M. (1998). Collaborative reasoning: Evidence for collective rationality. *Thinking and Reasoning, 4*(3), Aug 1998, 231-248.

Penner, B. C., & Voss, J. F. (1983). Problem solving skills in the social sciences: methodological considerations (ED242612).

Perelman, C. (1980). *Justice, law, and argument: essays on moral and legal reasoning.* Dordrecht, Holland: D. Reidel Pub. Co.

Perkins, D. N., Crismond, D., Simmons, R., & Unger, C. (1995). Inside understanding. In J. S. D. Perkins, M. West, & M. Wiske (Ed.), *Software goes to school: Teaching for understanding with new technologies* (pp. 70-87). New York: Oxford University Press.

Perkins, D. N. (1985). Reasoning as imagination. *Interchange, 16*(1), 14-26.

Resnick, L. B. (1991). Shared cognition: Thinking as social practice. In J. M. L. L.B.Resnick, & S. D Teasley (Ed.), *Perspectives on socially shared cognition* (pp. 1-20). Washington, DC: American Psychological Association.

Roschelle, J., & Behrend, S. (1995). The construction of shared knowledge in collaborative problem solving. In C. O'Malley (Ed.), *Computer-supported collaborative learning* (pp. 69-97). Berlin: Springer-Verlag.

Rosenthal, R., & Rosnow, R. L. (1975). *Primer of methods for the behavioral sciences.* John Wiley and Sons, Incorporated.

Saunders, K. M. (1994). Law as rhetoric, rhetoric as argument. *Journal of Legal Education, 44*(4), 566-78.

Scardamalia, M., Bereiter, C., & Lamon, M. (1994). The CSILE project: Trying to bring the classroom into world. In K. McGilly (Ed.), *Classroom lessons: Integrating cognitive theory and practice* (pp. 201-228). Cambridge: MIT Press.

Schrag, P. G. (1989). The serpent strikes: simulation in a large first-year course. *Journal of Legal Education, 39*, 555.

Spiro, R., Feltovich, P., Jacobson, M., & Coulson, R. (1992). Cognitive flexibility, constructivism, and hypertext: Advanced knowledge acquisition in ill-structured domains. In T. Duffy & D. Jonassen (Ed.), *Constructivism and the Technology of Instruction.* Hillsdale, NJ: Erlbaum.

Suthers, D. (1999). Representational support for collaborative inquiry. Paper presented at the *Hawaii International Conference on System Sciences,* Maui, Hawaii.

Toulmin, S. E. (1958). *The uses of argument.* Cambridge [Eng.]: University Press.

Toulmin, S. E., Rieke, R. D., & Janik, A. (1984). *An introduction to reasoning (2nd ed.).* New York London: Macmillan; Collier Macmillan Publishers.

VanLeeuwen, D. M. (1997). Assessing reliability of measurements with generalizability theory: An application to inter-rater reliability. *Journal of Agricultural Education, 38*(3), 36-42.

Voss, J. F., Blais, J., Means, M. L., & Greene, T. R. (1986). Informal reasoning and subject matter knowledge in the solving of economics problems by naive and novice individuals. *Cognition and Instruction, 3*(4), 1986, 269-302.

Voss, J. F., & Means, M. L. (1991). Learning to reason via instruction in argumentation. *Learning and Instruction, 1*(4), 337-50.

Wason, P. C. (1968). Reasoning about a rule. *Quarterly Journal of Experimental Psychology, 20*(3), 1968, 273-281.

Woxland, T. A. (1989). Why can't Johnny research? Or it all started with Christopher Columbus Langdell. *Law Library Journal, 81*(3), 451-464.

Zammuner, V. L. (1991). Children's writing of argumentative texts: Effects of indirect instruction. *European Journal of Psychology of Education, 6*(2), 243-56.

5 Enhancing Deliberation Through Computer Supported Argument Visualization

Tim van Gelder

Department of Philosophy, University of Melbourne, Australia; and Austhink

5.1 Introduction

As this is being written, the Governor General of Australia, Dr. Peter Hollingworth, has not resigned. Yet over the previous weeks and months he must have been thinking about it long and hard. He has been under intense pressure from various quarters, based on allegations that in previous positions of leadership he had not handled some sexual abuse incidents appropriately. In pondering what he should do, he must have been considering the many and varied arguments on both sides of the case. He must, in short, have been *deliberating* about his future.

Deliberation is a form of thinking in which we decide where we stand on some claim in light of the relevant arguments. It is common and important, whether in our personal, public or working lives. It is also complicated, difficult and usually poorly done.

This chapter contends that deliberation can be improved by visualization of the arguments, especially when the visualization is supported by newly-available computer tools. This point is supported in two ways. First, the chapter describes how computer supported argument visualization contributes to gains in general reasoning skills among undergraduate students. Second, it describes how real-time computer supported argument visualization can facilitate group deliberation in the workplace. The case studies are preceded by some clarification and discussion of the key concepts of deliberation and argument visualization, and of the relationship between argument visualization and prose.

5.1.1 What is Deliberation?

Deliberation, as the term is used here, is a process aimed at deciding whether some claim ought to be believed by considering the relevant arguments.[1] The claim might describe what one should do (i.e., be of the form *I/we should do X*) and so deliberation can be directed towards action as well as belief. The arguments considered will invoke further claims, and in some cases their truth must also be determined through deliberation; and so on. Thus deliberation often involves considering an extended hierarchy of arguments.

Deliberation is not the same as reasoning. Reasoning is tracing the web of inferential relationships among propositions; this can be done without intending to determine whether any particular proposition is true. For example, from *All As are Bs* and *All Bs are Cs* you can infer *All As are Cs* without caring whether any of these are true or even what they mean. This is reasoning but not deliberating. Deliberation obviously involves reasoning, however; indeed, reasoning is the means by which one deliberates. If reasoning is like running, then deliberation is like running to catch a bus or to win a race.

Deliberation also differs subtly from argumentation. The latter is defined by van Eemeren et al. as

> a verbal and social activity of reason aimed at increasing (or decreasing) the acceptability of a controversial standpoint for the listener or reader, by putting forward a constellation of propositions intended to justify (or refute) the standpoint before a rational judge. (van Eemeren et al., 1996 p.5)

and on this account, at least, involves rational persuasion: the point of argumentation is to influence others' attitudes by means of arguments. Deliberation, by contrast, is aimed at determining one's own attitude.

Deliberation is often, like argumentation, a collective activity. For example a group of friends may deliberate over which restaurant is best, or a group of historians may deliberate to determine whether the treatment of indigenous Australians by European settlers merits the term "genocide". These forms of deliberation essentially involve both reasoning and argumentation.

5.2   What is Argument Visualization?

An argument visualization is a presentation of reasoning in which the evidential relationships among claims are made wholly explicit using graphical or other non-verbal techniques. Argument visualization is producing such visual techniques.

All reasoning involves propositions standing in logical or evidential relationships with each other, and thus forming evidential structures. In any given case this "constellation of propositions" must be expressed or presented in some way in order to

---

[1]   As Webster's defines it, to deliberate is "to weigh in the mind; to consider the reasons for and against; to consider maturely; to reflect upon; to ponder; as, to deliberate a question." (Webster & Porter, 1913)

be comprehended or communicated. Overwhelmingly, this is done in prose, whether spoken or written. Argument visualizations can thus be seen as alternatives to prose as vehicles for presenting arguments.

To illustrate: consider the following piece of prose:

> Very few scientists have spent much time thinking about the end of the world, and those few have reached diverse conclusions. All scenarios for the end of the world are highly speculative. They cannot be tested or verified by observation or experiment. The beginning of the world in the colossal explosion that we call the Big Bang has left many physical traces that can be observed and analyzed. The science of cosmology is largely concerned with collecting tangible evidence of things that happened billions of years ago, going all the way back to the beginning. No such tangible evidence can exist for the ending. For this reason, most scientists consider that the end of the world does not have much to do with science (Dyson, 2002)

This passage presents some reasoning; the reasoning involves various propositions concerning matters such as science, observation, and the end of the universe. The propositions are listed in the text; part of the hermeneutic challenge for the reader is to figure out their evidential relationships to each other.

Here is similar reasoning, presented as a visualization:

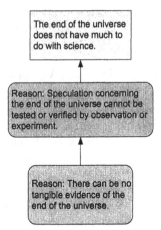

This uses some simple visualization conventions: the main conclusion is written in a white, square box at the top, and grey rounded boxes contain reasons; the arrows indicate the relations of supposed evidential support.

Note that it is not clear that the reasoning presented by the visualization is identical to the reasoning presented in the prose. This is mainly because it is hard to say what the logical structure behind the prose actually is; there is room for different interpretations. There is no such room in the case of the argument visualization; there, the logical structure is entirely clear and unambiguous, assuming one understands the conventions.

The paradigmatic argument visualization is a *visual* display, much like the familiar paper maps of towns, subway systems, treasure islands etc. A more abstract approach would define an argument visualization as any presentation of reasoning in which evidential structure is made wholly explicit or unambiguous, whether by visual means or some other approach. It ought to be possible to construct argument visualizations in which the structure is conveyed explicitly through other sensory modalities. Blind people, for example, might construct argument visualizations using chemistry sets, where claims are encoded using Braille on the balls and then joined up using sticks into argument structures. These could be unambiguously read by people with appropriate skills. The key point is that, if the argument visualization conventions are clear and appropriate, inferential or evidential relations can be "read off" the presentation in a more or less mechanical way. There is no need for sophisticated comprehension and reasoning skills in order to figure out the *structure* of the reasoning (though understanding and evaluating individual steps in the reasoning might take further thought).

The fairly minimal definition recommended here allows for enormous variety in argument visualizations. The point of argument visualization is to present complex reasoning in a clear and unambiguous way, and visualizers should use whatever resources work best in achieving this goal. Currently, argument visualizations are mostly "box and arrow" diagrams like the one above, but it may turn out that some different approach will work more effectively. For example, somebody may develop a clever way to present arguments in virtual 3D, or even in immersive "virtual reality" fly-through environments. As long as the presentation makes the structure of reasoning completely explicit and unambiguous, it will count as argument visualization.

5.3   Argument Visualization Versus Prose

Although prose is the standard way to present reasoning, it is not a good tool for the job. Extracting the structure of evidential relationships from reasoning as typically presented in prose is very difficult and most of the time we do it badly. This can be easily illustrated, in a kind of exercise we have done informally many times in workshops. Take any group of people sufficiently trained in reasoning and argument visualization that they are quite able to create argument visualizations to make explicit whatever reasoning they have in mind. Now give them a sample of *good* argumentative prose, such as a well-argued opinion piece from the newspaper. Ask them to figure out what the reasoning is, and to re-present it in an argument visualization. This usually takes about 20-30 minutes, during which time you can enjoy watching the participants strike various Rodinesque postures of intense concentration, wipe their sweaty palms, etc. Then compare the resulting argument visualizations. You'll find that you have as many different argument visualizations as there are people doing the exercise; in many cases the argument visualizations will be wildly different. This shows that the opinion piece failed to reliably convey the author's argument, whatever it was.

Argument visualizations are deliberately designed to overcome precisely this problem with prose. Exercises similar to the one just described show that they fulfil their intended role. Take any group of people sufficiently trained to be able to be read argument visualizations. (This training usually takes not more than a few minutes.)

Present them with an argument visualization, and ask them to identify the reasoning presented in it, and re-present it in whatever form they like (visualization, prose, point-form etc.). This is a very simple task and usually takes almost no time; indeed, it is so trivial that the hard part is getting the participants to go through the motions when no intellectual challenge is involved. Ask them questions designed to elicit the extent to which they have correctly identified the structure of the reasoning presented by the visualization (e.g., how many distinct reasons are presented for the main conclusion?). You'll find that they all understand exactly what the reasoning is, and ipso facto all have the *same* sense of the reasoning.

In short, a task – identify the presented reasoning – which was difficult, time-consuming and almost always fails in the standard prose format is easy, fast and almost completely reliable in the argument visualization format. The point here is really quite simple, although it often meets resistance. Representations deliberately designed to communicate reasoning easily, rapidly and reliably can achieve this goal. Representations not deliberately designed for this purpose fail to achieve this goal. Who should be surprised?

Why are argument visualizations so superior when it comes to presenting the structure of reasoning? The short answer, just rehearsed, is that unlike prose, they were *designed* to do the job well. More can be said, however. At least four main factors explain the superiority of argument visualizations. These points concern limitations of prose which are partly or wholly overcome in argument visualizations.

Prose Requires Interpretation

The most obvious problem with prose is that the reader has to *figure out* what the relationships among the claims are, using whatever clues (semantic, contextual, verbal) are offered by the text. This is hard work, and because every reader has different skills, background knowledge, etc., they will likely come up with different sets of relationships, i.e., different interpretations of the reasoning. In an argument diagram, by contrast, all relationships are made completely explicit using simple visual conventions. Readers have to do very little work in order to see how the claims are related (or, at least, how the claims are being *presented as* related by the person who produced the diagram). In practice, this removes a huge cognitive burden. Readers can then devote their mental energy to thinking about the argument itself rather than trying to figure out what the argument is.

Prose Neglects Representational Resources

The second problem with prose is that it makes use of an impoverished set of representational resources. It is just a monochrome stream of words, sentences and paragraphs. It generally makes little or no use of colour, shape, line or position in space to convey information about the structure of the argument. Yet we know that the brain can process large amounts of colour, shape line and space information very rapidly. It makes little sense to ignore those resources if they are available. In an argument diagram, for example, colour can be used to indicate in a matter of milliseconds whether a claim is being presented as reason or an objection. In prose, the reader has to *interpret* the claim and its context to figure out its role in the argument. Helpful authors will assist readers in the difficult process of interpretation by providing verbal cues (for example, logical indicators such as "therefore"), although it is quite astonishing how frugal most authors are in providing such cues.

Prose is Sequential, Arguments are Not

A third deep problem with prose is its sequential nature. Arguments are fundamentally *not* sequential. We take them to be directed acyclic graphs (roughly, tree structures), and others might claim that they are actually more complicated than that, but one thing is clear: arguments, like grammatical structures, are not just one thing after another. Prose, however, intrinsically imposes a sequential structure: all the sentences presenting all the claims making up the argument have to follow each other like carriages in a train. This means that prose necessarily introduces inappropriate juxtapositions: in some places claims which are not directly related in the reasoning must be concatenated in the prose. Sure, you can use verbal indicators, paragraph breaks, section breaks, etc., to help overcome the problem. But these are superficial or stop-gap measures, and cannot eliminate the fact that the reader, in order to understand the argument, must mentally reconstruct the non-sequential logical structure from the sequential sentential structure of the prose. This point was eloquently expressed by William Minto:

> In writing you are as a commander filing out his battalion through a narrow gap that allows only one man at a time to pass; and your reader, as he receives the troops, has to reform and reconstruct them. No matter how large or how involved the subject, it can be communicated only in that way. You see, then, what an obligation we owe to him of order and arrangement – and why, apart from felicities and curiosities of diction, the old rhetorician laid such stress upon order and arrangement as duties we owe to those who honor us with their attention. (quoted in (Minto, 1995) p.178)

Minto was wrong, however, in believing that one's subject "can be communicated only in that way." Minto wrote this well before the arrival of argument visualization as a feasible practice. These days, if one's subject is a piece of reasoning, there is another way to communicate it, a way which does not demand that the battalion file through the narrow gap. An argument visualization presents the entire argument, all at once, in its proper order, more like marching a battalion across a flat parade ground – and viewing it from a helicopter!

Prose Cannot Visually Display Metaphors

A fourth deep problem with prose is that it makes no use, in the form of presentation, of the deep metaphors in terms of which we naturally understand arguments. According to George Lakoff, human understanding essentially involves metaphors grounded in our basic bodily experience (Lakoff, 1987). This general principle applies to understanding arguments as a special case. It is no accident that so many of our metaphors for reasoning and argument are basic ones of space, force, size: how much *support* does the reason offer, what is the *balance* of considerations, how *strong* is that objection, and so forth. Indeed, it is an interesting exercise to try to describe fundamental aspects of reasoning, argument and evidence *without* using such basic metaphors. Using diagrams, we can to some extent take advantage of those mental schemas; e.g., we can place all the reasons over here and all the objections over there, or we can make stronger reasons bigger, or place them underneath (supporting) the conclusion, etc. None of this is possible in standard prose; thus argument diagrams can tap directly into our fundamental ways of understanding arguments in ways that prose cannot.[2]

5.4   New Tools for Argument Visualization

The basic idea behind argument visualization is remarkably simple. Everyone knows that good graphics are very effective for presenting complex structures; that we are much better at *visualizing* complexity than we are at *cognising* it. Argument visualization just applies this basic insight to complex reasoning.

Yet argument visualization has never really taken off as a practical tool for real argumentation or deliberation. Why is this? No doubt there are many factors, but one of the most important is surely that argument visualizations have not been easy to produce. Given available tools, standard practices, and people's abilities, it has been much easier to write out one's reasoning than to present it in a map, at least for reasoning of any complexity.

Now, however, we are seeing major changes in this regard. The arrival of the personal computer and printer has opened up a whole new range of possibilities for supporting thinking. A few decades ago, argument visualizations would have to be sketched by hand, and producing serious visualizations would require skilled draftsmen and highly specialised equipment. This is no longer true; even quite ordinary computer users can use standard desktop computers and inexpensive yet powerful software packages to create complex visualizations with a quite professional appearance.

The next major development will be tools designed specifically to support argument visualization. Using generic packages is still too slow and cumbersome, especially when major structural revisions to argument trees are needed. Dedicated tools will support argument visualization in much the way that PowerPoint effectively supports the process of producing overheads for a presentation.

Some first steps in this direction have already been taken. The primary function of software packages such as Araucaria,[3] Athena (Rolf & Magnusson, 2002) and Reason!Able (van Gelder & Bulka, 2000) is to support argument visualization. Using such software, one can now assemble argument visualizations easily and rapidly; and for certain tasks, such as reorganising reasoning, they can be superior to prose.

---

[2]   Joseph Laronge has been very creative in incorporating metaphors into argument diagrams; see, for example, his contributions to the argumap email discussion list (groups.yahoo.com/group/argumap).

[3]   See http://www.computing.dundee.ac.uk/staff/creed/research/araucaria.html

Packages in the current generation of argument visualization software are fairly basic, and still have numerous usability problems. Soon however there will be much more sophisticated packages designed from the outset to help people develop, modify and distribute argument visualizations. Working with reasoning in "argument visualization mode" will become easier than working in standard prose mode. Since argument visualization expands our capacity to engage in reasoning, such packages will be a major technological augmentation of our rational capacities; arguably, they will constitute the first major advance in this area in a very long time (Monk, 2001).

5.5   Enhancing Deliberation via Argument Visualization

The main thesis of this chapter is that argument visualization can substantially enhance deliberation. That is, we deliberate better when we use argument visualization to lay out reasoning, as compared with standard or traditional practice, which is to use prose. To deliberate better is, in the end, to make better judgements as to what is true and what is false. Such judgements can be better in two ways. First, they can be better-founded; more systematic, more balanced, more objective. Second, they can be more correct; they can better reflect the truth of the matter. Presumably if they are better in the first sense they will be better in the second.

The following sections provide two examples of how using argument visualization can improve deliberation by improving the quality of the reasoning which makes it up.

5.6   Argument Visualization in Critical Thinking Training

Deliberation is usually done quite poorly. An impressive piece of evidence in this regard is the study reported by psychologist Deanna Kuhn in her book *The Skills of Argument* (Kuhn, 1991). Kuhn and her team intensively interviewed hundreds of people, sampling from many age groups, occupations, educational backgrounds, etc., with a view to gauging their basic reasoning and argument skills. As I interpret the huge amount of data she presents, she found that over half of the population simply cannot reliably exhibit the basic skills needed in order to successfully deliberate over important issues of any complexity. For example, she found that while most people readily hold an opinion on an issue such as why many criminals repeat their crimes, over half, when asked for evidence to support that opinion, could not provide any at all. They would of course say a lot of stuff in response to the request for evidence; the trouble is that what they said wasn't *evidence* (let alone good evidence).

A natural response to this deplorable situation is to suggest that people ought to be *taught* these basic skills; and if ordinary education doesn't produce adequate general reasoning and argument skills, then there ought to be special courses in how to do it. And in fact, there are such courses, although not many people ever get to take one. Almost every university provides subjects such as Introduction to Logic, or Critical

Thinking, courses which are usually advertised as worth taking because they improve general reasoning skills. But is this true? Unfortunately there is not much evidence on the issue; only a handful of studies have been conducted. The evidence we do have suggests that such courses make little if any difference. Indeed, the gap between the available evidence and the strong claims made on behalf of such courses suggests that the philosophers and departments who offer such courses are guilty of misleading advertising. It is especially ironic that teachers of courses which focus on critically scrutinising evidence have made so little effort to critically scrutinize the evidence for their own claims.

Why do standard courses on reasoning fail (if they do) to substantially improve reasoning skills? I think there are three main explanations. First, they spend a lot of time teaching irrelevant material. Techniques of elementary formal logic, such as the theory of classical syllogisms and propositional logic, are of little or no use in real-world reasoning. Eminent philosopher Y. Bar-Hillel once said:

> I am reasonably sure that humanity spends more time on argumentation in natural languages than on the pursuit of scientific knowledge. It is therefore of vital importance to get better insights into the nature of argumentation in natural languages, and I challenge anyone here to show me a serious piece of argumentation in natural languages that has been successfully evaluated as to its validity with the help of formal logic. I regard this fact as one of the greatest scandals of human existence.

The forum of equally eminent philosophers to whom he said this was unable to meet the challenge (Bar-Hillel & others, 1969).

Second, reasoning is a skill, and skills generally improve through practice; however standard courses take a "theory first" approach in which improved performance is supposed to result from understanding the theory. Students spend their time wrestling with the theory and don't get nearly enough genuine practice.

The third explanation is most relevant to this chapter: insofar as such courses deal with real reasoning and argumentation, they do so in the standard prose format. This seems like an obvious and natural thing to do. As described above, however, prose is a poor medium for presenting arguments, imposing heavy and pointless cognitive burdens. Consequently, students' attempts to grapple with reasoning are confounded by the need to struggle with the prose presentation. This creates spurious difficulties which impede development of general reasoning and argument skills. If this is right, then students trained in reasoning using argument mapping ought to improve more rapidly than students in traditional courses.

The Reason! Project at the University of Melbourne has taken this approach. From the outset the goal was to develop a superior method for enhancing critical thinking, focusing on reasoning and argument skills. Its guiding inspiration has been what we call the Quality Practice Hypothesis, the claim that critical thinking skills improve through extensive amounts of the right kind of practice. The challenge is to set up a situation in which students will in fact do large amounts of such practice. As part of meeting this challenge we developed the Reason!Able software, which is a "quality practice environment" – a place where students can engage in reasoning tasks more effectively than in traditional contexts. The most important feature of Reason!Able in this regard is that it is very largely a matter of argument visualization; everything the students do with it takes place in that mode. The software supports rapid and easy construction, modification and evaluation of argument visualizations (Figure 5.1).

The Reason! method for enhancing critical thinking consists of students working through a large number of Reason!Able-based exercises. The efficacy of the approach has been intensively evaluated. Every time we run the one-semester subject, we pre- and post-test students using a number of different tests. On the California Critical Thinking Skills Test (CCTST), arguably the best available objective (multi-choice) test of critical thinking, students as a group reliably improve with an effect size of about 0.83 of standard deviation[4] (van Gelder, 2001). By this measure, a Reason!-based course is many times as effective as traditional critical thinking courses. To get a rough idea of the scale of improvement here, consider that an equivalent gain in IQ would be about 12 points in 12 weeks. Or, for another perspective, consider that the expected gain in critical thinking skills in the course of an undergraduate education, based on a wide variety of studies, is about 0.5 of a standard deviation.[5] Twelve weeks of training based on argument visualization improves reasoning skills, as measured by the CCTST, by an amount substantially in excess of the expected gain while at college.

For two years running we have also pre- and post-tested the same students using a written test of our own devising, requiring students to read some argumentative prose and to critically evaluate the reasoning. We had their written responses blindly scored by two critical thinking experts who are quite independent of our team. Although there was much more variation in scores, the overall magnitude of the gain was approximately equivalent to that found using the CCTST (van Gelder, 2001). This indicates that although the training was based on argument visualization, the students were improving their ability to handle reasoning in standard prose formats. In other words, the training effects transferred from the training tasks to other tasks in a more standard format.

How do we know that the improvement was due to argument visualization rather than to some other feature of the course? Perhaps the real causal factor was the large amounts of practice rather than the argument visualization medium. Indeed, we had designed the approach on the hypothesis that large amounts of quality practice is the key to improving skills. In order to test that hypothesis, we built mechanisms to log every move students made with the software over an entire semester. This data yielded crude measures of the total amount of time students spent using the software and the

---

[4]   There are various ways to calculate effect size, but we use one standard one: roughly, the average improvement divided by the standard deviation on the pre-test.

[5]   This estimate is by Earnest Pascarella, a leading authority on the impact of higher education. Pascarella gave this estimate in a manuscript under preparation for the revised version of *How College Affects Students* (Pascarella & Terenzini, 1991). The figure in the version eventually published may differ.

total amount of activity. We have also used questionnaires to interrogate the students as to their practice regimes. We took these figures as estimates of the amount of practice in reasoning they were actually doing. The Quality Practice Hypothesis predicted that there should be a correlation between practice and improvement. Much to our surprise and consternation, we have so far found virtually *no* correlation between the two.

Figure 5.1: Argument visualization using the Reason!Able software. The software supports rapid and easy construction, modification and evaluation of argument visualizations. The process helps translate abstract logical complexity into simple, colourful diagrams. When used with a touch-sensitive screen such as the SMART Board pictured above, the argument visualizations become manipulable in a very direct sense. Photo: Michael Silver.

This suggests that something else is the key difference between the Reason! approach and traditional approaches. Our hunch at this stage is that it is argument visualization. Exercises conducted in the argument visualization format give students a strong visual sense of the structure of reasoning and argument. Once this sense is acquired, further practice makes relatively little difference. If this is right, argument visualization is inducing a qualitative shift in students' abilities. Using the software, which translates complex arguments into simple, colourful and manipulable structures, students "click" as to how reasoning works. At this stage, however, this conjecture is untested. Our investigations in this area are still quite preliminary, and further studies are underway.

All this does not prove that argument mapping enhances deliberation per se. It is fairly convincing evidence that argument visualization substantially improves general reasoning and argument skills, and since deliberation is a matter of exercising those skills, it is plausible that deliberation would be improved.

5.6.1   Argument Visualization in Group Deliberation

Improving individuals' deliberative capacities is fine, but deliberation is often done in group contexts, especially when issues get really complex and important. Can computer supported argument visualization enhance group deliberation also?

Austhink has become increasingly involved in using real-time argument visualization to help groups deliberate about issues involving lots of complex arguments. The situations are quite varied, and so it is difficult to encompass the activity in a compact and comprehensive way. Rather, I will describe in detail one more-or-less typical example, and allow general considerations to emerge in that context.

A factory in Sydney producing domestic cleaning products had, a number of years previously, made a switch from their traditional "one person one job" (OPOJ) mode of operation to a multi-skilling mode in which each person was trained in, and rotated through, a number of different tasks. The change had been mandated from on high, and had produced a certain amount of discontent in the ranks. Over the following years there had been considerable grumbling and dispute, involving the multi-skilled workers themselves, supervisors, and human resource managers. These people of course brought quite different perspectives, interests, and educational backgrounds to the debate. No matter how much discussion took place, on the factory floor or in meetings, in small groups or large, little progress was made; arguments seemed to just go around in circles, and disagreement seemed only to become more entrenched. For every point somebody made there seemed to be a counterpoint, and in the thickets of disputation, everyone could find a way to hold onto their own opinion.

A human resources manager hoped to achieve some kind of rational resolution by bringing in some more effective way of handling the disagreement. The standard, prose-based methods just weren't working. Having read a newspaper piece about argument visualization, she decided to give it a go. Her goal was not to prove that any one perspective was right to the exclusion of all others. Rather, it was to try to lay out all the arguments so that everyone could better see how complex the issues were and that opponents were usually making at least some valid points. Ideally, from her point of view, the process would result in a solid consensus that some kind of middle road between OPOJ and complete multi-skilling was going to be best both for individuals and for the factory as a whole.

One morning, we gathered in a meeting room. Participants included workers (some of whom had just finished night shift) and managers, as well as one argument visualization facilitator. The facilitator brought along a laptop computer with visualization software loaded, as well as some introductory materials, including a few sample argument visualizations so participants could see roughly where the process was headed. A data projector and screen were set up, the laptop plugged in, and chairs set up in an arc close to the screen. There were approximately 20 participants, which is a good number for this kind of exercise; larger numbers mean that each person has less chance to be actively involved, which can lead to boredom and disengagement.

In what follows, the process we followed has been divided, somewhat artificially, into a series of distinct stages:

Stage 1: Introduce Argument Visualization

The first stage was a brief introduction to argument visualization. Usually, participants have never seen or even heard of the technique, but are able to understand what is going on pretty quickly. The "box and arrow" structure of an argument visualization seems to tap directly into an intuitive or metaphorical sense they already have that an argument is made up of "this piece over here and that piece over there". In the introduction, we spend more time explaining why you might want to use the technique than explaining how it works.

Stage 2: Identify the Central Proposition

Since argument visualization supports deliberation, and deliberation is aimed at determining the truth or falsity of a particular proposition, we next tried to figure out what that proposition should be. This involves a free-flowing discussion of the overall issue, and (non- visualized) debate over the merits of various candidates. Candidates are written in boxes on the screen so that everyone can see and compare without having to hold them in memory. This stage is critical to the success of the enterprise. Participants must accept the central proposition as being at the very heart of their disagreement, such that reaching some kind of consensus on that contention would constitute real progress. From a logical point of view, it should be clear, simple, specific, and an obvious target for the main arguments. In this case, we ended up with "The factory should return to one person one job," although in retrospect this was probably not the best one we could have used. Often you can only really tell how adequate the central proposition is after quite a bit of argument visualization.

Stage 3: Canvass the Arguments

In the third stage, we canvassed the arguments for and against, secondary arguments, etc. This is, loosely speaking, a matter of "brainstorming"; the idea is to get all the considerations which matter to any participant out and onto the visualization. As arguments are raised, new nodes are added to the argument tree and the sentences expressing the arguments typed into the nodes. With a skilled facilitator, this does not slow the flow of thought very much.

In this case, we followed standard practice and started by attempting to list all the major reasons which seemed to provide direct evidence for the proposition, such as "One person for one job is a simpler system to manage." However visualization usually proceeds in a "depth first" rather than a "breadth first" manner. That is, as soon as a reason is raised, those on the other side weigh in with objections or counterarguments, to which there are further responses, etc. (Figure 5.2). In order to help maintain a sense of the natural flow of the arguments, it is important to visualize these – to give them a definite place in the emerging argument tree – as they arise, rather than asking people to hold their point for later, when it may have been lost.

As the argument tree gets more complex, it becomes increasingly apparent that the process is not a matter of orderly accumulation of successive points. Rather, much time and thought must be given to reworking the existing tree. Claims which previously seemed OK have to be reformulated so that they are more precise, express the right nuances, or are more clearly distinct from other claims. Particular arguments, or even whole lines of argument may need to be relocated to another position on the tree. This is one place where good argument visualization software really proves its worth; indeed, real-time argument visualization would be practically impossible without such a tool.

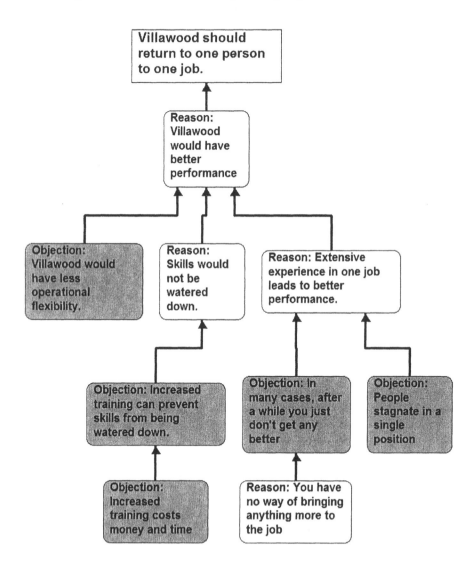

Figure 5.2: A small part of the argument tree-in-progress in Reason!Able format, much as it would have appeared to participants during the workshop. A cluster of argumentation bears upon a single primary reason to believe the main conclusion. This illustrates "depth first" elaboration

of the arguments. "Villawood" is the name used to refer to the factory, based on the neighbourhood where it is located.

Once all the primary reasons (with their supporting reasons, objections, and so forth) had been laid out, we turned to the primary objections. Work here usually goes a bit more smoothly than with the supporting reasons. This may be surprising, since objections are cognitively more demanding than reasons, and objections to objections (rebuttals) are far more demanding than objections to reasons. By this stage, however, participants are more experienced and comfortable with the process, and they start to pre-package their contribution so it can be entered directly onto the argument visualization. Also, many of the considerations relevant on the "con" side had already arisen in some form as the "pro" side had been elaborated, and so are better understood by this stage. (Such considerations can prompt a certain amount of effort reworking the tree so as to obtain the most elegant and conceptually satisfying structure for the overall argument.)

Periodically, the argument visualization was printed out, and copies were distributed to the participants. Although the projected image on the screen was large, it had a low resolution, and as the tree became more elaborate, we were faced with a choice – either the whole visualization was displayed, in which case the overall structure could be seen but the text of individual nodes was illegible, or we zoomed in to focus on particular parts of the tree, but the overall context was lost. A paper printout is much higher resolution, and although the writing is very small all the nodes can be read. (Of course, beyond a certain level of complexity, typical A4 printouts are illegible as well.)

The "canvassing" stage took about three hours. By that time participants were flagging due to the sustained effort involved. More importantly, they had run out of substantial new points; it seemed like most of the relevant arguments had been made. This is normal. In our experience, as a rule of thumb, roughly half a day suffices to extract all the significant arguments that a group of people can think of on any given issue, even when the issue is of some concern to them. This may be an interesting empirical fact about the level of complexity of typical debates. Of course there are contexts where people command argument structures which would take far more than half a day to lay out, and others where the known arguments can be elaborated in far less time. But under ordinary circumstances, participants in debates have available to them collectively a stock of a few score moves, and these can be visualized in a matter of hours.

Success in this third phase depends heavily on the skills of the facilitator. Of course he must have the standard repertoire expected of anyone facilitating group discussion. Beyond that, the argument visualization guide must be able to take the raw verbal material and rapidly massage it into a coherent argumentative structure. This means taking what a participant is saying and reformulating it in some text which is recognized by the participant as expressing her point, captures the essential underlying logic, and plugs appropriately into the existing argument tree. The participants have lots of "domain knowledge", but are often less able to translate that knowledge into coherent logical structures. The skilled facilitator knows little about the topic but is able to repackage contributions so that the participants feel that it is *their* arguments which are appearing on the tree. If the facilitator is a "one man show" and is also creating the visual map on the computer, he must be competent in using the visualization software and typing entries, and moving rapidly and easily back and forth between group facilitation and computer use. Many very able people would not be effective solo argument visualization facilitators because they are just too slow with the computer.

Stage 4: Review Arguments Seeking Rational Consensus
The aim of the whole exercise, remember, was to promote rational consensus on the main issue. The next stage, then, was to review the arguments as presented on the visualization and to see what this implied for the proposition that the factory should return to OPOJ. By this time however, something remarkable had already happened. As the negative case was being visualized, one argument emerged as conclusively establishing that the proposition was false. In a nutshell, it was that when each person is dedicated to a single task, if the one person responsible for a given task is sick or otherwise unable or unwilling to do their job, it can jeopardize the whole manufacturing process. We wrestled with this objection for a quite a while, trying to think of ways to soften its impact. Various suggestions were made, but none were convincing; this point was the knockdown argument for multi-skilling.

The remarkable part of this is not that this objection came to light, or that it was perceived as a strong one. In fact the point is pretty obvious and has always been a primary rationale for multi-skilling in the workplace. The remarkable part was that when this objection was laid out clearly in the context of all other relevant considerations, its overriding force was fully appreciated in a way it had never been when the arguments were rehearsed in standard ways. Opponents of multi-skilling had previously been familiar with this objection, but must have felt that they had adequate responses to it. Yet when the objection and the responses were laid out clearly for all to see, the strength of the objection and relative frailty of any counterarguments became unavoidably apparent.

Thus in the consensus phase there was little more to be said; the rational consensus among the group was that some degree of multi-skilling was essential, and that all objections to multi-skilling were so many hurdles or barriers to be overcome rather than a overriding case for a return to the bad old ways. There may continue to be grumbling and resentment, but whether the factory should continue to promote multi-skilling was no longer a topic for serious dispute.

Stage 5: Print and Display Visualization
By this time, participants had been viewing the projected argument visualization on the large screen, and had seen A4 printouts of drafts. As they walked out of the room, the complexity and arrangement of the full set of arguments would have to be held in their heads if it was to be retained at all. Yet we have very limited capacity to remember and to process complex structures of reasoning with our unaided brains. Even taking notes, in the traditional sense, wouldn't help much; the notes would probably not capture all the details, and in any case the note taker would have to mentally reconstruct the overall structure of the argumentation from the notes. The output of the visualization

process – the argument visualization – would have to be somehow made available to participants for review at later times.

Thus the final stage of the argument visualization exercise was producing a high-quality, poster-sized, colourful printed map of the entire set of arguments, for display in some prominent place in the factory. We took the final draft of the visualization away in electronic form, reworked the argument to clean it up, both within nodes and in its overall structure; then sent it off to be printed in A1 size (Figure 5.3). This poster was then laminated and sent back to the factory, where it was, at least for a while, pinned up on a public wall so that anyone could read it, review the arguments, and perhaps use it to help them rationally determine their opinion on the matter.

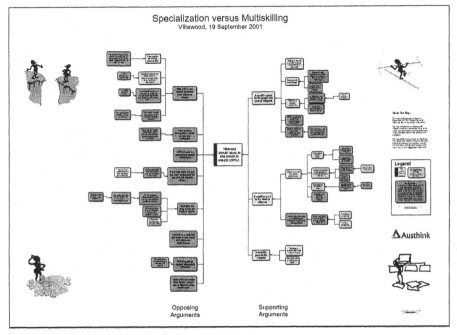

Figure 5.3: The revised argument visualization. This was printed in A1 size, laminated, and sent back to the workplace so that participants and others could easily review the arguments. Notice that even though the individual claims (text within nodes) are illegible, the main structure of the argument is clearly visible at a glance. For example, it is apparent that there is a larger number of primary objections (nodes immediately to the left of the central node) than primary reasons.

To return to the main theme of this chapter, how did computer supported argument visualization enhance group deliberation?

1　Most profoundly, the live argument visualization process expanded participants' sense of the full set of arguments, and where individual arguments belonged in the overall structure. They could, literally, *see* what was going on, in a way not possible with standard prose-based ways of handling reasoning; and, having seen the full argument, were better able to take relevant factors into account.

2   The evolving, projected argument visualization gave participants a *common* understanding of the arguments and their structure. In ordinary argumentative practices, people must maintain in their minds a sense of what the overall argument is. Since this is exceedingly difficult to do, they end up with partial versions and everyone has a somewhat different interpretation. When everyone is on a different wavelength, there is a great deal of confusion, needless disputation, and wasted time.

3   The argument visualization process gave participants a powerful sense that they had been *heard*, that their opinion had been registered. When they made a contribution to the overall debate, it was entered in a box and placed on the tree, and it stayed there for all to see for the duration of the workshop; and if it had not been responded to, this was immediately apparent in the visual layout of the argument tree.

4   The argument visualization process smoothed the path to rational consensus by *depersonalising* disagreement. In standard meetings or round-table discussions, positions tend to be identified with people, and debate becomes a personal contest as much as an objective considering of the arguments. When all attention is focused on the argument tree, however, personalities drop away and people are much better able to appreciate the force of the arguments, and to see gaps and weaknesses.

5   The poster-sized argument visualization is now a permanent part of that particular organisation's memory. On one day, the participants had achieved what was probably their highest-ever level of awareness and understanding of the arguments on a topic of considerable internal importance. If they were to rely unaided memory to store this "knowledge," or even had it written up and filed away in some kind of report, it would surely have been lost. The argument visualization both encodes that knowledge and makes it readily recoverable for anyone in future.

5.7   Conclusion

Deliberation is the primary means by which we strive for, and sometimes actually find, the truth on important, complex issues. Anything which enhances deliberation thereby enhances our ability to know the truth. Argument visualization can substantially enhance deliberation, relative to traditional practices. The emergence of new, dedicated argument visualization support tools will, I believe, enable argument visualization to become widespread practice in schools, and in the workplace, in domains as various as policy making, research, politics, the law, and dispute resolution. If all this is correct, computer supported argument visualization ought, in the long run, contribute substantially to human well-being. In this sense, our project is a extension of the Enlightenment vision of progress through the refinement and application of Reason.

5.8 References

Bar-Hillel, Y., & others. (1969). Formal logic and natural languages: A symposium. *Foundations of Language, 5*, 256-284.

Dyson, F. J. (2002, March 28). Science and religion: No ends in sight. *The New York Review of Books.* Retrieved on August 28, 2002 from http://www.nybooks.com/articles/15220

Kuhn, D. (1991). *The Skills of Argument.* Cambridge, Eng.: Cambridge University Press.

Lakoff, G. (1987). *Women, fire, and dangerous things:: what categories reveal about the mind.* Chicago: University of Chicago Press.

Minto, B. (1995). *The pyramid principle: Logic in writing and thinking.* Edinburgh Gate: Pearson Education.

Monk, P. (2001, March 16). Mapping the future of argument. *Australian Financial Review,* (pp. 8-9).

Pascarella, E. T., & Terenzini, P. T. (1991). *How college affects students: Findings and insights from twenty years of research.* San Francisco: Jossey-Bass.

Rolf, B., & Magnusson, C. (2002). *Developing the art of argumentation. A software approach.* Paper presented at the 5th International Conference on Argumentation, University of Amsterdam.

Van Eemeren, F. H., Grootendorst, R., Henkemans, F. S., Blair, J. A., Johnson, R. H., Krabbe, E. C. W., et al. (1996). Fundamentals of argumentation theory: A handbook of historical backgrounds and contemporary developments. Mahwah, N.J.: Lawrence Erlbaum Associates.

Van Gelder, T. J. (2001). How to improve critical thinking using educational technology. In G. Kennedy, M. Keppell, C. McNaught & T. Petrovic (Eds.), *Meeting at the crossroads: proceedings of the 18th annual conference of the Australasian Society for computers in learning in tertiary education* (pp. 539-548). Melbourne: Biomedical Multimedia Uni, The University of Melbourne.

Van Gelder, T. J., & Bulka, A. (2000). Reason!Able (Version 1.1). Melbourne: The Reason Group. Available from http://www.goreason.com

Webster, N., & Porter, N. (1913). *Webster's revised unabridged dictionary of the English language.* Springfield, MA: G. & C. Merriam company.

6   Dialog Mapping: Reflections on an Industrial Strength Case Study

Jeff Conklin

CogNexus Institute, and George Mason University, USA

6.1   Introduction

Earlier chapters have introduced the notion of "wicked problems" and the Issue Based Information System (IBIS) framework (Buckingham Shum, Chapter 1, van Bruggen Chapter 2), both of which derive from the work of Horst Rittel. Selvin (Chapter 7) proposes a generic framework for facilitated Computer Supported Argument Visualization (CSAV), and reports on case studies using the IBIS-based *Compendium* approach. Compendium itself is based on a facilitated CSAV approach called *Dialog Mapping*, the focus of this chapter. We begin by elaborating on the art and process of Dialog Mapping, before reporting on a particular business application, probably the longest-term case study available of CSAV adoption in an organization.

The case study reports on ten years of continuous usage of Dialog Mapping by a group of approximately 50 users in the Environmental Affairs division of Southern California Edison (SCE). More precisely, this group have been users of the *QuestMap*™ software system,[1] which is the software system underpinning Dialog Mapping. QuestMap provides some hypertext and groupware features which are quite powerful but are also can be difficult for new users to master. Such features often spell doom for the successful rollout of new collaboration technologies. The case study explores the some of the practical success factors for CSAV adoption as they apply to the case of the adoption and usage of QuestMap and Dialog Mapping at SCE.

6.2   IBIS: Issue-Based Information System

At the heart of the Dialog Mapping approach is the IBIS argumentation system. IBIS is

---

[1]   QuestMap is a trademark of GDSS, Inc., Washington, DC, USA

a rhetorical "grammar" which defines the basic elements of all analysis and design dialogs. IBIS consists of three basic elements: *Questions*, which pose a problem or issue, *Ideas*, which offer possible solutions or explanations to the Questions, and *Arguments*, which state evidence, facts, and viewpoints that either support or object to Ideas. Also called "pros and cons", arguments are often linked to evidential documents that back up their claim. IBIS was developed in the early 1970s as a tool to support planning and policy design processes (Kunz and Rittel, 1970).

For example, Figure 6.1 shows a small IBIS map for a meeting of a school board faced with a budget shortfall. Generally these maps are constructed from left to right; thus the "root issue" in this map is "What should we do about the budget?" There are three possible answers ("ideas") in the map so far, and there are additional questions about the first two ideas. There is an argument against the first idea, and an argument for the third idea. The links may seem to be backward, but they are not: new nodes are *about* existing nodes, and so point back to them.[2]

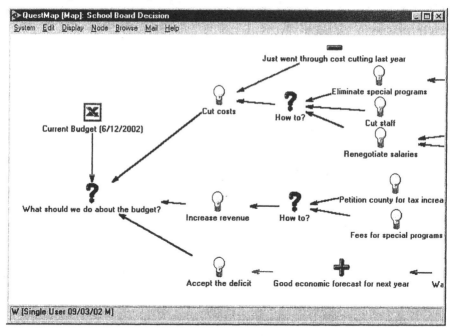

Figure 6.1: Dialog map segment showing all three IBIS elements. Note the spreadsheet program icon in the upper left which is a hot link to a background source document for the discussion.

The power of IBIS stems from three properties: (i) it maps complex thinking into *structured* analytic maps; (ii) it is based on asking the right *questions;* and (iii) it is simple

---

2   Thus the direction of the arrow is connected to the semantics of the link. For example, the idea "Cut costs" is about – "responds to" – the question "What should we do about the budget?" The impression that the link points backwards generally fades quickly.

and intuitive enough to be learned and used with *relatively low cognitive overhead*[3] (making it a good cognitive encoding formalism). Let's consider each of these claims in more detail.

First, IBIS captures complex thinking in structured analytic maps (i.e., diagrams). There is no limit to the size or richness of IBIS maps. A variety of linking and navigation mechanisms provide users with several ways to organize large amounts of information. One of the most basic is that a map can contain other maps (represented as map icons), so that information can be logically chunked. Often, the signal for a new chunk, a new map, is a major new question. For example, in Figure 6.1, the exploration of how to cut costs might lead to a larger and more detailed argument structure which would be better moved into its own map. This new "sub-map" would be hyperlinked to the top-level map.

Moreover, unlike most diagramming and mapping techniques,[4] IBIS has a grammar, imposing a formal structure (albeit a simple one) on IBIS maps. In English, you cannot say "John ball hit the." In IBIS, maps never start with an Argument node, for example, nor are Arguments allowed to link to Questions. The IBIS grammar imposes a discipline on IBIS maps, with two complementary consequences: it is harder to learn to use IBIS than to use free-form techniques,[5] and IBIS maps are more rigorous, more patterned, and more reproducible. For the analysis of wicked situations, the additional structure and rigor of IBIS creates an important baseline of order and reproducibility.

Second, IBIS invokes a discipline of finding the right *questions*. Recall that "IBIS" stands for "*Issue Based* Information System". Issues, stated as questions, are the heart of this method. One benefit of asking questions in a collaborative situation is that it can help to break up the "answer reflex," in which participants exchange answers without ever agreeing on the question. Also, the IBIS grammar allows a Question to be about *any* other IBIS element, so it is through asking new questions that IBIS maps grow. Finally, there are a small number of *types* of questions in IBIS (approximately five) – each type calls for different kinds of responses, and these types connect together in higher-level patterns, or templates. These patterns provide additional order and reproducibility in IBIS maps.

For example, there are Factual questions, such as "What is the expected budget shortfall?" There are Future questions, such as "What will the economy be like next year?" There are Meaning questions, such as "What are 'special programs'?" Each type of question has certain kinds of answers, and they fit together in regular patterns of reasoning.

The third important property of the IBIS grammar is that it is simple and intuitive. Numerous studies have shown that the potential advantages of rhetorical structuring

---

[3] Active use of any formalism will involve some cognitive effort. Typically one can become proficient in IBIS after a 2-day course and some practice, with the emphasis on practice: you become fluent in a new language only by conversing in it.

[4] For example, some consultants use the "mind mapping" approach and a tool that supports it, "MindManager" (for detail see www.mindjet.com/)

[5] "Free form" is equivalent to having a trivial or very simple grammar, e.g. circles and arrows.

techniques like IBIS are often offset by the increased "cognitive overhead" of applying them when engaged in a substantive task (Buckingham Shum and Hammond, 1994). In part, this overhead imposes a constraint on the expressive power of any formalism that might be adopted in the analysis process: candidate notations must be simple and intuitive enough that the "cognitive cost" of using them is very low. Years of practical experience have shown that more sophisticated and expressively powerful notations than IBIS are much more difficult to apply in a transparent way.

There is another way to meet the challenge of "cognitive overhead," and that is to recognize that lowering the cognitive cost of use is in part a matter of *fluency*. Although English is generally recognized as one of the more difficult languages to learn in the world, fluent speakers are unaware of the "cognitive overhead" of English when they are engaged in discussion. English is transparent to both speakers and listeners who are fluent. Similarly, as with a language or a musical instrument, practice and fluency render IBIS both transparent and powerful.

As simple as IBIS is, it can be broken down even further to increase its simplicity for those in the learning phase. One part of IBIS is Questions and Ideas/Answers, the basic constituents of dialog dating back to Aristotle. Virtually anyone can listen to a debate and quickly discern what the question is (or questions are), and what the positions or possible answers are. Moreover, the majority of comments in an analytic discussion are questions and answers, so you can map much of these interactions using only these two IBIS elements.

More challenging for IBIS students is the proper use of Arguments, the pros and cons for the various Ideas. Of course, the *concept* of Arguments is simple and intuitive. Most people are quite used to thinking in terms of tradeoffs, benefits and disadvantages, strengths and weaknesses, opportunities and a threats, and so on. These are the basic terms of critical analysis. However, there are subtle pitfalls for the unpracticed. For example, some arguments clearly object to an idea, e.g. "Management will reject this." But sometimes an argument supports an idea, but because it contains "negative words" it gets erroneously linked as an objection, e.g. "Rejection is unlikely." In applying Arguments clearly and correctly a background in logic can come in handy! In any case, it turns out that only about 10% of the nodes in open-ended and exploratory discussions are Argument nodes, and even less in more structured analyses, so, again, these are the least important of the IBIS elements (Selvin and Sierhuis, 1999).

In summary, distinguishing the three basic elements of IBIS – Questions, Ideas, and Arguments – can become, with practice, very natural. Indeed, many people report that, having learned IBIS, they find it very frustrating to listen to discussions in which the participants are not making these basic rhetorical distinctions! (We explore some ways of dealing with training costs and the learning curve later) Moreover, participants in meetings in which IBIS mapping is done on the fly, either with markers on a white board or with software on a computer projector, find the notation quite natural and obvious. No explanation is necessary, and any sense of mystery about what is going on generally vanishes quickly – assuming, of course, some level of fluency in the person doing the mapping!

One final note on IBIS: in addition to how simple and natural this notation is, it is also important to convey the *power* of IBIS as a mapping notation for complex analyses.

It is easiest to see this power simply by reflecting on what happens *without* such a notation. Different players have different ideas about what the issue is, especially in a wicked situation. Each player addresses their comments to *their version* of the issue, but it is often unclear how many versions of the issue there are, or what they are. Making the issues explicit in an IBIS map, as questions, adds a tremendous clarity to the discussion, as does being clear about which of those issues a given comment is addressing. Wicked problems often have dozens of interrelated issues involved, but human short term memory is limited, so unless one is extremely familiar with the all of the information related to all of the issues, the unaided exploration of these issues is confusing and error-prone. The power of IBIS as a notation is that it organizes all of the issues, positions, information, and assumptions so that all participants have the issue map as a point of reference, and they can refer to it instead of trying to keep it all in their head. Thus IBIS contributes to Dialog Mapping being a "cognitive aid" because it augments human cognition at one of its weakest points: the limits of short term memory.

6.2.1   Artful Questions

Much of the power of IBIS derives from its artful application, and nowhere is that art more evident than in the creation of *questions*. Artful questions must be simple, not compound. ("How big is the budget shortfall, and what should we do about it?" is a compound question – in IBIS it should be broken into its two component questions.) Artful questions do not try to "sneak" assumptions into their statement (e.g. "Given that we are already understaffed, what should we do?"). And artful questions are open, not closed. ("What should we do?" is open, "Should we cut costs to meet the budget?" is closed.)

A closed question is one for which the answer is "yes" or "no", or which lists the possible answers in the question (e.g. "Should we cut costs to meet the budget?"). Closed questions contain the answer and simply ask for verification. Years of experience have shown that IBIS discussions that start with open questions are more creative and rigorous. Closed questions seem to "stack the deck" and close the mind to new possibilities.

And yet, closed questions are very common in everyday speech. Many meetings have closed questions as their agenda, and occasionally facilitators are called on by their client to help a group address closed questions.

Fortunately, IBIS makes it easy to "open" the question up. Suppose the starting question is "Should we cut costs?" To open the question, simply locate the answer buried inside the question (in this case, "cut costs") and restate the question with the answer as an Idea: "What should we do?", "Cut costs". All of the analysis about cutting costs can then be attached to the idea "Cut costs" (see Figure 6.2).

Opening up questions is one simple example of how IBIS can support creative and rigorous analysis of a situation without putting the project group in a linear process or methodological straightjacket.

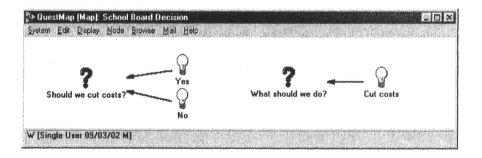

Figure 6.2: Opening up a question in IBIS. The forms are logically equivalent: the same arguments, issues, and evidence that apply to "Yes" on the left apply to "Cut costs" on the right.

6.3   Dialog Mapping

Dialog Mapping is a facilitation technique in which the Facilitator captures the group's discussion in real time in an IBIS map. Dialog Mapping can be done on a piece of paper or a flipchart pad, on a whiteboard, or using software such as QuestMap.[6] Dialog Mapping is a major aspect of the Compendium technique described by Selvin in Chapter 7; all of this chapter's discussion about Dialog Mapping applies to Compendium as well, but the focus here is on Dialog Mapping.

The role of the Facilitator has two component roles: one role includes engaging with the group in traditional facilitative ways (i.e. watching the clock and keeping the group on task), and the other role, also known as "technographer," focuses on listening and typing at the computer. Although one person can perform both roles, it is often preferable if two people work together, one as Facilitator and one as Technographer. In this paper we will refer simply to "the Facilitator."

In Dialog Mapping the group actively and collaboratively engages with the creation of the IBIS map. Central to Dialog Mapping is the notion of a "shared display", a projected computer display of hypertext software showing a map of the knowledge and reasoning of the group, unfolding in real time.

Dialog Mapping works because of the skill of the Facilitator. The Facilitator is sometimes referred to as a "chauffeur," because (unlike traditional facilitation) the Facilitator's job is to serve as an unobtrusive link between the group's conversation and the shared map. If group members are only speaking to each other and not looking at the shared map, then the Facilitator is not doing his or her job. Skillful Facilitation means listening to the comments of the group and capturing them in the map in a way that clarifies meaning and adds value to the conversation. The group learns to look at the map because, when it doesn't, it gets lost or goes in circles. The Facilitator is in charge of *listening*, and thus assures that there is a high quality of communication

---

[6]   Dialog Mapping is described here in the face-to-face meeting context; the process is similar, but with some differences, in facilitating a virtual meeting.

present in the session. In essence, the process of Dialog Mapping focuses a group on constructing a collectively owned model of their problem. With this visual model evolving as they speak, discussions revolve around agreeing on the model, which may of course include agreeing on points of disagreement.

Of course, sometimes the group doesn't pay much attention to the map, and occasionally the group wants the mapping to go faster or to go in a different direction. As with any group intervention, there are dozens of factors and parameters that contribute to the success or failure of a given Dialog Mapping session. One of the most important skills a Facilitator must learn is keeping the group focused on the map and maintaining the group's ownership of the map. Another critical skill is the ability to listen and type at the same time.[7]

Because Dialog Mapping is about the transparent crafting of a high quality map of the group's thinking, sometimes a Facilitator just listens, types, and edits the map. At other times more intervention is called for, including process guidance such as suggesting topics or calling for a break. The Facilitator must sense the needs of the group and make judgments about what kinds of process intervention and guidance, if any, are appropriate. Dialog Mapping does not work in every kind of meeting or with every kind of group. Sometimes the map ends up being nothing more than fancy meeting minutes.

To summarise, a common problem in collective work is sorting out what level of detail and abstraction the group needs to be focused on at any moment. For example, one of the most challenging collaborative tasks – in any field – is collaborative writing. In part this is because participants are working to create and organize the ideas (content) of the document at the same time that they are working on the expression of those ideas (style, wording, grammar, spelling, etc.). This often leads to unproductive disagreements (e.g. the "happy/glad" debate: whether to use "happy" or "glad" in a sentence) as participants stumble between content and style. Moreover, this kind of disagreement can mask a deeper lack of shared understanding about the issues and concepts, resulting in endless and irresolvable disputes over wording.

Dialog Mapping addresses this problem by providing a "pure content" framework – a semi-structured model – for the problem at hand. Participants can stay focused on the content level because it is starkly and graphically represented in the shared hypertext display. Moreover, disagreements over content are not mere verbal jousting matches – the Facilitator works with the group to bring the participants' best thinking to mapping out the opposing options and their respective arguments, and perhaps even introducing new options. While this emotional distancing does not make the debate disappear, it removes its fangs, and allows clearer heads to negotiate new meanings and formulate new options. In many cases, a clear "winner" emerges simply through the process of open dialog, and even when this doesn't happen, the Dialog Mapping model

---

[7]   There are many very good traditional facilitators who do not have great typing skills. It is important to bear in mind that Dialog Mapping Facilitation requires an unusual mix of skills, or two people: one to facilitate in the traditional sense and one to be the "technographer."

presents the options and tradeoffs clearly to the decision making authority (i.e. the chair of the meeting).

6.4   Case Study: A Decade's Deployment in a Public Utility

6.4.1   Background

In the Spring of 1992, Michael Begeman and I met with then Executive Vice President David Fogarty and Dr. Michael Hertel, the Director of the Environmental Affairs Division at Southern California Edison (SCE). Using screenshots of a research prototype,[8] we presented the plans for our new software product, CM/1 (now called QuestMap), explaining that it could be used to capture operational decisions and the rationale behind them, creating an "organizational memory." Early in the presentation, Hertel interrupted our presentation. "If you are telling me what I think you are telling me, " he said slowly, "I am very excited, because I have been looking for something like this for a long time."

That was a fateful moment for the new company, Corporate Memory Systems, Inc., because it was the beginning of the first installation (the "beta site") of our new IBIS-based CSAV system, and our first software sale. Starting with a 20-user license, SCE expanded over the years to its present installation of about 50 users, some of whom have been users of the system for the decade since.

From the tone of that meeting, and the apparent ease with which we had found this customer, the founders of Corporate Memory Systems, Inc. (CMSI) assumed that we had "struck it rich" by tapping into a large market of organizations who would pay well for tools that helped them to capture their organizational learning and memory. Alas, the market was not as ready as we had hoped. Five years later, in 1996, CMSI went out of business due to a lack of sales.

This case study attempts to capture some of the highlights of the SCE story, and to understand what factors have allowed the staff of that organization to continue for ten years to apply a structured argumentation method to the routine issues of environmental planning, regulatory compliance, and policy design.

---

[8]   The *gIBIS* (graphical-IBIS) system was developed during the late 1980s in the Software Technology Program at MCC in Austin, Texas, and was the subject of numerous publications in the hypertext and groupware literature (e.g. Conklin & Begeman, 1987, 1989). See also Buckingham Shum's historical review in Chapter 1.

6.4.2   Factors Impacting Success

In the workshop where this work was first presented,[9] four factors that impact the success or failure of a CSAV system were listed in the call for papers:
- Domain and argumentation knowledge
- Training in tools
- User interface design
- Motivation to use the approach

In a business application of a CSAV system like SCE's, we also want to consider:
- For what organizational purposes was the system used?
- What business problems did it address or solve?
- How was the system used in practice?
- For the people who used the system, why did they continue to use it?
- For those who didn't, why not?
- What if any technology features were especially useful?
- What features got in the way?
- Were there features that made believers of advanced users but were barriers to new users?

Moreover, there is the challenge of determining if indeed a CSAV system is a success. Sometimes in business situations one of the hardest issues is *"What are the criteria for success?"* I now discuss how the above factors had a bearing on SCE's use of QuestMap and Dialog Mapping.

6.4.3   Domain and Argumentation Knowledge

Staff members of the Environmental Affairs Division (EAD) are professionals with high levels of education and training in the areas of environmental and policy science. The EAD has 3 subgroups: a research group that focuses on environmental impacts, a services group focused on regulatory compliance and engineering assistance to facility operators, and an legislative policy group that designs policy and serves as a liaison to state and national environmental agencies. In addition, the EAD makes fairly heavy use of SCE's legal services group.

None of the EAD staff had any previous experience with an argumentation method such as IBIS. The initial training session for the user group was a 3-day course in both IBIS and QuestMap, with emphasis on the software. However, only person (Hertel) used the system following this training. To address this problem, additional training events focused on developing more proficiency in using IBIS as a "language" for thinking (Buckingham Shum and Hammond, 1994), and in coaching smaller work groups that were focused on a specific project and could commit to using the IBIS/QuestMap approach over a specific period of time.

---

[9]   *Computer-Supported Collaborative Argumentation for Learning Communities*, 11-12 Dec., 1999, Stanford University, CA <www.kmi.open.ac.uk/sbs/csca/cscl99>

Over the years, additional new users were trained in 2- or 3-day courses and there were refresher courses and advanced workshops for more seasoned users of the system. These courses attempted to cover three areas: the fundamentals of using IBIS as an argumentation structure, the fundamentals of using the QuestMap system, and practice with using IBIS and QuestMap. The issue of training is returned to later (section 6.4.7: Revisited), since it proved so crucial.

6.4.4   Training in Tools

Teaching QuestMap to new users is an interesting challenge. At the level of fundamentals, the software is easy to learn: "The software was incredibly easy to use. I think anybody who is facile with Windows can learn the scheme and use it effectively within an hour or less" (Seybold, 1993). On the other hand, QuestMap has some very sophisticated hypertext features, and the notion of a "virtual shared space", or Common Information Space (CIS – Bannon and Bødker, 1997), was and is only intuitive for more technical users. For example, if a user made a copy of a Question node, pasted it into another view, and edited it, the original node also changed: QuestMap's "Copy" operation was a "shallow" copy, creating a reference link to an underlying database object. Users who did not understand this shared object aspect continued to operate in a private desktop mode, sometimes wreaking havoc with other occupants of the CIS from the changes they made.

Some non-technical users who have been using QuestMap for *years* still do not understand how and when to use these sophisticated hypertext capabilities. Whether this is because of poor training or a poor user interface, there is not much evidence for successful training in using the "power tools" of the QuestMap system. In more recent years, newcomers to the EAD have picked up using the system more easily, perhaps because they are coming into an environment where it is an established way of working and there are many people who can answer technical questions.

6.4.5   User Interface Design

QuestMap was originally designed as a groupware CSAV tool for asynchronous collaboration, with additional provisions for "Reference" nodes and "Note" nodes that made it also an attractive CIS tool.[10] Creating and operating on IBIS structures is very easy in QuestMap.[11]

At SCE, two distinct applications of QuestMap have emerged in the past several years, exploiting two distinct sets of system features. The first is as a File Tracking System, in which users create maps dominated by sub-maps, Note and Reference nodes. The other application is as a Dialog Mapping tool during face-to-face meetings,

---

[10]   QuestMap won the award for "Best of Show" in the Group Information Sharing category at the first International Groupware Conference in San Jose in 1992, beating out such heavy weights as Lotus Notes.

[11]   For some users the mouse is overloaded: creating links and scrolling are both "Right Drag" operations, which is an unusual gesture in the Windows world.

where one person (often Hertel) "drives" QuestMap, capturing comments in the IBIS notation.[12] Hertel reports that this technique "works really well," because everyone is paying attention to the "shared display."

Thus at this site (as at others) there appear to be two primary applications of QuestMap, exploiting two aspects of its interface and functionality: as a CIS system for asynchronous information management and sharing, and as a meeting facilitation tool for face-to-face meetings. The former application makes light use of IBIS argumentation, the latter one makes very heavy use of it. The question is, could these be implemented as two separate applications, or is the convergence of synchronous and asynchronous use an essential aspect of its utility? This question is explored further below (section 6.4.10: Synchronous Versus Asynchronous CSAV).

6.4.6 Motivation to Use

The critical factor in the sustained use of QuestMap in EAD is clearly the commitment of Dr. Hertel, the Director. He has provided substantial levels of training, encouraged and occasionally even coerced his staff to use the system, and has been a role model by using QuestMap heavily, not only for visible Division functions but also as a personal note-taking tool when he is on the road at conferences.

Not everyone in the EA Division was successfully motivated to use IBIS and QuestMap. Some people reacted strongly to the early emphasis on having "virtual meetings" within QuestMap instead of face-to-face meetings. Some viewed it as just another "passing fad" of management. Some felt that IBIS was restrictive to the natural flow of conversations, and that using it for meeting facilitation slowed meetings down too much. A deeper study of EAD is planned to explore this resistance.

The other critical motivation to using CSAV has been having a clear business need for either the design rigour provided by embracing the CSAV discipline or the "audit trail" of the decision rationale, or both. In cases where there was a small, focused work group, including someone acting as the "view keeper",[13] there were many successful extended uses of QuestMap. These groups found that "it really does make it easy to put everything in one place and remember the thinking patterns that you went through to get to certain conclusions, such as why you decided NOT to take a path, which is almost always as important as why you decided TO take one ..." (Seybold, 1993).

---

[12] Using QuestMap in face-to-face meetings was a client (Hertel) innovation, which CMSI initially resisted (because we had developed QuestMap as an asynchronous groupware system). Fortunately, Hertel insisted, and in fact used large group policy design sessions as a way to introduce QuestMap and CSAV to his organization (Seybold, 1993).

[13] Most groups that collaboratively construct IBIS maps in QuestMap end up with very large and poorly structured maps. As a result, CMSI recommended that one participant in a project function as a moderator and gatekeeper for the map, to keep the map orderly and focused and the IBIS structures clean and well-formed. This role was dubbed the "View Keeper".

6.4.7   Training Revisited

Perhaps the most significant factor in the later success (and early failure) of Dialog Mapping at SCE has been training. It became apparent that teaching QuestMap and IBIS in the same course was trying to tackle too much at once. Feedback from participants, some weeks after the courses (at this and other QuestMap sites), revealed that many people had not acquired any fluency in using IBIS, while others had only the weakest grasp of the groupware capabilities of QuestMap. In more recent years we have run separate courses for the argumentation and software components (starting usually with the argumentation part), and this has resulted in much better sustained learning.

Indeed, for the past few years, I have given up on training people to use QuestMap altogether, focusing instead on raising IBIS "literacy" in client organizations. In the most recent version of this approach, Dialog Mapping, individuals and groups take the 2-day training course simply to learn a new method for "group problem solving and decision making" that focuses on creating "shared understanding" among the participants. The QuestMap software is provided at no cost, and with only one hour of software-specific training, as a part of the course.

Advanced practice sessions in early 1999 that focused primarily on IBIS and Dialog Mapping had a strong user uptake, particularly among new staff members who "did not have the baggage of the past" (Jim Young, EAD staff member, personal communication). In these sessions, a group of managers who had been trained in both IBIS and QuestMap observed while I facilitated the group in a 2-day strategic planning session (on a real problem of extremely high relevance to the group) using QuestMap. Several people reported learning more than they expected from watching me use the tools.

6.4.8   What is "Success"?

What would constitute "successful adoption" of a CSAV system in an industrial strength setting like SCE? What percentage of users would need to achieve what level of proficiency and sustained usage? What business outcomes would constitute success? How long would the usage of the CSAV system need to be sustained to say that it had "stuck"?

My assessment is that at SCE we have a qualified and perhaps "brittle" success of industrial-strength CSAV. It is qualified because not everyone uses it or is in favour of its use; it is not used routinely at every meeting, but there is an implicit sense of when it is appropriate to use QuestMap and IBIS on a project. It is brittle because it is not clear if, or for how long, the system would continue to be used if Hertel were not the Director of the Division.

QuestMap has many features, and can be described in several different ways: as groupware, as hypertext, as a Common Information Space, and as an IBIS-based CSAV system. This makes it harder to isolate factors specific to CSAV usage, because users may, for example, be simply tolerating the IBIS component of the system because of the value of the CIS or hypertext functionality. In any case, the CIS and meeting facilitation applications make very different use of CSAV.

Of the 50 staff in SCE's EAD, approximately 10 are moderate users of QuestMap (Hertel, personal communication). "The other 40 are not against the system, they simply do not see a need," Hertel said. "Not many people are willing to embrace the IBIS process and logic. It's probably like the percentage of people who are willing to go to law school and learn *that* thinking and analysis process. It's hard work!"

One way to measure success would be to look at statistics of system usage over the years. Who was using the system, how often, for what purpose? Selvin and Sierhuis (1999) report a statistical analysis of their QuestMap database. Unfortunately, it has not been possible as of this writing to gather that data from the SCE QuestMap database, which is now approximately 200 megabytes.

6.4.9   The Facilitator Issue

A principal distinguishing feature of the Dialog Mapping approach to collaborative technology is that it does not require everyone to learn new tools and methods. Instead, Dialog Mapping introduces a new player – the Facilitator – into the process, to act as the knowledge mediator, leaving participants free to focus on sharing their knowledge and completing the analytic task at hand.

One natural concern about Dialog Mapping's facilitation approach is, "Where do the Facilitators come from?" Typically, it starts with one enthusiast whose work impresses colleagues. They may of course then want to learn it themselves through informal practice and/or formal training, but a range of other options exist, which are being trialled in a variety of organisations affiliated to the Compendium Institute.[14]

- A contracting organization can be a source of Facilitators on an as-needed basis.
- One can offer Dialog Mapping training to managers and team leaders and let those for whom it is a good fit emerge as natural Facilitators. An issue to emerge from a recent workshop[15] is precisely how much training one needs to reap immediate benefits, and whether one could even envisage adept secretarial staff doing Dialog Mapping instead of just writing minutes.
- In a large organization one could include Dialog Mapping facilitation as one of the skills of the support staff. The Dialog Mapping Facilitator in this setting is simply another standard support function – just as you would always have IT staff to set up and maintain the IT and multi-media platform in a modern, high-tech "fusion" center, you might also have a cadre of facilitators equipped to facilitate using Dialog Mapping tool suite, integrated with the organisation's existing infrastructure.

---

[14] Compendium Institute <www.CompendiumInstitute.org>
[15] *HypACoM 2002: Facilitating Hypertext-Augmented Collaborative Modeling.* ACM Hypertext'02 Workshop, 11-12 June, 2002, Univ. Maryland, MD <cognexus.org/ht02>

6.4.10   Synchronous Versus Asynchronous CSAV

As we have seen, SCE uses CSAV in two very different ways:
- Synchronous: Dialog Mapping with QuestMap as a facilitation tool during group meetings
- Asynchronous: QuestMap as an organizational memory and file management tool, by individuals in their offices.

The original intent when the SCE Environmental Affairs group acquired QuestMap was to capture organizational memory in an asynchronous usage mode, and that was the "product" that Corporate Memory Systems Inc. was offering. Over time it became clear that, as beneficial as the organizational memory might be, the practical path to successful knowledge capture was by using the system in meetings, i.e., in synchronous mode. This observation accords well with earlier research suggesting that successful adoption of CSAV technology requires a short term payoff for the participants – it cannot simply be a long term payoff documentation effort (Burgess Yakemovic and Conklin 1990).

Ultimately, the practical success of CSAV will depend on an intimate and dynamic relationship between the synchronous and asynchronous modes of CSAV. CSAV tools provide an elegant way to knit two important aspects of knowledge work – individual work at one's desk and conversations during meetings – into a more seamless whole (Selvin, et al., 2002). For instance, Buckingham Shum, et al. (2002) report on how documents are written in the usual asynchronous mode, brought into a meeting and reviewed and modified there, and then new issues and action items captured in the system for further individual work after the meeting. From a practical standpoint, however, these are *very* different modes of work – they require different kinds of participation, have different tempos and social dynamics, and make very different demands on the supporting CSAV tools. For example, the skill requirements are very different for these two modes. In a meeting, only the Facilitator need be skilled in Dialog Mapping. In asynchronous work using a CSAV organizational memory, all participants must be skillful in the construction and evolution of argument maps. Integrating the practices and tools remains a major challenge for CSAV and for collaborative technology in general.

SCE's experience with working CSAV into everyday work provides some lessons and examples for this integration. For example, during meetings at SCE it is not uncommon to use QuestMap to locate the notes from an earlier meeting, or to locate a document. This is a case of using the organizational memory aspect of the system simply for retrieval during a meeting – no new nodes are created, no Dialog Mapping is done. Conversely, the groupware features of QuestMap allow a map that is under construction during a meeting to be emailed to a staff member with a question or request. Sometimes the staff member is able to quickly answer the question or request by adding new argumentation nodes directly to the map, causing the response to appear automatically on the screen in the meeting room.

The connection between synchronous and asynchronous work seems to focus on documents: how documents (reports, white papers, diagrams, budgets, requirements, etc.) are referenced and used during meetings, and how meeting notes become documents that evolve into other kinds of documents. For example, Selvin and Buckingham Shum (1999; 2002) report on the "representational morphing" of documents into IBIS maps, and then back to other notational formats such as data flow diagrams and requirements documents.

SCE's use of QuestMap as a document management system illustrates this connection between the informal knowledge typically captured in CSAV documents and the more formal knowledge of traditional documents, and also illustrates how useful the hypertext features of QuestMap were adapted to the document-centric nature of asynchronous work.

First, many environmental projects organize their project-related documents in QuestMap. The document file itself is stored in a folder in the corporate file system, usually in a subfolder named for the project. The person who saves the file also makes a link to it in QuestMap, by creating a "Reference node" that links to the file (contains the file's path name in the "File name" field of the node). He or she also creates a descriptive Label for the node, and might also enter a brief description of the document or its connection to the project in the Detail field. Finally, the Reference node is graphically linked to the IBIS node or nodes that it is about (see Figure 6.3). Although creating the QuestMap link is an added step, many EAD staff accept it as necessary because it captures the *context* in which the document is relevant to the project, because it allows the document to be more easily located using QuestMap's search engine, and because once linked the document's Reference node can be easily reused (transclusively linked) into other maps.

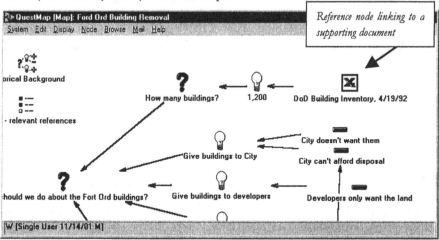

Figure 6.3: Use of a *Reference* node to link to an external document (spreadsheet) to back up an answer.

This is not to say that all relevant documents get linked into the appropriate project maps. Indeed, because it is extra work for busy people, relevant documents often do not get linked. Moreover, if a document is moved or renamed, or if new versions are created, the QuestMap links are often not updated. These are not new problems in document management, but they suggest an important set of requirements for extending CSAV tools into the asynchronous mode, to better support the organisational memory function.

Not all of SCE's asynchronous use of QuestMap is as a document management system. Sometimes staff members create argumentation maps asynchronously. One staff member might start a map, for example, seeding it with Questions. Other staff members, invited into the map by an internal QuestMap "email" feature, add new nodes to the map at their convenience (i.e. asynchronously), and reply to the QuestMap email with an indication that they have added to the map. Although this kind of process was the original design focus of QuestMap, in practice most argument maps are created in meetings using Dialog Mapping.

In a second, non-argumentation, use of QuestMap's hypertext features, EAD staff members have evolved a "time-line" map format that they use to organize all of the maps and documents associated with a project. The map consists of a horizontal axis along which major sub-maps are linked in chronological order, and vertical "ribs" extending from any of these major sub-maps with supporting sub-maps, notes, or documents (see Figure 6.4). The individual sub-maps represent CSAV notes of meetings or planning sessions, related maps from other projects, or occasionally time-line maps for subprojects related to the main project.[16]

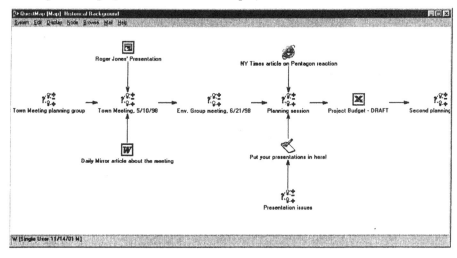

Figure 6.4: An example of how QuestMap's generic *Map* container for IBIS discussions has been adapted to other purposes, coupled with *Reference* nodes to external resources. EAD staff members have evolved a "time-line" map format to organize all of the maps and documents associated with a project, with time progressing left to right.

We have examined SCE's use of the QuestMap CSAV tool as a document management tool. Although this use is not Dialog Mapping, and does not necessarily involve the use of any argumentation, the integration of project documents with the

---

16 The timeline maps are referred to as "Jim Young style maps" at EAD, after the man who created and popularised this format in the group.

Dialog Mapping argumentation maps is so critical to the overall viability of CSAV at SCE that it bears careful study and further tool support.

6.5 Introducing Dialog Mapping into a New Organization

Based on years of Dialog Mapping in business and government contexts, one can distill out a number of factors that have impacted the likelihood of successful introduction. Against these criteria, the "ideal" pilot experiment for introducing Dialog Mapping to a group would most likely display the following characteristics:

1   The problem chosen should be "medium wicked." The issue or topic that the pilot group is working on should not be a "tame problem," one so simple that observers would say that it could have been solved by using *any* problem solving approach. Nor should the issue be so wicked that progress on it is virtually impossible due to entrenched positions and political implications. It is not that Dialog Mapping can't be used for such issues; it is just that they don't offer a fair initial evaluation of a new and unfamiliar methodology.

2   There should be a perceived need to increase the level of *shared understanding* among a group of stakeholders. That is, the ideal issue or topic is one in which there is some history, a wide range of positions and opinions, and some time in which to search for common ground on the topic. This eliminates presentational meetings (one person giving information to a group), and immediate decision meetings (a short time in which a final decision must be taken).

3   The Facilitator should be experienced and well prepared. Much of Dialog Mapping's value rests on the Facilitator; it is important that the person (or persons) filling this role be qualified, experienced, and skillful in all of the aspects of Dialog Mapping. (See Selvin, Chapter 7, for more on Facilitator skills.)

4   The pilot study should have organizational and management support. While there is much to be said for "bottom up" experiments and technology "pull," the ideal situation for a fair evaluation is that the pilot group's management is open to and seeking new ways to do business, and new opportunities for improved collaboration.

5   The experiment should involve a series of meetings. One of the greatest strengths of Dialog Mapping is *group memory*, the ability to capture and summarize a complex discussion and to carry it forward to future meetings, and for stakeholders who need to be briefed about the meeting. Thus, an ideal evaluation pilot would involve a series of three to six meetings over a period several weeks or months. This would allow the efficiencies of group memory to be demonstrated and evaluated.

6   The participants should care about resolving the issue, and be willing to share information. If the pilot session or sessions are attended by participants who

are only there because they were told to be, and who have no intention to collaborate, this is (again) an environment from which little new can be learned.

7   The participants should be open to new approaches and tools.

8   The meeting room should have good quality computer projection, and the seating should be arranged in a "U" that is open to the shared display screen.

9   The technology should not dominate the process. It is the mapping, and the group interaction to craft the map, that is the main value of Dialog Mapping. Indeed, sometimes it is better to start with "manual hypertext" — sticky paper on the wall, whiteboards, sticky notes, chart paper — whatever low-tech display technology is at hand, and then to transition the group to a computer display as the amount of material (and the process of maintaining it) becomes unwieldy.

These criteria are based not just on the SCE experience with QuestMap and Dialog Mapping, but also on experiments using Dialog Mapping in other contexts, including a meeting of analysts in an intelligence organization.

6.6   Conclusion and Future Directions

SCE's Environmental Affairs Division is a unique instance of successful long-term use of a CSAV tool in a business context. While the rarity of such cases points to the relative immaturity of the CSAV and collaborative technology fields, we have reviewed some of the features of SCE's case over the last 10 years that reveal important aspects of successful industrial adoption of CSAV.

Future directions for research include better training, better tools, and deeper understanding of the organizational and social context of CSAV use.

I have spent over ten years developing and refining training materials to teach Dialog Mapping, and I would say there is still much room for improvement and innovation. Being skillful in Dialog Mapping depends on fluency in IBIS, and that fluency, as with any language, comes from practice. Fluency in IBIS is the most challenging skill required, followed by the skill of creating and managing a map in a shared display such that the participants engage with, and own, the map. Naturally, the Facilitator must also know and use the software so well that it is transparent to them during the session. Structured materials and classroom sessions are certainly helpful and necessary, but in the end it seems that the only way to become proficient as a Dialog Mapping Facilitator is to "jump into the deep end and learn to swim," i.e. to set yourself up working on real (and often wicked) problems, and map participants' conversations in a shared display.

One way to make these skills more accessible would be to have a range of training videos from real Dialog Mapping sessions that could be used to illustrate common meeting situations and skillful ways of dealing with them. Another tool might be interactive exercises on the web or on CDROM that presented a meeting situation, allowed the student to create a fragment of a map, and then presented an idealized map along with the reasons for its structure.

If we can find ways to make it easier to learn the skills of Dialog Mapping, it can become more widespread, and that will in turn trigger new innovation and research.

Another front for further research is technology. Ultimately, CSAV is but a part of Doug Engelbart's bigger unfinished revolution to create tools for augmenting the human intellect, both individually and collectively (see Afterword). Many of the issues raised by the SCE experience with QuestMap have to do with integrating argumentation maps with the other aspects of knowledge work: easier and better linking to documents and document elements (figures, paragraphs, etc.), ability to email maps to others (especially colleagues outside of the organization and its firewall), and ability to publish maps and sets of maps on the Internet,[17] and to allow remote participants to contribute to those maps or discussions about them. Selvin, et al. (2001) describes some of the extensions to Dialog Mapping that are emerging as part of the Compendium approach.

Finally, much more research is needed in the social and organizational dimension. Argument maps are a new kind of document. They take a step in direction of being a kind of "living document" that serves as an especially dynamic boundary object among the members of a project team, as well as among subgroups, divisions, and organizations in large projects. As such, argument maps cross the boundary between two familiar metaphors of knowledge work: conversations and publication. During a meeting, a Dialog Map serves as a representation or model of the conversation as it is unfolding. The map is a snapshot of the conversation, but it is also an essential *part* of the conversation. After the meeting, it is natural to share that captured knowledge more widely, but the metaphor of publication, oriented as it is to more formal and stable kinds of knowledge, requires consideration of such issues as authorship, editing, vetting, validation, scope, and medium. What is the status of a published Dialog Map in a project? It seems to be something new, something more than minutes of the meeting, but less than a traditional report or white paper. What practices and tools are needed to allow social networks to engage with these artifacts in this gray zone between sense-making process and published knowledge representation? How can we make facilitation (in the Dialog Mapping sense) a more natural aspect of the rituals called meetings?

6.7 References

Bannon, L., & Bødker, S. (1997). Constructing common information spaces. In J. Hughes, W. Prinz, T. Rodden & K. Schmidt (Eds.). *Proceedings of ECSCW'97* (pp. 81-96). Dordrecht: Kluwer Academic Publishers.

---

[17] The Mifflin IBIS mapping tool, a next generation version of QuestMap under development by the Compendium Institute <www.CompendiumInstitute.org> and CoAKTinG Project <www.aktors.org/coakting>, provides powerful web publishing and interoperability with other collaboration tools.

Buckingham Shum, S., & Hammond, Nick. (1994). Argumentation-based design rationale: What use at what cost? *International Journal of Human-Computer Studies, 40*(4), 603-652.

Buckingham Shum, S., Motta, E., & Domingue, J. (2002, June). Augmenting design deliberation with compendium: The case of collaborative ontology design. In: *HypACoM 2002: Facilitating Hypertext-Augmented Collaborative Modeling.* ACM Hypertext'02 Workshop, University Maryland, MD. Retrieved August 10, 2002 from http://www.cognexus.org/ht02

Conklin, J., & Begeman, M. (1989). gIBIS: A tool for all reasons. *Journal of the American Society for Information Science (JASIS), 40*(3), 200-213.

Conklin, J., & Begeman, M. (1989, October). The right tool for the job. *Byte, 13*(10), 255-266.

Conklin, J., & Begeman, M. L. (1987). *gIBIS: A hypertext tool for team design deliberation.* Paper presented at Hypertext '87, Chapel Hill, NC.

Kunz, W. & Rittel, H. (1970). *Issues as elements of information systems* (Technical Report S-78-2). Universität Stuttgart, Institut für Gundlagen, Stuttgart, Germany.

Selvin, A. (1994). *Human interaction issues with group support technology in a software R&D organization.* Paper presented at the workshop on Human Interaction Issues in Technology Support Environments. CSCW'94. New York: ACM Press.

Selvin, A. M., & Buckingham Shum, S. J. (1999). Repurposing requirements: Improving collaborative sense-making over lifecycle. *Proceedings of International Conference on Product-Focused Software Process Improvement (Profes '99), Oulu, Finland,* 539-559. Retrieved Septermber 4, 2002 from http://www.inf.vtt.fi/pdf/symposiums/1999/S195.pdf

Selvin, A. M., & Buckingham Shum, S. J. (2002). Rapid knowledge construction: A case study in corporate contingency planning using collaborative hypermedia. *Knowledge and Process Management, 9*(2), 119-128. PrePrint available as: http://www.kmi.open.ac.uk/tr/abstracts/kmi-tr-92.html

Selvin, A., & Sierhuis, M. (1999, December). Relative amounts of argumentation in projects using differing structural conventions. In *Proceedings of the Workshcop on Computer-Supported Collaborative Argumentation for Learning Communities.* Paper presented at Workshop at the CSCL'99, Stanford University, CA. Retrieved September 4, 2002 from http://www.kmi.open.ac.uk/sbs/csca/cscl99

Selvin, A., Buckingham Shum, S., Sierhuis, M., Conklin, J., Zimmermann, B., Palus, C., Drath, W., Horth, D., Domingue, J., Motta, E., & Li, G. (2001). *Compendium: Making Meetings into Knowledge Events.* Knowledge Technologies 2001, March 4-7, Austin, TX. Retrieved August 10, 2002 from http://www.CompendiumInstitute.org/compendium/papers/Selvin-KT2001.pdf

Seybold, P. (1993, March). Southern California Edison's Experience with CM/1: Documenting the Decision-Making Process. *Paradigm Shift: Guide to the Information Revolution, 5*(1). Boston, Massachusetts: Patricia Seybold Group.

Yakemovic, K C. B., & Conklin, J. (1990). Report on a development project use of an issue-based information system. *Proceedings of CSCW'90.* New York: ACM Press.

7 Fostering Collective Intelligence: Helping Groups Use Visualized Argumentation

Albert M. Selvin

Verizon Communications, USA

7.1 Introduction

This chapter discusses lessons learned from applying visualized argumentation in real-time, face-to-face group settings. Using visualized argumentation in this manner requires special skills and considerations. Argumentation structures, especially when represented with software tools and manipulated in real time according to the needs and goals of the group using them, can be tricky to manage. Of special concern are the multiple issues involved in keeping the representations both coherent and tractable, both for immediate and later use (or re-use). This chapter focuses particularly on the role played by a *facilitator* – a person charged with managing both the creation and maintenance of the representation as well as the interaction of the group with it, and with each other and with the task at hand. The author has practiced such facilitation with hundreds of groups over a ten-year period and trained other practitioners in the art. The chapter provides a characterization of the practical, aesthetic, and ethical components of facilitating visualized argumentation for groups, with the goal of contributing to the development of improved means (tools, methods, and training) and to the wider spread of this competence and its benefits.

The chapter will first provide some background on the specific approach and experience that gave rise to the present reflections, then present a set of principles derived from that experience. Following this, the author provides several case studies illustrating the principles in action. I concludes by discussing how the principles can be further developed and promulgated.

7.2 Background

This chapter presents some reflections on lessons learned from nearly ten years of applying an argumentation-based approach – Compendium – in commercial and nonprofit settings. Compendium was first developed in 1993 as an approach to aid cross-functional business process redesign teams. It has been applied on more than one hundred projects in both industry and academic settings (Selvin, 1996, 1998; Selvin and Sierhuis, 1999). Its origins lie in the problems attending teams working over weeks or months to design business processes: keeping track of the plethora of ideas, issues, and conceptual interrelationships without needing to sift through piles of easel sheets, surfacing and tracking design rationale, and staying on track and "bought-in" to the project's overall structure and goals. The key feature of the early approach was the combination of an Issue-Based Information System (IBIS) concept-mapping tool (Conklin and Burgess Yakemovich, 1991), which supported informal and exploratory conversation and facilitation (see Chapter 2, Van Bruggen et al.), with a structured modeling approach (Selvin, 1999). This allowed teams to move along the spectrum of formal to informal communication as well as prescribed to spontaneous approaches as their needs dictated. It also let them tag data and add incremental formalization (Shipman and McCall, 1994) to it over the life of the project. The approach seemed to have great promise in helping groups come to grips with complex situations they faced at our company, itself enmeshed in fundamental and chaotic external and internal change. In that environment of disruption and discontinuity, I believed we had found an effective combination of IBIS facilitation techniques, engineering methodologies, and hypertext software that helped groups with both the "hard" and "soft" aspects of their sense-making efforts.

Compendium took argumentation as its starting point, but, as with some of the other techniques described in this book, what constitutes argumentation – explicit representation of the reasoning process or deliberation associated with an issue – is given a wide interpretation here. By working with a number of groups, I discovered that an effective way to view argumentation was as one of several explicit components of deliberate group discourse – a mode that can be invoked whenever helpful or indicated, rather than necessarily the central or only mode of discourse or representation. A central focus of the Compendium work was to create the opportunity for argumentation that was linked to well-understood and clearly represented issues and concepts that the group was working with. In this manner, the representation of a portion of a business process or a strategy alternative could become the seed for argumentation. Similarly, a classic IBIS discussion of alternatives could provide seeds for a requirements model, action item list, or concept map. The hypertext software and associated methods provide the means to interweave these modes and representations and keep the resulting large-scale structure coherent, manageable, and useful, even when the size exceeded dozens of individual "maps" and the time-scale stretched over weeks, months, or years.

Another view is that argumentation can be viewed more broadly than the systematic weighing of evidence in order to reach a right answer. The mapping of positions and exploration of interpretations can thus be seen as "argumentation" as well, as can the framing of good questions, exploration of alternatives, critical analysis and problem-solving. In the early years of Compendium I adhered more closely to a "traditional" view of argumentation, but as time went on I found that broadening our view in this manner made it more likely that the groups I worked with would embrace visualized argumentation as an effective mode of communication that helped them achieve their goals.

As Compendium was tested and refined, additional tools and methods were added. The early use of a commercial tool, QuestMap™, while effective, had a number of limitations. First, content often already existed in the form of documents or other textual materials (email messages, web pages, etc.), and it was not efficient to manually retype the material in order to transform it to hypertext nodes and links. Software was developed that analyzed document content and metadata, such as paragraph styles, and automatically generated typed nodes and links in the hypertext database. Participating teams wanted output in customized document forms, not just the outline format that the hypertext tool provided, so a tool was written to allow content to appear in multiple document formats, suited to the representational preferences of the audience (Selvin and Buckingham Shum, 1999). This was expanded to pictorial/graphic representations, such as data flow diagrams and ad hoc, user-defined representations. Next, teams desired rapid publication of the material to conventional web pages, so that minutes of meetings and analyses could appear instantly on corporate intranets.

Despite the success of Compendium for the projects it was used for, the development of a corps of skilled practitioners (facilitators) proved an elusive goal. This paradox of a highly effective, proven technique that seems resistant to adoption, is one of many that have emerged for my colleagues and myself in the years we've been working with Compendium. Some of them may just be due to the technique's immaturity, or to our own limitations as thinkers and practitioners. But some of them may be due to an incomplete understanding of the nature of communities of purpose and communication in problem situations, what kinds of tools and approaches could be helpful, and the depth and/or nature of the expertise required to apply them effectively.

To try to address this I next attempt to lay out some general principles of the context in which visualized-argumentation facilitation inherently occurs, starting with some general statements about the broad goals of facilitative interventions in general.

7.3 Principles of Facilitation

My starting point is to characterize the "audience" for visualized-argumentation facilitation. The types of groups of interest are collections of people who have come together to perform a task or pursue a goal in a change situation, or *communities of purpose* (also referred to as *task-based communities*). Communities of purpose differ from other types of groups in that their members need to communicate about a situation or event outside – to greater or lesser degree – the normal or expected set of situations, or they need to bring about a future situation that differs from the normal or expected in some way. In some way the group is faced with the need to change, or to make a change in some situation. How can such facilitation aid groups of people engaged in a problem situation, facing unprecedented challenges in the complexity and pressure of their environment, the lack of time, the crush of information. What enables such a group to accomplish their goals, to push together what needs to be pushed together? Conversely, what works against their abilities? What pulls a group apart, preventing it from reaching closure and effectiveness? Are there ways to enhance the enablers and diminish the disablers?

One way to think of the goal of facilitation is to help communities of purpose move toward increased functionality and effectiveness, to give them a superlative set of skills, to 'see' or visualize (both literally and metaphorically) their situation better. These skills can be summarized by Wilber's characterization of "vision-logic":

> The point is to place each proposition alongside numerous others so as to be able to see, or "to vision", how the truth or falsity of any one proposition would affect the truth or falsity of the others. Such panoramic or vision-logic apprehends a mass network of ideas, how they influence each other, what their relationships are. It is thus the beginning of truly higher-order synthesizing capacity, of making connections, relating truths, coordinating ideas, integrating concepts... a system or totality of truth-seeing at a single view; the relation of idea with idea, of truth with truth.... Self-seen in the whole... highly integrative structure (Wilber, 2000, p. 249).

Many factors can limit or block a group's effectiveness from emerging or being brought to bear on a problem. These insufficiencies can include:

- *Leadership:* Unclear or missing purpose, mission, direction, goals; the group isn't sure what to optimize its efforts around, what to do and what not to do.
- *Memory:* Not enough stories, tales, associations from the past; the group can't put things into context; can't see how its present situation relates to similar or familiar situations from the past.
- *Knowledge:* Not enough facts and associations are available; the group doesn't have enough ability to marshal and associate appropriate concepts and information.
- *Coherence:* The group and its consideration/apprehension of the situation is insufficiently "stuck together," the people and thinking are inconsistent, poorly connected, unordered.
- *Culture:* The group has an insufficient store of shared, unspoken beliefs, languages, understandings, and traditions. The elements of collectivity that need to be usefully implicit, built on top of, have instead to be said and explained explicitly; no foundations for statements and actions.
- *Trust:* Emotional bonds between the participants are weak or absent, no basis for knowing or believing people's motives, believing they will carry through on commitments and promises; insufficient grounds for believing people are being straightforward and present; belief that there may be hidden agendas, alliances, and priorities.
- *Expertise:* Insufficient ability to pull together the right concepts and ideas, to make the right connections in and between the specific subject matter domains at issue, to know how disparate things fit together and can be brought into service.
- *Time:* Even in the presence of all the other qualities, if there is too little time to accomplish the given tasks or understand the situation, it increases the

pressure on the group and reduces the opportunities for development of shared understanding and commitment.

A facilitator needs to be sensitive to the multiplicity of these factors. Meetings, no matter how apparently simple or straightforward their goals or subject matter may be, are inherently multidimensional events. The import or impact of any statement by a participant in a group also occurs on all these levels simultaneously, though not necessarily with the same force or meaning. We are all always multitasking – working, thinking, and operating at many levels at the same time. Thoughts, words, and actions are always occurring at multiple levels simultaneously. The levels include:

- *Emotional:* Personal feelings (both negative, such as confusion, anger, lassitude, frustration, distrust, or distraction, and positive).
- *Individual:* Our own (mostly) conscious agendas and goals, such as advancement of ourselves, our status, or more altruistically, for a particular set of beliefs.
- *Social:* Relations between the people present.
- *Organizational:* (could also be termed *Political*): Power and trust relationships among groups, subgroups, or roles.
- *Sectoral:* The particular core recurring issues of the subject matter domain(s) in question.
- *Historical:* The many layers of history that lead up to and inform the present situation. There are histories of all the other levels mentioned here as well as many others, such as *technical* (the evolutions of the techniques and technologies at work in the situation) and *policy* (evolutions of laws, rules, guidelines, conventions).
- *Societal:* Events and movements occurring in the broader society outside of the smaller dimensions mentioned above that have impact and purchase on the group's problem situation (even if indirectly).

All these levels include the previous discussions, encounters, and actions that the group itself (or portions of it) have had about the problem situation or aspects if it. In each of these discussions, people create and invoke associations and connections between ideas. This too happens with almost every statement, every pairing of subject and predicate. For groups, however, nothing is more forgettable or prone to error than these connections that they, or someone else, has previously made between ideas. These are even harder to remember distinctly and accurately than the individual facts themselves.

The above conditions characterize the environment in which facilitation occurs. I now turn to a conception of facilitation that responds to those conditions. I conceive the distinct role of a facilitator as a person who takes as her/his responsibility the support and guidance of a group to achieve its purposes, providing whatever the group needs that's missing in its own constellation of knowledge, understanding, trust, authenticity, engagement, inspiration, and efficiency.[1] The facilitator finds ways to bring focus, clarity, and coherence to the group if any of these are insufficiently present, drawing on the group's existing capabilities. Further, the facilitator watches for and avoids dysfunctions and weaknesses that can lead to collapse of necessary and helpful structure. The facilitator takes as her/his ethic that groups are always engaged in collective sense making. It is the facilitator's normative responsibility to view people in a situation through that lens, continually asking her/himself the question: *what is going to help this group at this moment make sense of their situation?*[2] It's my belief that visualized-argumentation facilitation, in general, provides a particularly effective set of structures and affordances that help achieve these goals. To do the job well, the facilitator must be competent at:

- *Listening:* To do this, facilitators must strive to put aside their own agenda and desires, making sure that they are truly listening to the group and paying close enough attention to the people and the situation so that they're able to determine what's going on, what's needed, and how what's needed should be provided.[3] Listening (and the setting aside of ego and agenda that it implies) is the core facilitator skill: when all else fails, just listen.
- *Determining style and level of intervention:* Listening enables the next core skill: the ability to determine what types of interventions into the group's normal way

---

[1] Facilitators do not have to be outsiders with special skills that are called in to work with a group. They can be members of the group itself. But in order for them to supply the kind of value to the group we described, they must also embody the types of principles described. It is often (but not necessarily) the case that group members find it difficult to step enough "outside" the situation and their normal methods of interaction to be able to perform in the manner described. For example, despite spending thousands of hours in the facilitator role with many purposive groups in many change situations, I still find it very difficult to step into that role when I am personally enmeshed in a meeting as a participant. The cognitive and emotional experience of facilitation involves stepping out of direct engagement with the issues in a way that seems at odds with direct participation and advocacy.

[2] Like other "helping professions", a facilitator is someone who can provide something necessary to those in the recipient audience that they can't, or are unable or unwilling, to provide for themselves. If the group is able and willing to perform the indicated service for itself, or if the service is not needed, then the facilitator isn't necessary, just as you don't need a lawyer present every time you transact business with another party, or (for most of us) a therapist present to mediate every family dispute (although it is also true that for some forms of business, lawyers are always required; there are situations where facilitators as we are describing them here may also always be required).

[3] Palus and Horth (2002) refer to paying attention as the "master competence."

of communicating and functioning will be effective at the particular moment. This includes knowing what level of abstraction, confrontation, or communicative style the group needs, what will help to unlock authenticity and engagement, what types of questions to ask. It requires flexibility along multiple scales: whether an intervention needs to be on a personal/emotional level or on a logic/structured level; whether an intervention should be informal or formal in character; whether the group needs closure versus exploration; and many others. Facilitators must always be asking themselves the questions "What is going on for this group at this moment? What will help them achieve their goals, improve their communication and coherence, leverage their capabilities, and prevent dysfunction and collapse?" But these are not helpful questions to explicitly ask the group. Helpful questions must be artfully situated in a clear understanding of the group's relationship to its subject matter, problem situation, and each other. Often they require "moving" the group to a different level from the one they are currently working in. The facilitator needs to be able (and remember) to question aspects of the situation, or the group's way of communicating about it, at any moment, and at any level, in the right granularity so as to be a useful intervention for the group. Further, the facilitator needs to be able to articulate the question in a useful, understandable, tractable (not too big or general) and generative form.

- *Navigation and improvisation:* Knowing how to choose these levels, pick the moments, and being able to articulate in the right manner can be compared to the function of a ship's navigator. A navigator must be able to "read" the general atmospheric conditions, the local undersea and coastal topography, the desired course, shoals and currents, the operating conditions and capabilities of the ship, the effect of possible changes and interventions (such as changes in course or engine speed) and a host of other background knowledge that informs every action they take. Their expertise inheres in their ability to comprehend this host of information and knowledge and choose the correct and effective actions on a minute-by-minute basis, especially under turbulent or adverse conditions. Similarly, facilitators must make minute-to-minute determinations of what's necessary, combining many functions and areas of expertise, including the skills and toolset, to some degree, of a therapist (able to read and understand the emotional climate of the group); a manager (able to determine when a group is on task and headed in the right direction); and an artist or performer (able to shape the right articulation or representation with the right form and nuance). The more turbulent, adversarial, or confusing a situation is, the higher a degree of improvisational skill – rapidly reading the situation and devising the right sort of intervention – a facilitator must have.

Providing conceptual frameworks and structures: Effective facilitator intervention, though, is not all subjective, ad hoc, and improvisational, although it certainly requires competence in those modes. Substantial help can also be found in the ability to understand and apply structures and conceptual frameworks of various kinds – a priori collections of principles and abstractions organized into forms that can help organize and manage discourse in a change situation. IBIS is one such framework. Facilitators must be fluid in thinking with, knowing about, and applying such frameworks in useful ways, as well as adapting existing frameworks to the current needs of the group (while preserving a framework's conceptual integrity) and even developing new framework as required. Frameworks can be as simple as categories or attributes – a level of information that describes or organizes the information the group is working with (as opposed to the information itself). For example, brainstorming a set of ideas about how to solve a problem would be considered "raw" information; if the ideas are then grouped into named categories, the procedure for grouping and categorizing itself could be considered a framework. Applying basic IBIS structures to discussions of such ideas would be a higher-level framework. Even more complex frameworks are those that are derived from a structured, repeatable understanding of how to approach a problem – for example, a medical diagnostic procedure that can be described separately from any actual patient.

- *Working with electronic information:* Because so much critical information is created and stored electronically, a further requisite facilitator skill is the ability to understand, reach into, and manipulate information stored in, created, or otherwise available in electronic form (see Chapter 9, Buckingham Shum et al.). Similar to other forms of discourse, facilitators need to understand the particular nature of electronic information and be fluid in retrieving it and bringing it to bear at the right moment and in the right form to be useful to the group. Fluidity and expertise in the many forms and levels of working with electronic information has become as much a core discourse mode as verbal speech and pictorial representation. Facilitators must also be oriented toward and skilled in making sure that information is preserved in such a form that it can an effective resource for subsequent use.

7.4 Tools and Representations

We now turn to general characteristics of helpful tools that facilitators can use to assist groups in change situations. The first characteristic of such media is that they support the facilitator in carrying out their primary functions – listening, paying attention, making interventions, pulling together and representing information, and preserving information in a useful form to serve as a future resource. The media should afford ways to do these so that, at minimum, they do not distract facilitators from performing their primary functions, and at best so that they augment and extend it, allowing facilitators to do things that they otherwise couldn't (or that would be prohibitively expensive and difficult).

7.4.1 Putting Something in the Middle

The second characteristic is appropriateness and effectiveness in creating artifacts that can serve as "something in the middle" (Palus and Drath, 2001) – a representation or object that mediates between members of the group as well as between the group and their task or subject matter.[4] The media should serve the purposes of enhancing or creating) dialogue:

> Dialogue is a process which occurs by putting meanings to be explored and re-constructed in the middle of a group. Placing a mediating object in the middle, under the right conditions, is a way to enhance the experience of dialogue. (Palus and Drath, 2001)

Not just anything can be put in the middle; it needs to be something that will enhance what the group is trying to do or the way that it does it. For example, if a group has two camps locked in a debate about what team should take on what tasks for an upcoming project, often simply seeing a visual representation of the overarching business problem, phrased as a question, with the two alternatives depicted as possible answers to that question, will defuse the tension and pave the way for constructive discussion. There should be value both in the object itself – i.e. it should contain sufficient meaning, information, and representational effectiveness to be useful to the task at hand – and in the encounter of the group with the object. This means that the something in the middle does not necessarily need to be a well-constructed, richly meaningful object (although being such is certainly not a disadvantage), but that regarding, considering, discussing, and working with the object must provide value to the group. An object that does not allow, facilitate, and invite such actions (which can, of course, take a myriad of forms) will not completely serve.

7.4.2 Familiar or Vernacular Language

To meet the aforementioned, the media should not require participants to learn new languages or complicated abstractions before being able to regard, comprehend, and work with the object (or at least, such learning and unfamiliar abstraction should be kept to a minimum lest it consume and deplete the mental energy and motivation of the group).[5] Excessive complexity or arcane language in the shared display works against this (see Chapter 2, van Bruggen et al) Helpful media need to be rich enough to embody complex relationships, but accessible enough to communicate such relationships in the vernacular. Many media, representational styles, and languages used by a particular expert culture are impenetrable to outsiders, although they may be

---

[4] This is also related to the idea of "shared display" – cf. Jeff Conklin, "The Dialog Mapping Experience," http://cognexus.org/dmepaper.htm

[5] It is fine, though, if the *facilitator* had to learn these beforehand in order to work with the media, but the participants should not need to, any more than filmgoers need to learn the principles of lenses, light, and sound in order to enjoy a film, even though filmmakers must have working understandings of these in order to manipulate the media.

consistent, coherent, and highly expressive to those who understand the visual, verbal, and conceptual elements they are created with. To be useful in the kinds of pressurized contexts we are discussing, media should both easily fit into as well as augment or extend a group's normal discourse – or at least at a level of discourse that is both comprehensible and useful to all members of the group.

7.4.3   Easily Manipulable Representations

At the same time, the media must be capable of supporting representations that are lightweight enough to be constructed and manipulated quickly and at multiple levels. Representations shouldn't require heavy, slow, or ponderous manipulation. Unmaking or taking apart should be rapid. Addressing and changing pieces should not require having to take on or worry about the whole (although facilitators need always to understand how parts of a representation relate to the whole, and need to be able to bring that awareness to the participants when necessary or helpful). The media must provide "handles" to manipulate its form and content in many ways and at many levels. Media that only allow facilitators to manipulate the representation indirectly don't provide sufficient support. Manipulation may need to occur on small parts, on large structures, on the totality of the representation, or on longitudinal or latitudinal samples or sections.

The media also need the means to contain and support many layers of meaning and information, but allow the group to focus on particular, small subsets of these – even one at a time – without losing or forgetting the larger set of connections in which the particular item temporarily in focus resides.

This means that the media must also provide and/or support different techniques and practices. Because a group's sense making and task achievement needs can be so many and varied, the media must support a requisite variety of techniques without forcing the group to jump from one tool to another. It is much more difficult to maintain the connectedness and continuity of information when changing tools, moving information from one medium to the next, etc.

7.4.4   Representational Sufficiency

Representations need a minimum level of *sufficiency* to be useful. Looking deeper into conventional notions of such as ease of use, learnability, and reusability, sufficiency here means that which qualifies a particular medium or representational strategy to meet the criteria and needs we have posited throughout this chapter. The most important dimensions of representational sufficiency are:
-   *Reframing:* The representation must support the group's ability to recontextualize some element of their problem situation, such as attaching a new set of explanatory reasons to justify a proposed action, or a new way of understanding the nature of their problem situation and possible sphere of actions.
-   *Preservation:* The representation needs to support the group's ability to preserve both the information they develop and work with as well as the connections

they've made between elements and the ways they've learned or developed to work with the information and keep track of it (this can also be summarized as preserving both the data and the metadata, or the information as well as the conceptual frameworks used to work with the information).

-   *Rigor:* The representation must support applying rigorous methods that can be understood, explained, and reproduced. This is important for the group to work in the present as well as to feel and demonstrate that they are approaching their subject and tasks with integrity and exhaustiveness. It also enables subsequent or future auditors and other groups to be able to understand, inspect, and respect the work the group has done – both the process and the product. The media must support the use of the work product as evidence of the rigor with which the group has approached their work.[6]

-   *Repeatability:* Closely related to the rigor dimension is the aspect of repeatability. Both for all the reasons covered under rigor, as well as for efficiency and productivity reasons (not having to reinvent the wheel, being able to hit the ground running, etc.), the media must afford easily repeatable methods, must allow the group to move smoothly from one task to the next (once the situation and subject matter is well enough understood to be tractable for such repetition).

-   *Affordance* (Norman, 1990): The media must make it clear and obvious how and in what ways manipulation, inspection, and other operations on the representation can occur. In the same manner that a fire exit should be clearly marked, and its opening mechanism designed in such a way that it's obvious what a person must do to open the door correctly (such as a push bar). Representational media designed for group understanding must make clear and obvious in what ways they should be worked with in order to yield the desired results.

-   *Dimensionality:* In order to support multiple coherences, the representation must be capable of holding information in multiple dimensions, including *time* (how various pieces of information have developed and changed with the passage of time) and *context* (the multiple situations, moments, relations, or views[7] in which a particular piece of information has been made relevant by the group, its members, or other predecessors). This can include pieces of

---

[6] It does not mean that "rigorous" methods are either always applied or that only certain a priori methods, such as empirical analysis, count as "rigorous" – but rather that the media must include and support such methods. Choice of appropriate methods to apply at a particular moment is a facilitator function; it's the medium's requirement just that it supports the requisite variety.

[7] A "view" is a particular "holder" of information, such as a document or the results of a database query.

information that have their origin in electronic documents or other parts of the infosphere.

- *Permeability:* This refers to the ease and readiness with which the representation can be "entered into" for different purposes and in various manners.
- *Continuity:* To enable the kinds of continuity spoken of above, the representation and its elements need to be able to be manipulated in the present while retaining links to past formations, and also the presence of particular pieces of information in the past contexts, so groups can see what roles particular elements played in past coherences (as an aid to forging the correct current coherence). Just as importantly, the media needs to allow new information and relations to be created, represented, and stored in forms that reach forward in time – that is, that are in such a form that they will easily and usefully be available for subsequent actors and uses to draw into future coherences.
- *Depth of palette:* This refers to the richness of the representations that can be created and manipulated in the media. Rich representational palettes are those that contain a large number of representational elements, gradations, subtleties, and techniques, such as those found in an image created by a professional artist. Limited representational palettes are those which have only a subset of such means and options to work with. Depth of palette represents a trade-off of expressive depth and variability with the speed and skill required to make and manipulate the representation. Properly understood and applied, however, a limited palette can actually be a boon to group understanding as well as efficiency. It raises the accessibility (one doesn't need to be as skilled an artist to create effective representations) and can even boost the creativity of a group or facilitator, by requiring representation by implication and metaphor rather than "naturalistic" means. Many of the argumentation visualization approaches discussed in this book employ such limited palettes, with Horn's approach a notable exception (See Chapter 8, Horn).

7.4.5   More on Structure

Through much experience, we have found that groups can benefit by communicating within a priori structures, as much as (and sometimes more than) they can in free discussion. Both modes have value, but the value of structured group interaction and guided discussion is often underrated[8] and misunderstood.[9] (See Chapter 5, van

---

[8]   Which may also be due to its misuse. Incorrect structure, or structure improperly applied, leaves a bad taste in most people's mouths.

[9]   This is often due to the fact that structures which make sense to a particular community of practice can be foreign or alien to outsiders. For example, many fields employ such structures as part of their normal ways of operating, such as law, engineering, etc. People within those fields are quite comfortable communicating in

Gelder). Well-designed formalisms and structures can help bring coherence, both in their ability to aid in organization, cross-referencing, and efficiency in generating, capturing, and categorizing information, as well as in the sense that they can make a mass of information more accessible and tractable as "something in the middle". They make it easier to see the connections between information and to work with collections of connected information than if the information appears as a mass of disconnected data. Formal structures can aid in the affordance and manipulability dimensions spoken of earlier. Properly applied, structures can actually enable and generate expressive freedom. In our experience, argumentation structures can be used quite effectively for visualizing many sorts of concepts, such as models and process flows.

7.4.6 Interweaving

The media must be able to interweave information from heterogeneous sources. This means that, since coherences many need to draw from widely divergent origins in order to effectively address a discontinuous situation, the media must be able to assemble information from any relevant source, time, person, or method. It must be able to reach into, retrieve, and manipulate information and bring it to bear for the group. In addition, since both groups and their members spend time connected to networked and local electronic information, the media (as the means for groups to work together) should not be separated from the means for individuals to work. That is, both products of, inputs to, and the representation itself should be available electronically for individual, and collective, work.

7.4.7 Venues

Finally, the media should enable a continuum between face to face (physically proximate) and virtual (via software and networks) group gatherings, as well as between same-time (synchronous) and asynchronous meetings. The general principle is that the media should provide bridges between all manner of group and individual action and collaboration, so that spatial and temporal boundaries are no more hindrances than the linguistic, emotional, and existential boundaries spoken of above.[10] In addition, the media should be useful in situations ranging from highly formal and structured (such as an off-site workshop or training session) to informal and opportunistic (such as an ad hoc informal meeting). The problems that this raises for asynchronicity – keeping multiple sessions on track and in sync – can be at least partially addressed by a

---

their familiar structured ways, using constrained and highly specific vocabularies and representational conventions. But those same people will react with suspicion and annoyance when forced to use structures common to other fields or domains.

[10] This isn't saying that all this needs to be available and present in the same tool, merely that it all needs to be easily accessible and integratable within the set of chosen media.

facilitator, who can integrate, synchronize, and maintain linkages between the views and materials from the various groups and sessions.

7.5   Examples in Practice

What follows is several examples to illustrate the above principles. The intent is to begin to show the wide range of skills and techniques that can be necessary in different situations. The examples are given in increasing order of the degree of explicitly visualized argumentation, with an emphasis on the moment-to-moment facilitative choices made and actions taken.

I'll start with an instructive counter-example – counter in the sense that it shows what an experienced facilitator might do in a situation that turned out not to require active facilitation.

7.5.1   A Counter-Example

The context was a meeting between a company's systems development group and a group from one of that company's long-time external vendors. The two groups were essentially competitors since both were retained by business groups within the company to do systems work in the same subject matter domain. The particular meeting had been called by the company's senior executives in an effort to resolve a confrontation between the two groups over the technical direction for a particular set of systems. The issues at stake were who would "own" and control the large amount of development work necessary to evolve the systems. Previous meetings had been difficult and contentious, with both groups arguing from entrenched and opposed positions. Management had arranged the meeting and framed it with the goal of "come up with a way to work together; pretend you are on one team." Each group was told to prepare a "full disclosure" set of information about their own approaches and goals, with the aim of enabling the other group to propose how it would help achieve those goals. The facilitator was brought in from the outside, with little background on the specific issues and systems the groups were to discuss.

The meeting began with presentations from both sides on their background activities and approaches to the various business and technical problems. The facilitator began capturing the flow of the surrounding discussion, issues raised, and pros and cons voiced. As the meeting proceeded it became evident that both sides had taken the management direction seriously and had come prepared to listen and be flexible and constructive. The groups discussed the detailed technical issues with a high degree of knowledge and sophistication in both sides. The discourse was engaged, but polite. The mood was receptive and forward-looking. Side conversations, grandstanding, and recycling of issues were minimal. The participants stuck to the agenda and reached points of decision and closure efficiently. By the end of the day they had created a new agenda of possible collaborations covering many dimensions of the various business problems.

After several hours the facilitator realized that capturing and representing discussion in the argumentation tool was unnecessary. The immediate issues and discourse were cared for; there were no conflicts, knowledge gaps, power trips, impediments, or inarticulateness that required facilitative intervention. Members of the groups were capturing and recording the discussion, issues, and decisions in conventional ways. Since everyone else in the room besides the facilitator had a much greater degree of shared knowledge of the technical language, acronyms, and other arcane aspects of the discussion, the facilitator's representation of them as hypertext argumentation would have been much slower, less accurate, and less useful than their own. While this is not an exhaustive list of criteria for using an argumentation approach, it does point to a value-for-effort trade-off that experienced facilitators can make in certain situations.

This example is certainly not universal. Many groups do not have the requisite combination of factors to have discussions of such clarity, usefulness, and efficiency and could benefit from some level of, at minimum, a shared display of their issues and deliberations. But it does point to a central issue for facilitators: to know what is useful in a situation and what level of action and intervention to take. If the parameters of a situation are known and the conditions are set, then specific, a priori techniques can be effectively applied. The less true this is, the more creativity, flexibility, and skills on the part of the practitioner are necessary.

The next example was one in which a much greater degree of facilitator intervention and range of techniques were not only indicated but crucial to the success of the group's goals.

7.5.2 Team-Building and Problem Exploration in a Constrained Timeframe

The next example shows the range of facilitative techniques used in an exploratory, workshop setting.[11] I focus on illustrating a set of making-sense-of-complexity techniques as applied during a two-day leadership development workshop.

The workshop had two sets of goals. The first was to mutually explore, and then begin to solve, selected urgent – but frustratingly complex – challenges facing a business unit. The second was to develop leadership capacity within this group, including enhanced sensemaking competencies, and an enhanced leader-to-leader

---

[11] The work described in this example was performed as part of a collaboration between Verizon Communications and the Center for Creative Leadership about how to help leaders face and resolve complex challenges. A principle part of that effort has been experimentation with tools and process for better sensemaking – that is, for paying attention to diverse and often chaotic information about critical challenges, and creating shared understanding in support of mindful action.

network of relationships.[12] Participants were executives from different geographic regions and functional groups within a business unit of a large corporation. Many of the participants had never met face-to-face before the session. By the end of the workshop, two action-learning teams were formed to address targeted aspects of the challenges thus explored.

One of the initial exercises is called Visual Explorer™ (VE).[13] Participants, who had done pre-work around identifying a key challenge they're facing, were instructed to walk around and look at around approximately two hundred 21.6 X 28 cm. pictures spread out on the floor in the hallway outside the conference room, looking for pictures that seems to speak to them in some way – not literal illustrations, but rather ones triggering some metaphorical or emotional resonance. Each person was asked to select two pictures – one representing the current state of the challenge, and one representing a pathway for taking action. After the individuals selected the pictures, they brought them back and discussed them in small groups according to a structured protocol: first the selector explains what they see in a picture, why they selected it, and how it seems to speak to their challenge, then others in the group say what they see in the picture, then the selector has final comments, then it moves on to the next person.

The facilitator then brought the images into the Compendium software tool. Each of the VE images has a serial number, tied to a file name of thumbnail images stored on the laptop computer, which also had the Compendium software installed. The practitioner created a map with each participant's name linked to two Question nodes: "Present state?" and "Future state?" (Later, a digital photo of each participant can be added). These were then linked to the associated VE image. The entire map was projected on a shared display.

The practitioner made this map to serve as a reference for later use, both in the two day session and in subsequent individual work, documents, and future sessions. It was only shown briefly during the workshop, at several times, but is likely to serve as a starting point for subsequent work by the participants later on.

The facilitators then led the participants in a dialogue about their collective challenges.[14] That was captured in real time, the first time that Compendium was seen

---

[12] For our understanding of the leadership sensemaking competencies useful for complex challenges, see Palus, C .J., and Horth, D. M. (2002). *The Leader's Edge: Six Creative Competencies for Navigating Complex Challenges.* San Francisco, CA: Jossey-Bass.

[13] Visual Explorer is a trademark of the Center for Creative Leadership. See Palus, C. J. and Drath, W. H. (2001). Putting Something In The Middle: An Approach To Dialogue. *Reflections, 3*(2).

[14] See Isaacs, W. (1999). *Dialogue and the Art of Thinking Together.* New York, NY: Random House.
Palus, C. J. and Drath, W. H. (2001). Putting Something In The Middle: An Approach To Dialogue. *Reflections, 3*(2).

by the participants on the screen in the front of the room. At this point of the proceedings, the practitioners and facilitators only intermittently directed the participants to look at the screen. This was only done when it seemed as though the group would benefit from clarifying a particular point ("does this capture what you said?") or to refocus the discussion by tying it to an already voiced question or idea. Most of the time the Compendium practitioner typed continuously, forming participants statements into question or idea nodes and deciding on his own what to link them to, as well as what and how to capture. This went on for quite a while, surfacing many issues and assumptions that were facing the organization as a whole (see Figure 7.1).

The dialogue was started by posing a set of organizational challenge statements that the organization's president had outlined earlier in the year. Part of the point of the exercise was to bring those abstract statements ("top down") into relation with the immediate, tangible and tactical challenges that the participants were facing ("bottom up").

At this point the facilitator made minimal attempts to guide or shape the conversation, emphasizing the verbatim "capturing" of the participants' statements more than shaping or active construction. There were several reasons for this. One was to simply get a record of the discussion. Another was to capture the discussion as it happens in such a form as that its elements will be available for later use. Another was to use the display as one aspect of the facilitation for this particular session. Yet another was that each participant is validated by having his or her comments added to the display. This approach to the mapping involves aesthetic and technical choices appropriate to the situation. At other times and for other reasons, practitioners can employ much more deliberate shaping, using pre-established structural templates for example.

At this point of the workshop, the participants divided their visual attention between the screen and each other. They watched as the practitioner entered their words (or close paraphrases) in nodes, sometimes calling out corrections either to the current node or to a previous node as the meanings became refined or changed in the discussion, sometimes in a 'review' mode as either the practitioner, one of the facilitators, or one of the participants read out loud through some portion of the discussion. Most of the time, though, they looked at each other.

At one point, one of the facilitators asked if any of the chosen VE images spoke to any of the points raised in the general discussion. The participants identified such images and these were added to the map in context, as were the copious points made in the ensuing lively discussion. Note that this is a matter of reusing a node already created in the individually chosen images map – an instance of knowledge element reuse, on the fly.

At times in a live session, it is useful to show participants that an idea they have created or referenced in one context has been used in another. In the example above, the image selected had already been discussed by one of the small groups of participants in the earlier VE exercise. Compendium has a special interface for displaying in which views a particular node appears.

In the afternoon of the first day, the facilitators had the participants review the Compendium discussion map as a prelude to reframing their challenge statements. The practitioner read through the map while the participants listened and watched the screen. The facilitators checked to make sure that the review seemed to match what the participants remembered, and had captured the sense of the morning's discussion, correcting the map where necessary.

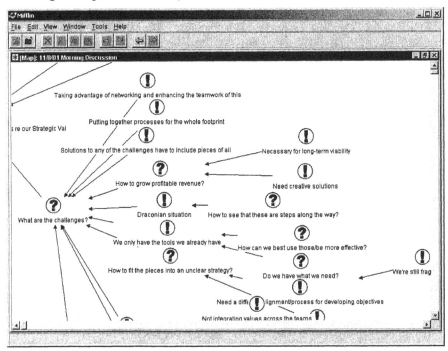

Figure 7.1: Map showing portion of an open, minimally structured discussion.

The facilitators then conducted a "reframing" session, in which the participants would come up with alternative ways of talking about their major challenges, incorporating the dialogues they had had during the VE exercise and the subsequent Compendium discussion session. The purpose in reframing was to identify better ways of stating the essential challenges, thus leading to more robust solutions.

To introduce this, the facilitators presented some material about how to reframe challenges in order to achieve more robust results. Then they conducted a brainstorming-style Compendium session where participants were asked to call out new challenge statements in the form of questions, starting with "How to ..." (abbreviated as "H2"), "How do we ..." ("HDW", "In what way ..." ("IWW"), etc. Participants were asked to pay attention to the screen and directly engage with how their questions were being captured and displayed. The practitioner captured each question in real time. He employed only minimal arranging, to keep more or less regular columns of questions on the screen. The exercise was not conducted as an open discussion; if new ideas were suggested by another participant's question, the facilitators encouraged the participant to state the idea as another question.

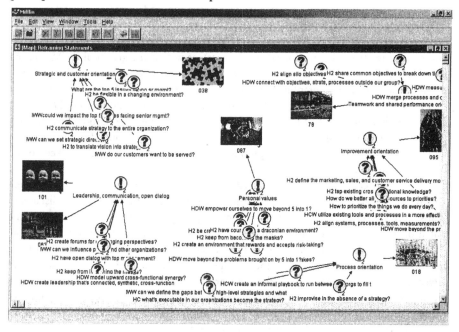

Figure 7.2: Map showing results of brainstorming, grouping, and labeling exercise.

When the screen was filled with brainstormed questions (38 in all), the facilitators had the participants get up from their chairs and form a standing circle near the screen. They asked the participants to point to the screen and move around the brainstormed questions into groups that seemed to hang together (similar to "affinity group" exercises traditionally conducted with sticky notes or index cards). During this, the participants were encouraged to "touch" the nodes, going up to the screen and "physically" "moving" the nodes, instructing the practitioner exactly which nodes to move and where. When the participants were satisfied that they had created a set of more or less stable and coherent groups, the facilitators asked them to give names to the groups, then to select images from the VE exercise that seemed to characterize the themes of each group. Figure 7.2 shows the state of the screen at the conclusion of this exercise.

Following this, the group held a lengthy discussion of how to present the newly created information at a session with the group's president the following morning. It was decided to present a "cleaned-up" version of this last map, with individual participants taking the president through each of the themed groups. The practitioner agreed to create the cleaned-up views, while assuring the participants that the "messy" views they had worked on would be left in their original state, unaltered, for future reference.

While the participants were working on other exercises led by the facilitators, the practitioner created the "cleaned-up" maps, HTML exports of the maps, and Word documents with the complete notes of the discussion and reframing exercises to be given out to the participants.

The next morning, all the participants were given the Word document with the complete notes from the previous day (13 pages), as well as the graphical HTML output with the cleaned up versions of the reframed challenge questions. The group's president was given the graphical HTML printout to refer to during the subsequent two-hour dialog session among all the participants, facilitators, and himself. During the session, individual participants presented the grouped reframed questions by referring to the "cleaned-up" maps on the screen. The president then responded to the questions and the resulting discussion was captured on the screen in a new map linked to the challenge question.

As in the preceding example, the facilitator was able to create considerable reusing and restructuring of the knowledge maps during the session. The original discussion maps were preserved while at the same time copying them into new maps where the initial dialogue was sorted into themes and modified by deeper reflection. Unlike the next example, though, the entire workshop was conducted mostly in an improvisational manner. The structures used by the Compendium practitioner were not set up in advance or "programmed in" to the software (with the exception of the VE images already being present on the hard drive); no templates were created or applied. Compendium was not imposed on the workshop; rather, it reflected and responded to what was happening, including unanticipated twists and turns.

7.5.3 Applying a Range of Techniques with Multiple Teams over Time

The Year 2000 Contingency Planning (Y2KCP) project comprised an intensive analysis effort to identify the resources in a large telecommunications company's core business processes that would cause the highest degree of risk if they were to fail for some reason related to the Year 2000 computer problem. The output was to be used both as the content of a contingency plan document that could be given to external stakeholders, and as a validation check against the departmental-level contingency plans generated in an earlier phase of the project.

Participants were grouped into five teams of 8-20 people and charged with creating process maps of the business processes (Call Completion, Ordering and Provisioning, Maintenance and Repair, 911 (emergency calls), and Billing). For each work step in the business processes, the participants were then to identify which resources (people, systems, equipment, locations, etc.) were used in the step. Following this, they were to rate each resource in terms of the competitive, legal, and operational risk to that work step if the resource were to fail for Y2K-related reasons. Resource/task combinations rated as "high risk" were then subject to a separate contingency planning effort. Further, the project's sponsors required that the output be customized for different audiences in various document and diagrammatic forms.

Prior to the start of the facilitative work described here, a team of external consultants had spent several weeks recruiting participants and holding meetings attempting to kick off the analysis process. When these kickoff meetings proved difficult and contentious as to purpose and process, a Compendium facilitator was asked to help provide a structure and database for the rest of the effort.

The first meeting that the facilitator attended was intended to be a regrouping and planning session for the consultant team. The consultant team had a depth of experience with risk assessment and contingency planning but had been frustrated in their earlier attempts to run meetings for the process teams. Competing agendas, arguments about approach and priorities, complaints about time taken away from other duties, and other distractions had stymied the consultants' attempts to get the risk assessment process moving.

For the first hour or so the facilitator did little but listen to the discussion to get an understanding of the basic situation, desired outcomes, difficulties, and personalities. Even within the consultant group, there were disagreements as to the right level to conduct the meetings, the right pace to set, the right frameworks to apply, and the right level of management "stick" to use. There seemed to be some level of tension as to which of the consultants was most senior and which had what role with regard to setting approach and direction. Once he discerned the basic issue, the facilitator begin to create a representation on the screen. After he had assembled about a screen's worth of nodes and links, he asked the group to look at the map on the display screen while talking through what he thought he had heard. The group almost immediately seemed to embrace the shared display as a way to get some clarity and order in their own discussion. The facilitator then offered the notion of a template of questions to use in the next process team meeting, and the rest of the afternoon was spent working on the template, surfacing pros and cons to different questions to include in it.

The next meeting of one of the process teams took place a few days later in New York City. One of the consultants introduced the process and then the Compendium facilitator took over, using the template developed in the previous session (see Figure 7.3). One of the participants, a subject matter expert in both contingency planning and the particular business process under review (Call Completion), took to the approach immediately, jumped up, and spent the balance of the meeting not only contributing ideas but directing the facilitator to correct text and move around nodes and links on the projected display to make sure everything was correct (see Figure 7.4).

Feedback from the team and reflections after the session prompted the facilitator to refine the templates. He then used the templates in subsequent sessions with the remaining groups, with continuing refinement and improvement based on the results of those sessions. Over the next few weeks, several dozen meetings were held around the Northeast USA to continue the mapping and analysis process. As the templates improved, the effort picked up speed. After three or four sessions, the process moved into a consistent mode: the facilitator would introduce the project, problem, and approach; do a high-level process flow on paper or whiteboard to make sure that the group achieved buy-in to the right "level" to model the business process on; enshrine the agreed-on high-level flow in Compendium software tools; apply the process template to identify which resources pertained to each subtask; when all the resources had been identified attach the risk assessment template to each resource so that the team could assess the operational, competitive, and legal risks attendant to that resource for that task.

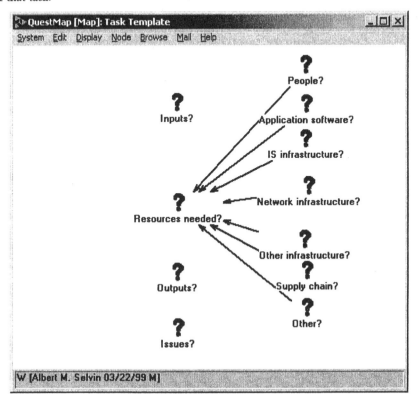

Figure 7.3: Task template from Y2KCP Project.

A key success factor was to weave the elements of one group's analysis into all the others', so as to get correct risk assessments for the same resource from all the perspectives. As the teams got deeper into the analysis, they were able to leverage each other's work. This function would not have happened without the facilitator's knowledge of each team's work and deep familiarity with the software tools and how to manipulate the database. For example, several of the teams identified the same systems, roles, and tasks, often adding more description or definition in the process. The facilitator systematically used only one node to represent a resource (people, systems, equipment, locations, etc.), for example, "the LMOS system", in multiple views in the database. Thus, teams could leverage the work that other teams had done by re-using the same node in multiple contexts. The use of "transclusive hyperlinking" (Nelson, 1993) meant that each team could add corrections or descriptive information to a resource, and know that it was immediately updated in every process map and risk assessment where it appeared. In addition, since the facilitator created and displayed "libraries" of the various resources, the teams could save time by simply copying icons from a list into their current analysis map. The result was that one could find all the maps in which a resource appeared, helping to answer key questions such as, "in what contexts is this factor relevant?", and "who are the stakeholders?"

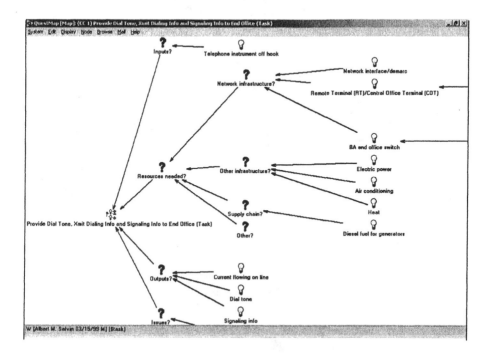

Figure 7.4: Early call completion process map using the task template.

Due to the tight timeframes and high pressure on the project, there was no time available for the more exploratory discussion of the many issues involved. The facilitator focused the discourse on completing the analysis tasks and politely but firmly discourage other sorts of discussions.

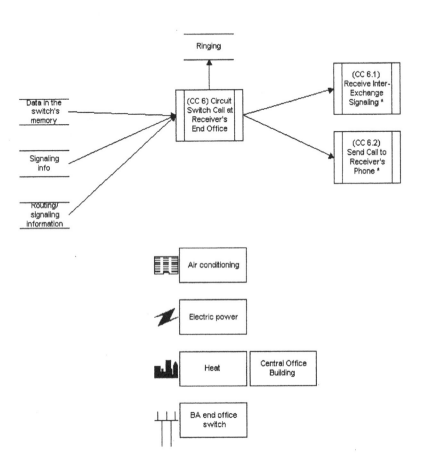

Figure 7.5: Auto-generated diagrammatic output.

By using a visual map continuously created and cross-referenced in real time by the facilitator, with all the content provided by team members, validation of the database's content could occur as it was being created. The facilitator had to know how particular sorts of changes (for example, editing a resource's description) would ramify, changing the meaning or usefulness of that object, not only for the database itself but for the various reports and other output. Participants saw the maps of hypertext nodes and links being created, and informed the facilitator if there were inaccuracies or omissions. A second "round" of validation occurred when documents and diagrams were circulated. The project's sponsors required that the output be customized for different audiences in various document and diagrammatic forms. The facilitator configured the Compendium software to generate five different tabular reports and more than 500 process diagrams for immediate feedback and review (see Figure 7.5).

The level of interweaving of all of these discussions, meetings, people, representations, output, and outcomes could not have happened without the facilitator's knowledge and skills. These covered a broad range, including: sufficient group process facilitation experience to keep the large-group meetings productive and efficient in the tight timeframe; the ability to manipulate the data and the representation quickly enough in real time to both capture the flow of the process and risk assessment analyses and keep the shared display "fresh" and relevant without slowing the meetings down; knowledge of what sort of representational and metadata conventions would lend themselves to the automation of document and diagrammatic output without such automation having been designed and developed in advance; and the willingness to step in, intervene, pull the discussion back from side issues, and take over control of the meetings when necessary.

7.6 Discussion and Conclusions

This chapter has presented a number of dimensions required for facilitating visualized argumentation in real time with groups, and provided several case studies that illustrate how many of those dimensions can coexist for a single group or within a specific project setting. Although Compendium as a methodology, Mifflin and QuestMap as particular software tools, and the skills of the particular facilitators referred to in the case studies are presented as examples of how these multidimensional requirements can be fulfilled, a gap remains between these examples and their widespread realization by a large body of similarly skilled practitioners. Left open is the question of how teachable, learnable, and transferable such skills are to a critical mass of people. This chapter doesn't attempt to answer this question, except to point out that the question itself is a promising area for further research and inquiry.[15]

Through my years of experience with Compendium, I built up sufficient experience and expertise to believe that I could add value to almost any group in a problem situation, by drawing on the techniques and skills discussed in this chapter. My experience has been that such approaches can be tremendously effective and add value in many ways, but that the expertise required to achieve that effectiveness has been difficult to disseminate. Often the practitioner is regarded as a "wizard", with participants or observers making statements like "That looks hard" and "I'm glad you're here, we'd never be able to do that for ourselves." Although the elements of the approach are relatively simple, combining them and putting them into practice, in real

---

[15] In what may be the beginning of such attempts, a workshop in "Facilitating Hypertext-Augmented Collaborative Modeling" was held at the 2002 ACM Hypertext Conference in College Park, Maryland: http://cognexus.org/ht02/

time, working with a real group of people watching every move the facilitator makes, has proven to be an intimidating challenge – one overcome, at this point in time, by relatively few people. Despite conducting many facilitator training sessions (150+ participants estimate) and much proselytizing for the approach, the number of effective practitioners has remained very small – less than a dozen at last count, and most of those infrequent at best. So this chapter is part of an ongoing attempt to characterize the practice of visualized-argumentation facilitation so that its elements and affordances can be better understood, and to pave the way for future work to understand how to better instruct new practitioners, construct tool support, and otherwise make this powerful practice easier to adopt.

Although the examples presented in this chapter have all been with Compendium, the intent of the chapter is actually agnostic regarding tool or method of choice. Rather, the intent is to instill a sense of the requirements for, and potential of, collective sensemaking and group intelligence if such tools and skills become so well understood, and well embodied in future tools and practices, as to become routine, or at least commonplace (as opposed to the province of a relatively few researchers and zealots). One step in that direction is to set expectations higher than is conventional for the potential of people to work with high collective intelligence and productivity when they come together to work on problems. We should learn to have low tolerance for time-wasting, unproductive, unsatisfying meetings. In this future state, visualized argumentation would be a resource available to teams and workgroups at any time. Continuing to evolve and improve tools, methods, and training and apprenticeship approaches, coupled with a commitment to set the bar high for acceptable team productivity and intelligence, may bring this future state about sooner rather than later.

7.7 Acknowledgements

I thank my many colleagues in the development and practice of Compendium, most particularly Maarten Sierhuis, Jeff Conklin, Simon Buckingham Shum, Steven Vedro, and Chuck Palus.

7.8 References

Conklin, E. J., & Burgess Yakemovich, K. C. (1991). A process-oriented approach to design rationale. *Human-Computer Interaction, 6*(3,4), 357-391.

Nelson, T. H. (1993) *Literary machines*, (1993 ed.). Sausalito, CA: Mindful Press.

Norman, D. A. (1990). *The design of everyday things*. New York: Doubleday.

Palus, C. J., & Drath, W. H. (2001). Putting something in the middle: An approach to dialogue. *Reflections, 3*(2), 28-39.

Palus, C. J., & Horth, D. M. (2002). *The leader's edge: Six creative competencies for navigating complex challenges*. San Francisco: Jossey-Bass.

Selvin, A. (1996). Leveraging existing hypertext functionality to create a customized environment for team analysis. *Proceedings of the Second International Workshop on*

Incorporating Hypertext Functionality Into Software Systems. Bethesda, MD. Retrieved on July 1, 2002 from
http://www.cs.nott.ac.uk/~hla/HTF/HTFII/Selvin.html

Selvin, A. (1998). Facilitating electronically: Using technology to help Maria, (Special Issue on Automated Meeting Support). *The Facilitator*.

Selvin, A., & Sierhuis, M. (1999, December). Case studies of project compendium in different organizations. *Proceedings of the Workshop on Computer-Supported Collaborative Argumentation*. paper presented at CSCL'99, Stanford, CA.

Selvin, A., and Buckingham Shum, S. (1999). Repurposing Requirements: Improving Collaborative Sense-Making over the Lifecycle. paper presented at the International Conference on Product-Focused Software Process Improvement (Profes '99), Oulu, Finland.

Selvin, A. (1999, February). Supporting collaborative analysis and design with hypertext functionality. *Journal of Digital Information, 1*(4). Retrieved on July 15, 2002 from
http://jodi.ecs.soton.ac.uk/Articles/v01/i04/Selvin/

Shipman, F. M., & McCall, R. (1994). Supporting knowledge-base evolution with incremental formalization. In *Proceedings of CHI'94: Human Factors in Computing Systems* (pp. 285-291). New York: ACM Press.

Wilber, K. (2000). *Eye to Eye: The Quest for the New Paradigm* (3rd ed.). Boulder: Shambhala Press.

8 Infrastructure for Navigating Interdisciplinary Debates: Critical Decisions for Representing Argumentation

Robert E. Horn

Stanford University, USA and Saybrook Graduate School, USA

8.1 Differences Among Types of Debates

There are differences between those argumentation mapping schemes that focus on supporting real-time disputes and those which support carefully crafted, heavily edited representations of the intellectual history of some of humanity's most significant and enduring debates. Table 8.1. suggests some of the important distinctions:

Table 8.1: A comparison between real-time and historical debates.

Debate Types	Audience	Purposes
Real-time Debates	Those currently involved in the debate	- capture debates and evaluations on the fly - document a project's decisions - support the development of the debate - serve as a tool for teaching critical thinking
Historical Debates	Educators, researchers, students	- display the intellectual history of the debate as well as the current status - provide a navigational framework for whole academic subfield - serve as a tool for teaching critical thinking

Other chapters in this book describe approaches to the requirements for real-time debates. All of these approaches to argumentation analysis (historical and real-time) attempt to help people manage complexity and sort out differences of opinion and point of view.

8.1.1   Critical Decisions Must be Made Before Software is Designed

This chapter will focus on the detailed sets of analytic and design decisions that need to be made to create effective argumentation maps on great debates, especially for use in teaching and learning. These are critical because once structure and graphic commitments are made, software is costly and difficult to change. I will organize our approach by showing how we solved a series of analysis and design problems that are relevant to any computer-assisted collaborative argumentation work.

8.2   What Level of Detail?

Stephen Toulmin's pioneering book *The Uses of Argument* (Toulmin, 1958) was our inspiration.[1] (for an example see Buckingham Shum's Chapter 1) My initial impression was that he had solved all the problems. So I immediately attempted to use his diagrammatic approach (Toulmin et. al., 1979) with such public policy questions as the use of nuclear weapons (Horn, 1989, 200-203). But there was a major problem with the Toulmin approach: using it for a large, complicated argument created a huge tangle. It was fine for 5 to 10 sentences, but it became spaghetti for more. After experimentation we found that we were interested in portraying argumentation analysis at an overview level. Thus, argumentation mapping had at least two levels. There was the Toulmin level which worked the debate sentence by sentence. And there was a "higher" overview level of summary of the debate. It was this latter that we used in our first major project (described in case number one below).

8.2.1   Preliminary Assessment of Overview Approach

Our preliminary assessment of the overview approach is that it is quite useful and that

---

[1]   Our project began in the mid-80s. The work I had done on the Information Mapping method of structured writing and analysis is a successful attempt to carefully delineate a taxonomy and later a lifecycle document-creation methodology for relatively stable subject matter (Horn, 1989, 1992a, 1992b, 1993, 1995). Relatively stable subject matter is that which doesn't change much and about which there is little dispute. Information Mapping's method is widely used in industry and government for writing documentation, training, procedures and policies, and reports. Information Mapping is a registered trademark of Information Mapping, Inc. See <www.infomap.com>

the next layer down in detail would be the actual words of the protagonist in the argument, either an excerpt or the complete article or chapter. In our web version, we plan to include such links to source material. Toulmin sentence-by-sentence analysis could also be included at a "deeper" level.

Little has been done by the Intellectual historians so far rather slow to use these argumentation methodologies. Instructors of history and philosophy of artificial intelligence and cognitive science have used the maps to a greater extent. (Horn 1998c, 2000)

8.3 Case Number One: Mapping Great Debates: Can Computers Think?

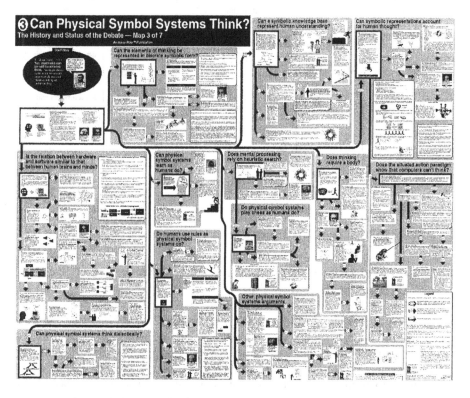

Figure 8.1: This is one of seven maps in the Mapping Great Debates: Can Computers Think? Series. Reproduced by permission of MacroVU Press. www.macrovu.com

We wanted to do a major philosophical debate, one that would test the robustness of the overview level of argumentation analysis. I had the vision that it would be a contribution to our common intellectual heritage if we could "map" the great debates both current and past. We picked the Turing debate as to whether computers will ever be able to think as a debate that both had a considerable history since 1950 and appeared to be ongoing. As we analyzed the large, sprawling debate – which turned out to have over 800 claims, rebuttals, and counter-rebuttals – we began to call what we were doing "argumentation mapping" because (as I shall discuss later) the graphic elements loomed large in display. (see Figure 8.1 for an example of one of these 7 maps)

8.3.1   Claims, Supports and Disputes

To trace the threads of the arguments we crafted "claims boxes" that contained claims, rebuttals and counterrebuttals. We linked them with arrows that contained the words "is supported by" and "is disputed by." (see Figure 8.2 for a closeup of a thread of linkages.)

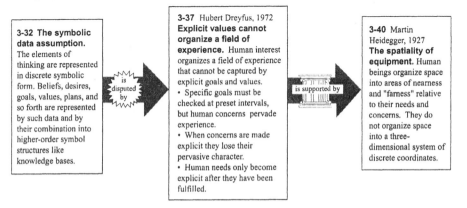

Figure 8.2: This is a closeup of one of the threads of arguments from the Mapping Great Debates series. Reproduced by permission of MacroVU Press. www.macrovu.com

8.3.2   How to Display Both the History and the Status of the Debates at the Same Time

We started out with the goal of showing the status of the debate. That part was relatively easy. All we had to do was read the current articles and see who was answering whom. But we were soon faced with the question of whether to show any current statement of previous claims and rebuttals or to find out who had made the claims first. So within the classification of argumentation analysis described at the beginning of this chapter, there are two criteria that need to be made clear. Criteria one: use the earliest statement of a "move" in the debate. This gives a new type of authentic intellectual history. Criteria two: use the best, or the only available, statement of a "move," which gives a rough-and-ready statement of the argument Both have value depending on your purposes. We chose the earliest-statement criteria so as to satisfy our own wish to provide intellectual history.

8.3.3 Criteria for Inclusion of "Moves"

Over a considerable period of time, we developed criteria for the Mapping Great Debates series. Such criteria for inclusion and exclusion of moves are essential to the integrity of an argumentation map. Our final group:

Use only Published Arguments
We decided to include only "moves" that were published in an established print or electronic medium: journals (including reputable electronic journals and white papers), magazines, and books. Arguments made in Usenet newsgroups, electronic forums, e-mail exchanges, or in interpersonal debate were excluded as too ephemeral and as representing positions still in development.

Use only Arguments that lie Within the Scope of the Map
The major claim – that machines can or will be able to think – determines the scope of these maps. We excluded any threads of arguments that drifted away from the central issue into such related territories as the mind–body problem, functionalism, and the philosophy of science.

Seek out the Historically Earliest or Best-Known Version of an Argument
When different authors make similar arguments, we chose the version which was historically earliest. In a few cases, we used the best-known version of the argument. When the best-known version was used, the historically earliest version is usually mentioned in a note. In the few cases in which differing versions of an argument are sufficiently unique or separately disputed, each is summarized separately.

Avoid Loosely Drawn Arguments
Sometimes an author makes an argument loosely, at the end of a paragraph, as an aside, or in a footnote. In general, such arguments are not included unless they are developed further in follow-up articles or are the focus of further debate.

Avoid Repetitive, Nitpicking, or Duplicative Arguments
One goal of the maps is to facilitate productive debate. *Ad hominem* arguments, redundant rounds of back-and-forth, and tediously nitpicky arguments were left out.

Avoid Forbiddingly Technical Discussion
There is a significant domain of highly technical arguments in logic and mathematics (mostly having to do with the Godel debates), which are based on extensive symbolic notation and formalisms, that could not be represented easily with the cartographic conventions we developed, or at the scale at which we chose to work. This was a difficult decision to make. I do not think that such highly mathematical arguments are in principle impossible to characterize in argumentation maps. However, it was difficult to map them within the limits of our paper poster format. Our compromise solution to this problem was to write *summaries* of many technical and symbolic discussions. Only the most forbidding (perhaps 2 or 3) had to be excluded entirely.

Summarize the Author's Published Claim

Many authors hold views today that are different from those they expressed at the time they entered into the debate. To be historically accurate, we included authors' claims as published. If an author later changed his or her position and *published* the change, the new claim was included, and the change of position was noted.

Avoid Tentative Arguments

The tentative style of some academic writing often makes it extremely difficult to understand exactly what is being argued. Authors had to be definitive in their arguments to qualify for inclusion on the map.

Include some Rather Ancient Historical Arguments

In order to properly situate the debate in its historical context, we included a sampling of notable historical philosophical supports for contemporary arguments such as arguments from Leibnitz and Descartes.

Include some Experimental Results

To situate the debate in a context of concrete experimental and computational results, we included some implemented systems and empirical results. Again, we only included a small sample of such results, sticking to famous and notable computer models and experiments. See Figure 8.3 for an example.

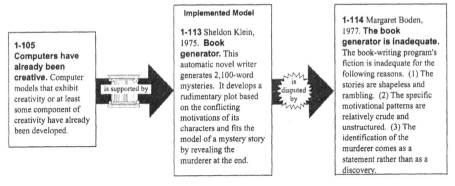

Figure 8.3: This is an example of claims boxes showing how claims about experimental results were used in argumentation maps. Reproduced by permission of MacroVU Press. www.macrovu.com

Include a Small Sample of Outrageous and Humorous Arguments

Some of the stranger claims were worth including just to liven things up and have some fun. Such claims also provide potential "targets" for lively threads of response.

8.3.4   How Exactly to Phrase Arguments

Claims can be written with great clarity or can be hopelessly confusing. We found that writers need to be continuously reminded to write the claims in simple declarative sentences. It is very easy for academic writers to hopelessly complicate sentences. This does not make for good argumentation mapping. Many is the time that our writers remarked that they wished that the debate protagonists whom they were summarizing would have written in such a succinct style.

8.3.5   How to Design Large Displays

As it turned out, we decided to use paper posters for our initial display. Each of the seven posters measures 3 x 4 feet. Initially, we didn't know which method of spreading out the claims and rebuttals would be better for display. Our criteria here was: How easy is it the initial learner to "get into" the maps. We tested several versions. Top down? Bottom up? Center outward? Which way should the arrows go: left-to-right or right-to-left?

Start-at-the-top and go-left-to-right appeared best. We tried several linking words and chose "is disputed by" and "is supported by" as our best option for clarity. These words effectively link the claims, supports, and dispute boxes, and also remind the reader of how to read the arrows.

Each of the seven maps present 100 or more major claims, rebuttals and counterrebuttals, each of which is summarized succinctly and placed in visual relationship to the other arguments that it supports or disputes. Claims are further divided into more than 70 issue areas, or major branches of the arguments, each organized around a question. (See Figure 8.2) Arguments by nearly 400 cognitive scientists, philosophers, AI researchers, and mathematicians, and a half-dozen other specialties who have weighed into the argument in a significant way are represented on the maps.

This approach appears to continue to have value. We have built two conference rooms at Stanford University that have large wall-size computer-managed display screens. They are different from the usual projection devices in that every place on the wall has the resolution for approximately 10-point type. This resolution makes it possible to display large argumentation maps of the kind we have created. One early experiment with computer display showed the value of putting the maps on such screens.

The didactic opportunities abound. One can create software commands that say, "Show all of arguments by protagonist (x)." "Show the arguments in a single timeline instead of 70 issue-area timelines." "Show all of the arguments by protagonists from worldview (y)." These and many more computable variations will make the argumentation map a very flexible tool for educational situations. We hope to implement these in the near future.

8.3.6   How to Graphically Design the Claims?

In extremely complex arguments, it is essential to use all the graphic tools available to clarify the debates and, thus, help the reader maneuver through the web of claims and rebuttals. The essential tool is a short title in boldface type for every claim and rebuttal. This improves initial scanning of the argument and also aids retracing one's steps through the debates. Earlier research (Horn, 1989, 1992; Hartley and Trueman, 1983; Reid and Wright 1973) has shown that these kinds of subheads or titles provide "Prechunking" that helps the reader overcome human shortcomings of working (or short-term) memory.

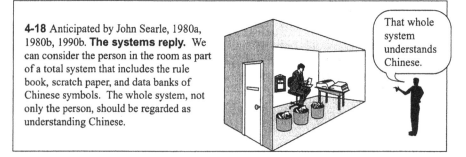

Figure 8.4: Examples of illustrated claims boxes   from the Mapping Great Debates series. Reproduced by permission of MacroVU Press. www.macrovu.com

Our graphic approach is constructed on the syntactic and semantic analysis found in Horn 1998b. We used illustrations to (1) aid exposition of difficult topics, (2) serve as examples and (3) aid navigation. First, for some difficult topics, a diagram provides exceptional clarity and ease of understanding. Secondly, graphic illustrations that provide examples of the sometimes abstract and abstruse arguments give the reader welcome assistance. These graphics must be used if the maps are to achieve maximum usefulness to learners. Thirdly the rich use of visual icons, illustrations, and examples significantly aids readers' navigation of the argument. During the evaluation period, we frequently heard: "I remembered the drunken Norwegian argument's icon." "I could remember where the argument fit in and where to go back to find it."

It has become our practice to write the claims and rebuttals first, and then to add graphic illustrations. But one should not conclude from this sequence that the visuals are not tightly integrated with the verbal elements. Rather, this is simply a work process simplification, and often in this process, the verbal elements are modified to synchronize with the graphic elements.

In the final version of the *Can Computers Think?* maps, we used several hundred icons and illustrations and about 60 photographs. Figure 8.4 shows examples of some kinds of illustrations we used to enhance the claims boxes.

8.3.7 How to Structure Massive Arguments?

An argument with 800 major moves defies most human ability to comprehend and manage. It became clear early in our process that the arguments clumped around themes. Our strategy was to let the data determine the clumps. That is, we worked from the bottom up rather than trying to impose a scheme of logically delineated themes.

6-76 Dieter Birnbacher, 1995
Consciousness might still be necessary. Just because there isn't a perfect correlation between thinking events and consciousness events doesn't mean that consciousness is unnecessary for thinking. Consciousness might still be necessary for thinking in general, though not necessarily attached to each thinking event.

Figure 8.5: Example of a focus box from the Mapping Great Debates series. Reproduced by permission of MacroVU Press. www.macrovu.com

At several points we found that there were references in the articles we were reading to "those who claim (x)" – offered without citation. In fact it happened so often that we had threads of debates – claims, rebuttals, counterrebuttals – with no one to attribute the initial claim to. We finally assumed that much of the debate we were tracing was woven around conferences, meetings, and live debates where individuals asserted these major claims but no one bothered to put them in writing. Yet, for the linking together of arguments about a given theme, something more was needed. So we had to violate our "use only published sources" criterion to give the map regions sufficient coherence. At last, we invented what we call the "focus box" which was a statement of a claim for which we did not actually find a statement by some specific protagonist. These focus boxes were then used to initiate issue areas (Figure 8.5).

For several years during the time we were making these maps, we simply used words like "emotional arguments" or "creativity arguments" to clump the debates. As we began the final designs of the maps, it was suggested by a colleague that we translate the themes into questions to act as headlines for the regions (e.g. Can computers be creative? Can computers have emotions?). This has become our standard practice.

8.3.8 How to Represent and Incorporate Worldviews

One of the difficult aspects of understanding great debates like this one is that the protagonists come from quite different points of view. They bring vastly different assumptions about the nature of reality. Often, in a specific article, the protagonists do not reveal their assumptions or their affiliation with a specific camp of thinkers. We have tried to provide a tool for learners here also. The basic clue was provided by Simon and Newell's listing of their postulates for the representationist point of view, which they call the physical symbol system hypothesis. (See Table 8.2) We then wrote sets of postulates for nine other major points of view and have included them on the various maps. We identified, where possible, which participants on the maps could be regarded as being part of a specific camp, thereby providing students with an insight as to why particular arguments might be taking place.

For us, it is still a research topic as to how to incorporate these postulates usefully onto web versions of the maps. It is also a creative project for our field to try to imagine a different sort of graphic display for worldviews than our lists of postulates.

8.3.9   How to Incorporate Ancillary Information?

In developing the argumentation maps as a teaching and research tool, we recognized that the bare-bones, stand-alone argumentation map is insufficient. Students new to the area need supplementary information to enable them to fully comprehend the arguments. They need, for example, definitions and historical background. They need to have a Turing machine explained to them. We imbedded a variety of sidebars onto the maps to provide access to this information. The definitions have the visual look and feel of a dictionary entry. In the end, we included 50 definitions and 32 sidebars on the 7 maps. These are located at strategic spots in the maps close to where the topics and terms are introduced. As we have migrated some of the maps onto the web, these have become clickable topics. It is very important in developing such ancillary blocks of information to clearly label them by type (e.g. definitions, historical notes, etc.)

Table 8.2: Example of Postulates. Reproduced by permission of MacroVU Press. www.macrovu.com

Postulates of the Physical Symbol Systems Hypothesis

1. A physical symbol system
   - is physical (that is, made up of some physical matter)
   - is a specific kind of system (that is, a set of components functioning through time in some definable manner) that manipulates instances of symbols.

2. Symbols can be thought of as elements that are connected and governed by a set of relations called a symbol structure. The physical instances of the elements (or tokens) are manipulated in the system.

3. An information process is any process that has symbol structures for at least some of its inputs or outputs.

4. An information processing system is a physical symbol system that consists of information processes.

5. Symbol structures are classified into
   - data structures
   - programs.

6. A program is a symbol structure that designates the sequence of information processes (including inputs and outputs) that will be executed by the elementary information processes of the processor.

7. Memory is the component of an information processing system that stores symbol structures.

8. Elementary information processes are transformations that a processor can perform upon symbol structures (e.g., comparing and determining equality, deleting, placing in memory, retrieving from memory, etc.).

9. A processor is a component of an information processing system that consists of:
   - a fixed set of elementary information processes,
   - a short-term memory that stores the input and output symbol structures of the elementary information processes, and
   - an interpreter that determines the sequence of elementary information processes to be executed as a function of the symbol structures in short-term memory.

10. The external environment of the system consists of "readable" stimuli. Reading consists of creating internal symbol structures in memory that designate external stimuli. Writing is the operation of emitting the responses to the external environment that are commanded by the internal symbol structures.

Adapted from Newell and Simon (1972, chap. 2).

Proponents include Jerry Fodor, Allen Newell, Herbert Simon, John McCarthy, Zenon Pylyshyn, early Marvin Minsky, Doug Lenat, Edward Feigenbaum, and Pat Hayes.

8.3.10 How to Incorporate Secondary Links?

We found, for example, that many of the arguments used for and against the von Neuman architecture (the kind of internal design of ordinary computers on our desks) and the arguments for and against connectionist networks (computers that are built around a structure similar to that of interlinked neurons) were quite analogous. Yet the arguments about connectionist architecture of computers took up half of map 5 and the sprawling arguments about von Neuman architecture covered maps 3 and 4. It seemed important to somehow show these similarities of argumentation threads to learners. There were other situations like this that appeared widely separated in the argumentation networks. We developed a set of secondary links which help readers tie together such important connections. On the paper versions, they were simple statements. For an example, see Figure 8.6. It is much easier to develop these secondary linkages in a software hypertext environment.

3-45 Joseph Rychlak, 1991
Learning is process of interpretation. Most AI theorists model learning on a Lockean paradigm that takes repetition and contiguity of perceptions as the primary way in which new concepts are learned. For example, we learn how to spell by repeatedly seeing how words are spelled and which letters are contiguous to each other. But such a model does not pay sufficient attention to the role of meaning in learning. Learning occurs when a mind that reasons dialectically and predicationally interprets what it perceives in terms of the meaning of what it perceives. Because computers don't work with meanings, interpretation and the relevant kind of learning is impossible for them. Note: Rychlak's further arguments about artificial intelligence can be found in the "Can physical symbol systems think dialectically?" ◄───── **Secondary Link**
arguments on this map.

4-28 The man in the Chinese Room doesn't instantiate a program. A human being (or a homunculus) shuffling symbols in a room is not a proper instantiation of a computer program, and so the Chinese Room argument does not refute AI.
Note: For more multiple realizability arguments, see the "Is the brain a ◄───── **Secondary Link**
computer?" arguments on Map 1, the "Can functional states generate consciousness?" arguments on Map 6, and sidebar, "Formal Systems: An Overview," on Map 7.

Figure 8.6: Examples of secondary links from the Mapping Great Debates series. Reproduced by permission of MacroVU Press. www.macrovu.com

8.3.11 What Happens when there is a Variation of a Claim?

In some instances an author makes a distinctive and crucial shift in the definition of an issue, yet is clearly arguing with a specific protagonist. We had to indicate that a major shift in ground had taken place. When such a distinctive reconfiguration of an earlier claim was made, we used a different icon on the arrow with the words "is interpreted as." (See Figure 8.7 for an example)

2-69
The Turing test provides a behavioral/operational definition of intelligence. The Turing test defines thinking in terms of overt, measurable behavior. It offers a behavioral/operational definition of our ordinary concept of thinking. Disputed by "A Box of Rocks Could Pass the Toe-Stepping Game," Box 7.
Note: A similar debate takes place in the "Is passing the test decisive?" arguments on this map, which deal with the question of what can be demonstrated by successful simulation.

is interpreted as

2-83 Anticipated by Ned Block, 1981
The behavioral disposition interpretation. A system is intelligent if it is behaviorally disposed to pass the Turing test. In this interpretation, neither passing the test nor failing the test is conclusive, because intelligence doesn't require passing but only a disposition to pass.

Figure 8.7: Example of "is interpreted as" link from the Mapping Great Debates series. Reproduced by permission of MacroVU Press. www.macrovu.com

8.3.12 Value of CSAV in Interdisciplinary Navigation

Our work on the *Mapping Great Debates: Can Computers Think?* series has opened up the development of a new field for the understanding of intellectual history. Among other advances, it illuminates the important history of how new concepts and distinctions in intellectual endeavors arise out of debate. Still to be worked out on the web-based versions are how to build instructional modules around the argumentation maps which would serve as the navigational core. However, the argumentation structure aids students, as well as researchers and scholars from outside a field, who, of course, become students once they enter an unfamiliar field.

8.3.13 Pedagogical Implications

Complexity Requires Structure
The argumentation maps are beginning to be used in a wide variety of ways in the classroom. It requires considerable rethinking for the instructor to change familiar classroom lecture and question routines to implement them to full use. But they offer the opportunity for innovative assignments ranging from (1) (relatively easy) choosing one of the 70 major branches of the debate and writing a paper agreeing or disagreeing; to (2) (moderately more difficult) asking students to rank order the strength of different debates on a given branch and consider why they give the weights they do to the different arguments; to (3) (more advanced) asking students to come up with at least one new argument at the end of one of the branches, which represent the frontiers of the debate; to (4) (even more advanced) asking students to write a paper that shows why two or more of the eleven philosophical camps described in postulates on the maps are debating a particular issue.

One professor told me that he had always had difficulty explaining to graduate students about how to select and narrow down topics for philosophy dissertations. With the maps he was able to show the amount and depth of coverage quite easily simply by waving his hands over parts of the maps.

Opportunity to See Major Disagreements
The biologist Lewis Thomas wrote, "College students, and for that matter high school students, should be exposed very early, perhaps at the outset, to the big arguments currently going on among scientists. Big arguments stimulate their interest, and with luck engage their absorbed attention... But the young students are told very little about the major disagreements of the day; they may be taught something about the arguments between Darwinians and their opponents a century ago, but they do not realize that similar disputes about other matters, many of them touching profound issues for our understanding of nature, are still going on, and, indeed are an essential feature of the scientific process." The maps provide major insights for the challenge that Thomas highlights. Over the next few years perhaps the biggest impact for teaching and learning from the use of argumentation maps will be in this area.

Provide Context and Visible Structure
As I noted in Horn (2000): We live in an age of information overload and specialization. The sheer numbers of argumentative "moves" in the maps(over 800); the number of authors represented on the maps (380); the number of sources that we consulted (over 1,000) and the sources that contained original arguments used in the maps (over 400) are overwhelming to the student undertaking study in this area.

One graduate student in the philosophy of mind said: "These maps would have saved me 500 hours of time my first year in graduate school. For almost two semesters, I had to keep reading article after article without enough context to see how they fit in to the bigger picture. The maps would have made my whole experience a much more rewarding one."

It was also interesting to hear from a professor of philosophy of mind who had begun using the maps in her teaching. She reported that: "The maps have, in fact, prompted me to reorganize my Philosophy of Mind course to cover certain issues and problems from a particular approach, using the commentaries of thinkers noted on the maps – e.g. the Chinese Room in more depth, and connected more explicitly to the question 'Can Computers Think?' (Wagner, 1998)

Evaluations Needed
At this point, the evaluations of classroom use of our argumentation maps has been limited to observations by teachers and anecdotal feedback. The maps have been laminated and hung on walls in classrooms. They have been put in the library on reserve. They've been spread out on the seminar room table. A recurrent recommendation has been that they would be more frequently used if they were in some electronic form. But almost as soon as a professor suggests electronic form they take back the recommendation with the words "of course, then you wouldn't get the

benefit of seeing the structure of the arguments that the maps provide." This can only be solved by larger screens.

8.4   Case Number Two: Genetically Modified Food

8.4.1   Science and Science Policy

Society needs to be able to continuously evaluate new potentially disruptive knowledge and technologies. We were commissioned by *New Scientist* magazine to look into the question of how to create a web display of our maps on a science policy project. We were given the topic of the debates about genetically modified food and requested to investigate a prototype.

What was interesting was the arrangement of the top level – how the topic was "framed" by the questions asked. How the top level framing of the policy questions look on the web is shown in Figure 8.8.

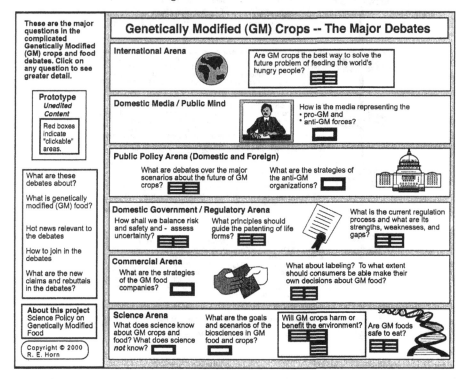

Figure 8.8: The top level window of the Mapping Great Debates series on Genetically Modified Food.

8.4.2   How to Display Extensive Argumentation on the Web?

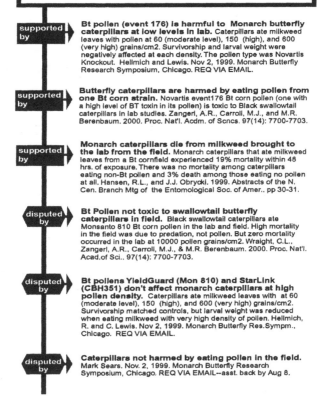

What harm, if any, happens to Monarch butterflies fed Bt corn pollen?

Monarch butterfly caterpillars can be killed by pollen from GM corn containing insecticidal toxin Bt. Caterpillars only eat milkweed, which grows near corn. In the lab, 56% of caterpillars died in 4 days when they ate milkweed leaves dusted with Bt pollen, compared with zero mortality in two control groups (no pollen and non-Bt pollen). Caterpillars consumed 65% less and grew half as much when Bt pollen was present. Larva feed when pollen is shed (late June to mid-Aug.), and pollen is spread by winds at least 60m. Losey, J.E., Rayor, L.S., and M.E. Carter. 1999.*Nature* (ENG)399: 405.

supported by ▶ **Bt pollen (event 176) is harmful to Monarch butterfly caterpillars at low levels in lab.** Caterpillars ate milkweed leaves with pollen at 60 (moderate level), 150 (high), and 600 (very high) grains/cm2. Survivorship and larval weight were negatively affected at each density. The pollen type was Novartis Knockout. Hellmich and Lewis. Nov 2, 1999. Monarch Butterfly Research Symposium, Chicago. REQ VIA EMAIL.

supported by ▶ **Butterfly caterpillars are harmed by eating pollen from one Bt corn strain.** Novartis event176 Bt corn pollen (one with a high level of BT toxin in its pollen) is toxic to Black swallowtail caterpillars in lab studies. Zangerl, A.R., Carroll, M.J., and M.R. Berenbaum. 2000. Proc. Nat'l. Acdm. of Scncs. 97(14): 7700-7703.

supported by ▶ **Monarch caterpillars die from milkweed brought to the lab from the field.** Monarch caterpillars that ate milkweed leaves from a Bt cornfield experienced 19% mortality within 48 hrs. of exposure. There was no mortality among caterpillars eating non-Bt pollen and 3% death among those eating no pollen at all. Hansen, R.L., and J.J. Obrycki. 1999. Abstracts of the N. Cen. Branch Mtg of the Entomological Soc. of Amer.. pp 30-31.

disputed by ▶ **Bt Pollen not toxic to swallowtail butterfly caterpillars in field.** Black swallowtail caterpillars ate Monsanto 810 Bt corn pollen in the lab and field. High mortality in the field was due to predation, not pollen. But zero mortality occurred in the lab at 10000 pollen grains/cm2. Wraight, C.L., Zangerl, A.R., Carroll, M.J., & M.R. Berenbaum. 2000. Proc. Nat'l. Acad.of Sci.. 97(14): 7700-7703.

disputed by ▶ **Bt pollens YieldGuard (Mon 810) and StarLink (CBH351) don't affect monarch caterpillars at high pollen density.** Caterpillars ate milkweed leaves with at 60 (moderate level), 150 (high), and 600 (very high) grains/cm2. Survivorship matched controls, but larval weight was reduced when eating milkweed with very high density of pollen. Hellmich, R. and C. Lewis. Nov 2, 1999. Monarch Butterfly Res.Sympm., Chicago. REQ VIA EMAIL.

disputed by ▶ **Caterpillars not harmed by eating pollen in the field.** Mark Sears. Nov. 2, 1999. Monarch Butterfly Research Symposium, Chicago. REQ VIA EMAIL--asst. back by Aug 8.

Figure 8.9: The vertical format of the Mapping Great Debates series on Genetically Modified Food.

Displaying extensive argumentation on the web within the confines of small screens is difficult. Initially we tried simply to put our maps on the web as they were presented print format. But debates of more than a few moves produced much difficulty for the reader to stay oriented. Once into the middle of the visual space, the reader had difficulty tracing the arguments back. As this chapter goes to press, we are experimenting with a vertical format illustrated in Figure 8.9.

The genetically modified food project did not receive any formal evaluation as it was done as a prototype project. We are in the process of seeking support to evaluate its use in public policy development.

8.5 Case Number Three: Consciousness Research

8.5.1 How to Display Different Entry Points?

We received a grant several years ago to create prototype argumentation maps in the rapidly expanding discipline of consciousness studies. This presents a different problem from that of the Turing debates. The debates are all focused on the same phenomena – consciousness – but different disciplines start with quite different questions. What this has meant for mapping the debate is that there can not be a single determining question, such as appears in the Turing debates (i.e. Can Computers Think?). So, we have provisionally decided to simply cluster questions. Our first group of questions are the philosophical ones, and as a top-level web page can be seen in Figure 8.10. Part of our detailed argumentation map is shown in Figure 8.11.

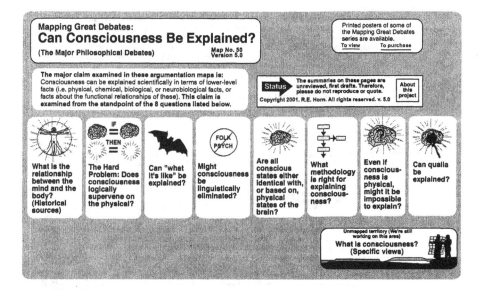

Figure 8.10: The top level of the Mapping Great Debates series on Consciousness.

It is clear that questions emanating from neuropsychology will start from quite different places.

 What is the relationship between mind and body? (Historical Sources)

Map No. 51
Version 1

 Status The summaries on these pages are unreviewed, first drafts. Therefore, please do not reproduce or quote.

Rene Descartes, 1641a
Cartesian Dualism. The mind and body are two distinct substances. The essential attribute of body is that it is extended in space. The mind is not extended in space and it cannot be found in the physical world. Meditations on First Philosophy. Transl. by John Cottingham. Cambridge: Cambridge U. Press, 1996.

 is supported by

Rene Descartes, 1641b
The Divisibility Argument. Bodies are always divisible, but the mind is simple and indivisible. Therefore mind and body are distinct substances. *Meditations on First Philosophy.* Transl. by John Cottingham. Cambridge: Cambridge U. Press, 1996.

is disputed by

Stephen Burwood, Paul Gilbert, and Kathleen Lennon, 1998.
No sharp distinction between the mental and the physical. Descartes' dualistic picture relies on a sharp distinction between the mental and the physical. But there is no reason to suppose that the body cannot have some of the features of mentality and intentionality that Descartes considers to be the domain of the mind. If mind and body are not separated in the sharp way that Descartes presupposes, the mind/body problem might not even arise. Burwood, Stephen and Gilbert, Paul and Lennon, Kathleen. 1998. *Philosophy of Mind.* UCL Press.

is supported by

Gilbert Ryle, 1949
The Myth of the Ghost in the Machine. Since Descartes, consciousness has been understood as akin to a spiritual "ghost" in a physical "machine." The idea of the ghost in the machine categorically misrepresents the assumed distinction between the physical and the mental as a distinction between facts about the body and facts about a private, inner realm of consciousness. Mental facts are really facts about the behavior and dispositions to behave of the physical body. Ryle, Gilbert. 1949. *The Concept of Mind.* University of Chicago Press.

 is supported by

Rene Descartes, 1641c
The contents of thought cannot be doubted. If I undertake to doubt everything that can be doubted, I can doubt that there is an external world corresponding to my ideas, but not that those ideas themselves exist. *Meditations on First Philosophy.* Transl. by John Cottingham. Cambridge: Cambridge U. Press, 1996.

 is supported by

George Berkeley, 1710
Berkeleyian Idealism. Ideas are the only things we can know at all. Therefore the world is made of ideas: for a thing to exist is for someone to have an idea of it. Things that are unperceived by humans are ideas in the mind of God. Berkeley, George 1710. *Of the Principles of Human Knowledge.* Roger Woolhouse, ed., Penguin Books, 1988.

 is supported by

Immanuel Kant, 1781a
Transcendental Idealism. We can only know and experience the world as conditioned by the form of our minds. For instance, space and time are not ultimately real: they are conditions under which we know the world. The world, as it is in itself, independently of our conditions of knowledge, is unknowable. Note: Although Kant's view is a version of Idealism, he does not hold, as Berkeley does, that the world is made of ideas. Immanuel Kant, 1781. *Critique of Pure Reason.* Translated by Norman Kemp Smith. New York: St. Martin's Press, 1965.

Figure 8.11. The vertical format of the Mapping Great Debates series on CONSCIOUSNESS.

8.5.2   How to Build Infrastructure Collaboratively?

As this chapter is written, I have begun to work on the issue of how to involve graduate students in collaboratively creating maps. Clearly there needs to be a course to help bring students into the conventions and criteria used in the mapping. In addition we need to provide some kind of content and editorial review of their summaries of moves. We are not interested in developing a chatroom. The content review needs to be done by specialists. The editorial review needs to be of two kinds: the writing of the actual sentences summarizing claims, and the linkages. How this will all be managed on the web is yet another research problem. We imagine using some form of annotation functionality in the software[2].

8.6   Conclusion: Our Vision

We envision the ability over time to witness the creation of vast webs of argumentation maps on the web that cover many fields and that show us how humanity working together has asked, debated, and sometimes even answered the Great Questions.

8.7   Acknowledgements

I want to salute the members of my team – Jeff Yoshimi, Mark Deering, (University of California, Irvine) and Russ McBride (University of California, Berkeley) – without whose dedicated effort and creative thought these maps would not be what they are today. I also want to thank the publishers, MacroVU, Inc. and the Lexington Institute, for their generous support of the Can Computers Think? project. I further salute Paul Livingston as the primary writer in our project on consciousness. I further want to thank The Consciousness Studies Program of Arizona University for support (through a grant from the Fetzer Institute) of the Consciousness Project. Thanks, too, goes to Terry Winograd of The Computer Science Department of Stanford University for his enthusiastic encouragement of our work. And finally, I want to express appreciation to *New Scientist* magazine (especially its editor, Alan Anderson) for support of the Genetically Modified Food project, and to project analysts Ben Shouse and Shirley Dang.

8.8   References

Hartley, J. and Trueman, M., (1983) The effects of headings in text on recall, search

---

[2] The *ClaiMaker* system (Buckingham Shum, et al., Chapter 9) is a promising tool for modelling claims in Great Debates.

and retrieval. *British Jounral of Educational Psychology, 53*, 205-214.

Horn, R. E. (1989) *Mapping Hypertext.* Lexington, MA: The Lexington Institute.

Horn, R. E. (1992a) *How high can it fly? Examining the evidence on information mapping's method of high performance communication.* Lexington, MA: The Lexington Institute.

Horn, R. E. (1992b) Clarifying two controversies about information mapping's method, *Educational and Training Technology International, 2,* 29, 109-117.

Horn, R. E., (1993, February). Structured writing at twenty five. *Performance and Instruction,* 11-17.

Horn, R. E., (1995). Structured writing as a paradigm. In A. Romiszowski & C. Dills (Eds.), *Instructional development: State of the art.* Englewood Cliffs, NJ: Educational Technology Publications.

Horn, R. E. (1998a). *Mapping great debates: Can computers think? 7 maps and Handbook.* Bainbridge Island, WA: MacroVU. Available from http://www.macrovu.com

Horn, R. E. (1998b). *Visual language: global communication for the 21st Century.* Bainbridge Island, WA: MacroVU.

Horn, R. E. (1998c). Using argumentation analysis to examine history and status of a major debate in artificial intelligence and philosophy. In F. H. van Eemeren, R. Grootendorst, J. A. Blair & Willard, C. A. (Eds.) *Proceedings of the fourth international conference of the international society for study of argumentation,* 375-381.

Horn, R. E. (2000, Fall). Teaching philosophy with argumentation maps. *American philosophical association newsletter on teaching philosophy,* 153-159

Reid, F., & Wright, P. (1973). Written Information: Some alternatives to prose for expressing the outcomes of complex contingencies. *Journal of Applied Psychology, 57*(2), 160-166

Thomas, L. (1981, July). Debating the unknowable. *Atlantic Monthly,* 49-50.

Toulmin, S. (1958). *The uses of argument.* Cambridge, MA: Cambridge University Press.

Toulmin, S, Rieke, R., & Janik, A. (1979). *An introduction to reasoning.* New York: Macmillan.

Turing, A. (1950). Computing machinery and intelligence. *Mind 59*, 434-460.

Wagner, E. (1998). Personal communication. Available from http://www.macrovu.com

9   *Visualizing Internetworked Argumentation*

Simon Buckingham Shum, Victoria Uren
Gangmin Li, John Domingue, Enrico Motta
Knowledge Media Institute, Open University, UK

9.1   Scholarly Publishing and Argumentation: Beyond Prose

In this chapter, we outline a project which traces its source of inspiration back to the grand visions of Vannevar Bush (scholarly trails of linked concepts), Doug Engelbart (highly interactive intellectual tools, particularly for argumentation), and Ted Nelson (large scale internet publishing with recognised intellectual property). In essence, we are tackling the age-old question of how to organise distributed, collective knowledge. Specifically, we pose the following question as a foil:

> In 2010, will scholarly knowledge still be published solely in prose, or can we imagine a complementary infrastructure that is "native" to the emerging semantic, collaborative web, enabling more effective dissemination and analysis of ideas?

We are neither trying to replace textual narrative as an expressive medium, nor its products such as books and peer reviewed publications. We seek instead to augment them by exploiting globally networked information in ways that – precisely because of its historical pedigree – the venerable prose publication cannot support. Conventional scholarly publications are the way they are through a co-evolution of notational form with print publishing technology, but are not designed in any way to take advantage of today's information infrastructure. Still at a relatively early stage, our project is bringing to bear on this challenge a *networked representational environment* (a digital library server based on an argumentation ontology (Buckingham Shum et al., 2000)), *semantic web services* (e.g. ontology-based reasoning, Li et al., 2002), and recent work on *distributed collective practices* (why and when individuals in a community of practice are willing to subscribe to a shared repository, and role of formalism, Buckingham Shum et al., 2002). All of these must be interacted with via a variety of *user interfaces*, of which a key component will be renderings of the network of *argumentative claims* – the focus of this chapter.

We start with some background needed to understand the rationale for this work, and refer the reader to other sources for more detailed treatments of technical and social issues. We then focus on challenges associated with designing visual interfaces onto a shared repository, in order to construct what we call "claims" about research contributions. Finally, we conclude by outlining the agenda for future work.

9.2   What's the Problem?

Researchers are benefiting from more rapid access to research documents as resources such as new digital libraries and eprint archives go online almost by the week, but researchers (like almost all other professions) are also drowning in this ocean, with less time to track growing numbers of conferences, journals and reports. But beyond tracking new results, there is the whole dimension of analysing a literature. Researchers are interested in questions such as, *How does the expert community perceive this theory, model, language, empirical result? Where did this idea come from? What kind of evidence supports it, and challenges it? Are there different schools of thought on this issue?* These are of course questions about the *meaning* of a research contribution. Such questions operate at a different level from that addressed by conventional metadata or ontological markup, which normally seek to iron out inconsistency, ambiguity and incompleteness (clearly undesirable for details such as bibliographic or other uncontentious details). In contrast, principled disagreement about significance, conflicting perspectives, and the resulting ambiguities and inconsistencies are precisely what define a field as research; they are the objects of explicit inquiry. It in this context that structured argumentation has a contribution to make. In sum, there remains a yawning gap in the researcher's digital toolkit: tools to track *ideas* and *results* in a field, and to express, analyse and contest their *significance*.

As well as characterising this problem, the Scholarly Ontologies (ScholOnto) project is developing a system to support scholarly interpretation and argumentation, investigating the practicality of publishing explicit conceptual structures (grounded in conventional documents) in a collective knowledge base. The *ClaiMaker* system enables researchers to make *claims*, that is, to describe and debate, in a network-centric way, their view of a document's key contributions and relationships to the literature. It thus provides an interpretational layer above raw resources (such as documents, datasets, and tools).

We hypothesise that this will be of value to a variety of end-users: filtered views for students onto major debates in their field (as pioneered on paper by Horn: Chapter 8); tools for information analysts/librarians to conduct literature analyses; alerting services for researchers working across inter-disciplinary boundaries in which it is impossible to track all relevant research; visual browsing of concept networks to locate relevant documents. We turn now to the argumentation scheme that underpins the making of claims in the system.

9.3 The Discourse Ontology

"Ontologies" are the term used in knowledge modelling and agent research, and increasingly within the semantic web community, to describe an abstract (implementation-independent) specification of concepts, attributes and relationships (Gruber, 1995). Typical semantic web work develops an ontology to control interpretation or semantic annotation in a specific domain of inquiry (such as an ontology of problem-solving methods) or to model a particular aspect of the world (such as organisational functions), enabling machine-to-machine interoperability and interpretation. In contrast, we propose an ontology for scholarly discourse, primarily for *humans* to communicate through as a medium for publishing and discourse (although we envisage agents as protagonists and claim-makers at some point), with the express goal of supporting multiple (often contradictory) perspectives. In this sense it is as much an ontology for *principled disagreement*. Of course, it requires consensus in the sense that participants subscribe to the ontology as a reasonable language for "making and taking perspectives" (Boland and Tenkasi, 1995), but they need not agree at all on the actual issues under debate.

The requirements for the ontology that we aimed for are summarised in Table 9.1.

Table 9.1: Motivating requirements for the research discourse ontology.

Requirements for a scholarly discourse ontology
1 **Mimic natural language expressions to reduce the cognitive gap.** An underlying structure based on a noun/verb metaphor with the relations taking the role of verbs seemed appropriate. Making arguments in pseudo-natural language should make the scheme intuitive for contributors.
2 **The scheme must permit the expression of dissent.** The ScholOnto project is fundamentally about argumentation and, more broadly, scholarly discourse (not all of which is argumentative). The ontology is not there to impose a single domain model, but to support the contesting of *perspectives*.
3 **Ownership of public content is critical.** Contributors must take responsibility for the claims they make. ClaiMaker's content could be filtered via a formal peer review process, but in early versions we depend on the social control of peer pressure to motivate high quality claim-making. Ownership also has a key role in ClaiMaker as digital library server: claims would be "backed up" by a link to a published paper. There is an analogy here with Toulmin's (1958) warrants.
4 **Social dimensions to being explicit.** ClaiMaker invites researchers to consider making explicit what is normally implicit in the text of a paper (an issue discussed in Buckingham Shum et al., 2000). Discourse relational types vary in strength, which has both computational and social dimensions. Consider a relation *refutes*. This is a forceful term and therefore can carry greater weight in computation than, for example, *takes issue with*. From a

social perspective, some contributors might prefer to use the less extreme term when linking to concepts created by eminent figures. Providing these soft options recognises the social dimensions to citation, and aims to remove a possible barrier to adoption.

5   **A concept has no category outside of use.** A key precept of conventional approaches to ontologies is that objects in a scheme are typed under one or more classes. While this is acceptable for non-controversial attributes (or where an interpretation can be imposed), this cannot be sustained when we are talking about the *role* that a concept plays in multiple arguments in research: after all, an idea that is a *Problem* under debate in one paper may be an *Assumption* in another. The scheme must therefore allow the same concept to take on different types in different situations: meaning derives from context, where context is the forging of a connection between two ideas. It may even be impossible, or too much cognitive effort, to try and classify the concept (e.g. whether something is classed as a *Method, Theory, Language,* or all three, may not be of real interest).

6   **The   scheme   should   recognise   disciplinary   differences   in argumentative style.** We are trying to identify a core set of argumentation relations that are useful in many disciplines. However, the precise language used for making a case will differ from one research community to another. We tackle this using the idea of *dialects.* Drawing on Cognitive Coherence Relations,[1] we define a core set of relational classes, with properties such as type, polarity and weight, but these may be reified with natural language labels in many ways. For instance, a community in which it would be strange or unacceptable to *refute* your colleagues could change the label to something they felt more comfortable with (e.g. *is inconsistent with; challenges; raises issues with*), but the notion of a negative relation that challenges a concept would remain unchanged. This method would let us configure ClaiMaker for different communities without altering the underlying engine.

Based on our intuitions as researchers, and drawing on related computational linguistics work on "coherence relations" (Mancini and Buckingham Shum, 2001), plus earlier work on hypertextual argumentation (e.g. Newman and Marshall, 1991; Trigg and Weiser, 1983), a prototype discourse ontology was devised to satisfy this list of requirements. It had two basic object types: data and concept. The most important type of data object is a set of metadata describing a document in a digital library, these provided the backing, every claim being grounded in a published document (a quality-control policy decision – more open policies could be adopted). Concepts are stored as

---

[1]   Cognitive Coherence Relations (e.g. Knott and Mellish, 1996; Knott and Sanders, 1998) is a field in psycholinguistics which investigates the question of whether there is a core set of cognitive relationships that underpin written language. This field is summarised and related to the ScholOnto project by Mancini and Buckingham Shum (2001).

short pieces of free text succinctly summarising a "contribution" (at whatever granularity the researcher wishes to express this), for instance: *<Data> Undergraduate chemistry exam performance is doubled after training on the ChemVR system*. This is now an object that others can connect to, whether positively or negatively. A claim is a triple (Figure 9.1) of two objects connected by a link.

Each link is drawn from a general class (e.g. *Problem-related; Taxonomic; Causal*), has the properties type, polarity and weight, and a dialect label in natural language. A concept may optionally be assigned a type (e.g. *Data, Language, Theory*), stored as part of the link connecting it. By storing the concept type in the link, rather than binding it intrinsically to the concept, the typing of concepts is made context dependent. Researchers may of course disagree on the concept's type, a common focus for discussion some fields (e.g. is this *Language* also a *Theory*? Is this based on *Opinion* or *Data*?).

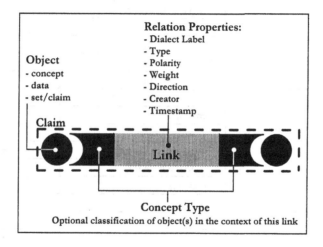

Figure 9.1: Structure of a *Claim* in the discourse ontology.

Elsewhere we have described the iteration from the first to the current version of the ontology (Buckingham Shum et al., 2002), a process which itself was supported by the IBIS approach for capturing team deliberations (described by Conklin, Chapter 6 and Selvin Chapter 7). The current scheme is summarised in Table 9.2. Our goal is to provide a given research community with a dialect that will cover the most common claims that they make (there may well be exceptional kinds of contributions that fall outside the expressiveness of the vocabulary, but the generic *Other Link* is available for those situations). We are aware that the scheme could be much more expressive, rigorous and formal. However, as we discuss elsewhere (Buckingham Shum et al., 2000), we are walking the tightrope between usability and formal rigour, and important lessons have already been learnt about over-formalizing interactive systems for untrained users (Shipman and Marshall, 1999).

Table 9.2: The revised discourse ontology following a first iteration and use analysis.

Relation Class	Dialect label	Polarity/Weight
General	is about	+/1
	uses/applies/is enabled by	+/1
	improves on	+/2
	impairs	− /2
	other link	+/1
Problem Related	addresses	+/1
	solves	+/2
Supports/Challenges	proves	+/2
	refutes	−/2
	is evidence for	+/1
	is evidence against	−/1
	agrees with	+/1
	disagrees with	−/1
	is consistent with	+/1
	is inconsistent with	−/1
Causal	predicts	+/1
	envisages	+/1
	causes	+/2
	is capable of causing	+/1
	is prerequisite for	+/1
	prevents	−/2
	is unlikely to affect	−/1
Similarity	is identical to	+/2
	is similar to	+/1
	is different to	−/1
	is the opposite of	−/2
	shares issues with	+/1
	has nothing to do with	−/1
	is analogous to	+/1
	is not analogous to	−/1
Taxonomic	part of	+/1
	example of	+/1
	subclass of	+/1
	not part of	−/1
	not example of	−/1
	not subclass of	−/1

To summarise, we propose that the kinds of connections shown in Table 9.2 are expressed at a level which most researchers would not only recognise, but indeed, would naturally use when summarising part of a literature.[2] Our internal testing shows that with a little practice, fluency in thinking in these terms is not hard to acquire, although of course, we will only know how generalisable this finding is as we study the system in wider use.

9.4 Making Claims Requires Mental Mapping

Given this underlying language, we now turn to the specific challenge of making claims structures visible in a coherent manner, whether at the point of creation, or when browsing/searching. We implemented the first *ClaiMaker* user interface as rapidly as possible in order to understand the authoring process, evaluate the ontology and populate the knowledge base. Now in its second main design iteration, this is a web forms/menu based design, is illustrated in Figure 9.2.

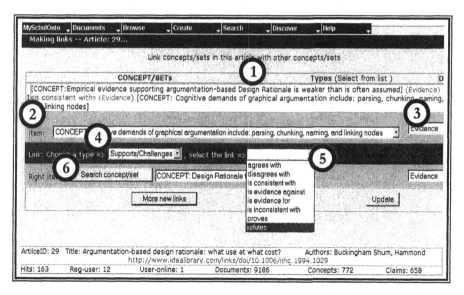

Figure 9.2: User interface to ClaiMaker, showing how a researcher can build a set of claims. Key: (1) A claim that has already been constructed, ready to submit; (2) the Concept to link from, which has (3) been assigned the type Evidence, and (4) linked via the Relational Class Supports/Challenges, (5) more specifically, refutes (selected from the dialect-specific menu). (6) The user then searched the knowledge base for a target Concept, Set or Claim to which they wish to make the connection.

---

[2] One strand of the ScholOnto Project is analysing the text of research publications, and shows some promise that we can indeed highlight phrases that correspond to claims in ClaiMaker. This would assist in the submission of new claims to ClaiMaker.

Although this supports claim-construction at a technical level, and menu-based form-filling is a familiar activity to web users, we are also exploring a complementary user interface approach. Making claims is essentially literature modelling, a cognitive task that requires the mental construction of a network structure. In our experience, externalising this through conceptual maps (sketched or diagrammed in software) is the most intuitive way in which to manage the cognitive load, and leading typically, to iterative refinement of the model as concept names and types, link types, and granularity are revised (cf. earlier empirical studies into the cognitive demands of graphical argumentation, Buckingham Shum et al., 1997). Figure 9.3 shows an example of the cognitive map that is typically produced when a researcher starts to think about how to describe a literature in terms of claims. It is also the kind of representation that one often constructs *prior to* using ClaiMaker, a signal that the tool is not supporting all phases of important cognitive work: to clarify one's thinking prior to adding claims in the forms/menus interface, one first sketches visually.

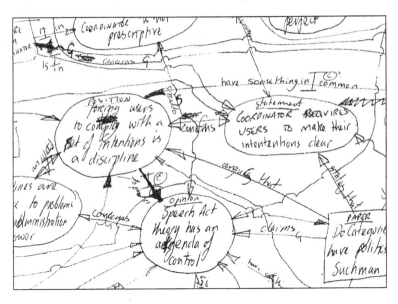

Figure 9.3: Sketching is a requirement for managing the cognitive task of modelling complex claim structures in a literature.

We are now developing a concept mapping user interface, screens from an early version of which are shown in the following section.

9.5   Visual Construction of Argumentative Claims

In the spirit of practising what we preach, let us take as a local example: the very book that you are now reading. What would it mean to represent the key contributions of each chapter, and the connections (both inter-concept, inter-chapter and to the roots and wider literature in the field) as an explicit claims network of concepts and associated argumentation? What kind of user interface could we provide to map out this structure, and what representational issues arise in the process?

Figure 9.4 shows a claims analysis of Chapter 7 by Selvin.[3] We have adopted a vertical layout convention, with a primary concept at the top ("primary", of course, by our reading of the chapter, and in order to make a specific point with our map; different readers might produce different maps). Under this we unfold the supporting argument that is presented.

The map of van Gelder's Chapter 5 (Figure 9.5) illustrates not only individual claims (concept-link-concept), but claim-link-claim structures (highlighted), in other words, arguments supporting other arguments.

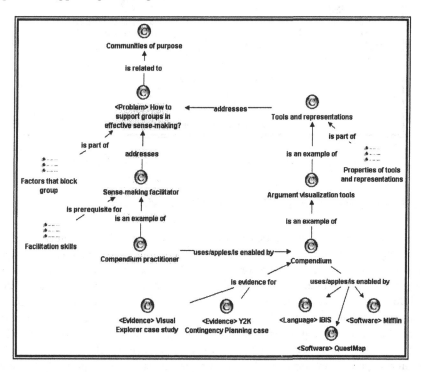

Figure 9.4: Visual claims analysis of part of Chapter 7 by Selvin.

---

[3] The modelling has been done in an adaptation of the *Mifflin* tool for IBIS argumentation <www.compendiuminstitute.org/tools/mifflin.htm>

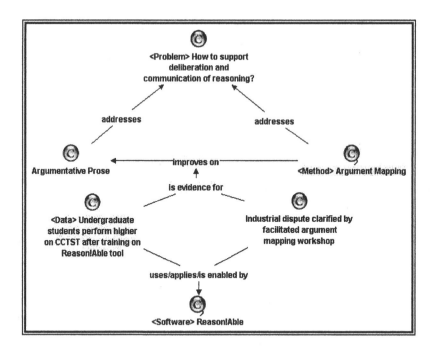

Figure 9.5: Visual claims analysis of part of Chapter 5 by van Gelder.

8.5.1   Representational Issues in Claim-Making

In any argument mapping approach (or for that matter, any conceptual modelling approach) there are always representational decisions to make about naming, classifying and linking objects, managing the coherence of the overall structure, and working at an appropriate level of granularity. Being able to make such "meta-decisions" is a critical skill for real time collaborative argument/issue mapping approaches (van Gelder, Chapter 5, Selvin, Chapter 7), given the time and group pressures to maintain momentum; speed of capture is a major driver towards "lightweight" notations such as IBIS. The pressure is less intense in a use context such as ClaiMaker, in which a researcher/student/analyst is working in a more reflective mode, probably (although not necessarily) on their own, distilling the essence of a piece of work into a succinct map. We can, therefore, afford a richer notation offering more expressive choices. A persistent design concern, however, is to walk the tightrope between overwhelming the user with subtly different link (and optional node) types that they cannot differentiate, and straitjacketing them into a frustratingly small vocabulary in which they cannot express themselves.

Turning to visual claim-making specifically, the use of an open, networked environment with "live" concepts that may be used by numerous researchers (as opposed to static concept mapping in a closed application), places a premium on the *re-use* of concepts and claims wherever possible: the same idea should be expressed in the same way, as far as possible. This should be relatively simple for "concrete concepts" such as the names of specific theories, methods, algorithms, software tools, and so forth. A quick search should reveal the concept if it has been created, so the user can just re-use it. In contrast, complex ideas will comprise claims or sets of claims of an unpredictable structure (for instance, it may be impossible to know in advance how an idea such as *the internet is forcing the publishing industry to reinvent itself* will be expressed). A keyword search may reveal a good candidate for re-use, or a researcher's own knowledge of the field may take them to a document they know, whose claims they can inspect and re-use or adapt. A research group may publish a public library of concepts and claims representing their major publications, recommending that to cite their work, others should use this library (in the process, greatly assisting automated analysis of that group's research impact). These are scenarios that we can envisage, but which depend on the complex interplay of the technology and its adoption.

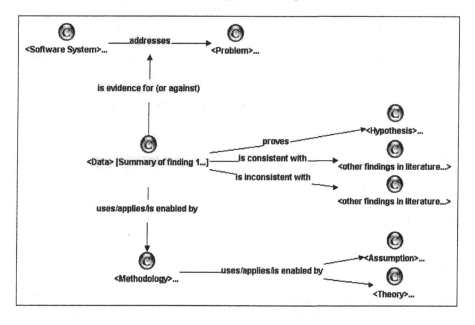

Figure 9.6: A claim-making template for a stereotypical *empirical software evaluation* paper. The structure provides scaffolding for authors to think about their work, and perhaps for reviewers to evaluate it by making it easier to trace concepts with which they are less familiar. The highlighted structure shows the expected core contribution of an evaluation paper: evidence about the effectiveness of a software system.

Another representational decision that must be made is how to lay out the structure. We can give a blank canvas for the user to lay out their arguments as they please, or provide a library of templates to "fill in the blanks" for canonical genres of paper in a given field. This may help beginners given the evidence from educational concept mapping that some "scaffolding" can be helpful (Reader and Hammond, 1994). Genres in the field of *Human-computer Interaction* would include *system description paper, evaluation paper* (e.g. Figure 9.6), *theoretical paper,* and *literature review* (reflected in the categories of submission that major HCI conferences often call for). These papers have different structures, and are refereed according to different criteria; indeed it has been suggested to us more than once that authors could be required to complete a template such as Figure 9.6 to accompany their submission, also assisting referees. (The use of spider diagrams to teach students different genres of writing is of course a long established technique related to this idea of templates for conceptual, discourse-oriented publishing.)

9.6   Analysis and Visualization of Claims Networks

Thus far, we have considered the construction of claims to populate the repository. As the network of claims and arguments grows, however, support will clearly be needed to manage the complexity. The discourse ontology has been designed to provide a language for filtering and querying. We begin this section by looking at the use of non-semantic graph theory to provide coherent views onto the network, and then illustrate the additional power gained from working from the semantics of the structure.

9.6.1   Graph Theoretic Analysis of Claims Networks

Graph theory offers mechanisms for exploring the topography of networks. In the ClaiMaker repository, the structure that grows as claims are made can be viewed as a graph with the concepts providing vertices and the relations providing edges. We are beginning to apply techniques based on graph theory to see what phenomena of interest they can detect in a claims network. Studies on random graphs (Erdos, 1960) suggest that if you have more than half as many edges as vertices a giant component will emerge. This is a connected piece of graph that includes most of the vertices. For instance, at one point, the claims made in our early trials comprised almost as many links (531) as concepts (556), making it likely that there was a giant component. Additionally, it is possible that any giant component will be an example of a 'small world' network (Watts, 1999), which are relatively sparse (they have few edges) and are clustered. As a result they have small diameter; if directionality is ignored, a user can reach most nodes from most other nodes in a few steps (provided they know the right route). Identifying and highlighting such "short cut" routes could play an important role in a visual browsing interface.

We hypothesise that in ClaiMaker there may be concepts that are sufficiently important that they will be used by several disciplines. For example, the concept *Small Worlds* might be linked to analysis of telecommunications networks, graph theory, and to studies of food webs. Starting a browsing session at *Small Worlds* would be helpful to a user, who could move quickly to several different regions of the graph. A first step to finding short cuts across the graph is therefore to identify clusters of highly linked documents. One way to do so is to browse filtered views of the network visually, as illustrated in Figure 9.7. Using established graph layout algorithms, augmented by interface technologies such as hyperbolic trees browsers (e.g. Inxight[4]), one may be able to visually spot "hub" concepts with above average numbers of links to and from them, suggesting an important concept.

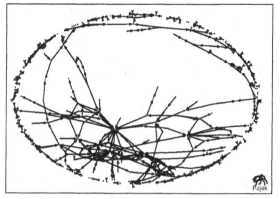

Figure 9.7: A birds-eye view of a large claim network gives a sense of gross structure such as visual cues to dense clusters of potential interest, but conveys little semantic information.[5]

Figure 9.8 "zooms in" to show a subgraph of Figure 9.7, filtered to show only "significant" concept nodes (defined as having three or more claim links).

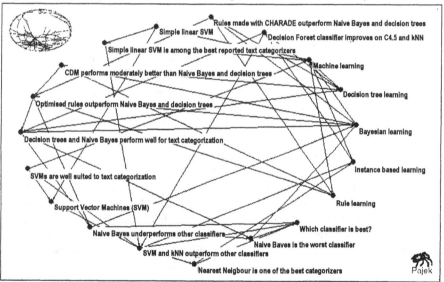

Figure 9.8: A 3-core cluster extracted from a network of claims and argumentation links. From hundreds of nodes modelling literature on text categorization, only those which connect to at least 3 other nodes in the cluster are presented (with link labels switched off). A flavour of key issues in the field is given without overwhelming the viewer.

---

4   http://www.inxight.com/products/core/star_tree/
5   Network visualization using the Pajek (2002) program for large network analysis.

Another approach we are experimenting with is to adapt a method from scientometrics, the quantitative study of publication and citation patterns. Scientometrics uses *citations to articles* as its basic unit of measurement, to derive "performance indicators" of journals, individual authors, organisations, and national research efforts, or to analyse literatures for potentially significant patterns. ClaiMaker presents an opportunity to do similar analysis but at a *finer granularity*: we substitute papers with optionally typed concepts, and citations with typed relations. In doing this, we draw on work presented which demonstrates a method for treating citation networks as partially ordered graphs (Egghe, 1990). The method used for discovering highly inter-linked clusters was based on the Research Fronts method used at the Institute for Scientific Information (Garfield, 1994). This approach assumes that an interesting topic is marked by a cluster of highly cited papers, which in turn cite each other. A prototype clustering algorithm has been tested and does identify coherent topics.

The work summarised in this section encourages us to believe that graph theory and scientometrics are two of a palette of potential methods for exploring the topography of a claims network (taking no account of the semantics of the nodes and links). We turn now to analytical services which exploit the vocabulary of the discourse ontology.

9.6.2   Semantic Analysis of Claims Networks

Example 1: Perspective Analysis ("What arguments are there against this paper?")
Consider a common question that many researchers bring to a literature: *"What arguments are there against this paper?"* Despite the centrality of such a notion, there is not even a language in which to articulate such a query to a library catalogue system, because there are no indexing schemes with a model (ontology) of the world of scholarly discourse. There is no way to express the basic idea that *researchers disagree*. If we can improve on this, then we have a good example of the argumentation ontology adding value over existing retrieval methods.

How can we realise such a query? First, we are looking for *arguments against*, which map to the ontology as negative relations of any type (recall that all relations have positive or negative polarity). At a trivial level, *this paper* corresponds to the currently selected document in ClaiMaker.[6] More substantively, *this paper* refers to the *claims* that researchers have made about the document, specifically, the *concepts* linked to it. Moreover, we can extend this to *related concepts*, using the following definition: *the extended set of concepts linked by a positive relation to/from the document's immediate concepts.*

For the given document, this discovery service does the following:
1   finds the concepts associated with that paper;
2   extends the set of concepts by adding positively linked concepts from other papers;
3   returns claims against this extended concept set.

---

6   If not already in the database (e.g. we are working with journal publishers), one can manually enter document metadata, or more conveniently, upload one's personal library of bibliographic metadata in a standard format such as Refer or Bib.

Typical results are presented in Figure 9.9.

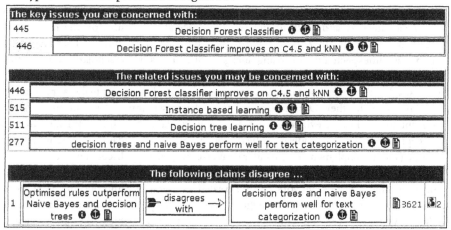

Figure 9.9: Arguments that contrast with the concepts in a research paper by Chen and Ho (2000). Key: clicking ❶ displays concept metadata; ❶ sets the concept as the focal concept, to show incoming and outgoing relations; 📄 links to the document metadata/URL. 👤 links to information about the concept's creator.

ClaiMaker then supports further structured browsing; for instance, having discovered that one of the concepts related to the article is challenged by *Optimized rules outperform Naïve Bayes and decision trees*, clicking on the ❶ icon sets this as the focal concept of interest, showing its immediate neighbourhood (Figure 9.10).

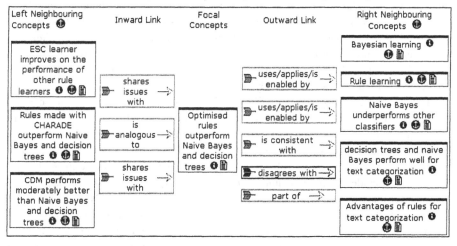

Figure 9.10: Examining the 'relational neighbourhood' around a focal concept. The concept *Optimized rules outperform Naïve Bayes and decision trees* (discovered in Figure 9.9) now occupies the centre in order to show incoming and outgoing links. Any concept displayed can then be made the focal concept by clicking on its ❶ icon.

Example 2: Lineage Analysis ("Where Did This Idea Come From?")

A common activity in research is clarifying the lineage behind an idea. Lineage is essentially ancestry and (with its inverse, the descendant) focuses on the notion that ideas build on each other. Where the paths have faded over time or been confused, uncovering unexpected or surprising lineage is of course a major scholarly contribution. We have a more modest goal to start with in ClaiMaker: to provide a tool pick out from the "spaghetti" of claims, candidate streams of ideas that conceptually appear to be building on each other. Our lineage tool tracks back (semantically, not in time) from a concept to see how it evolved, whereas the descendants tool tracks forward from a concept to see what new ideas evolved from it. Since descendants are the inverse of lineage (and are implemented as its literal inverse) we will only discuss lineage.

So, let us consider a new query: *Where did this idea come from?* We have already suggested that a claims network can be treated as a graph, with concepts as vertices, and the links between concepts as edges. A path in a graph is a sequence of connected edges. A lineage can be conceptualised as a path in which the links suggest development or improvement. The problem of finding lineage in ClaiMaker can then be formulated as a path matching problem, a well known problem in graph theory for which algorithms exist.[7]

To provide lineage analysis as a ClaiMaker service, path queries are constructed from link-types using a set of primitives. For example, we can search for paths that may be of any length, and which contain (in any order) any of the positive links that have type *similarity* in either direction, or the two general links *uses/applies/is enabled by* or *improves on*, going in the direction away from the target concept of the query. The *improves on* link type is included to reflect the notion of progress implicit in lineage, while *uses/applies/is enabled by* has a weaker implication of "building upon." The *similarity* links are included because if a new concept is like another that *improves on* a third, then the new concept may well also be an improvement. *Similarity* links are acceptable in either direction because *similarity* is a naturally symmetrical relation (if A is like B, then B is like A). Figure 9.11 shows examples of acceptable paths that could be returned by this lineage analysis.

The search can be tightened by filtering the paths returned to ensure they contain the *improves on* relation, after which only the second of the paths in Figure 9.11 would be retained. Conversely, one can relax the conditions to broaden the search, for instance, to permit the inclusion of any Problem-related links (see Table 9.2), since *addressing* or *solving* a known problem usually represents progress of some sort. One could also include Taxonomic links, since if a *part of* some innovation *improves on* another approach then it implies there may be improvement overall. Note that in these cases, the direction of the link is fundamental: it is only problems that the new concept *solves* that are of interest, and even if a whole innovation is an improvement, there is no reason to assume that every *part of* it is also. One advantage of the path matching approach is that it facilitates the use of directional elements in queries.

---

[7]   A semantic web standard based on graphs is the *Resource Description Framework* <www.w3.org/RDF>. In the analysis presented here we use the *Ivanhoe* path matching tool available in the *Wilbur* RDF toolkit <wilbur-rdf.sourceforge.net>.

The results of this kind of structural query can then be rendered in a variety of forms back to the user. Figure 9.12 shows a visualization of the structure extracted from the claims network in response to a lineage query about a concept.

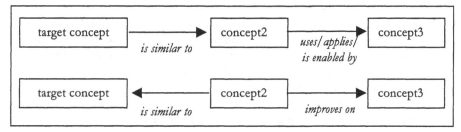

Figure 9.11: Examples of paths that could be returned by a lineage analysis on a target concept (see text for the specification of the query).

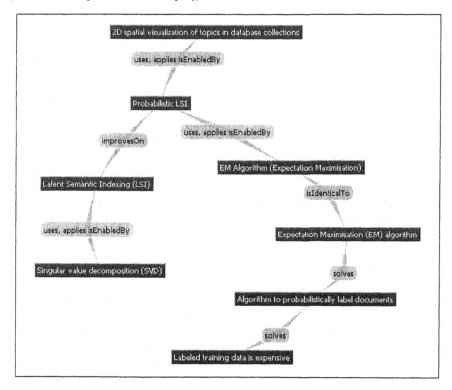

Figure 9.12: Visualization of the results of a *lineage analysis*, a representation of the claims in the network on which the top concept explicitly and implicitly builds, or alternatively, a guide to the local context in which a concept is embedded.[8]

---

[8] Graph visualization courtesy the *Ceryle Project* by Murray Altheim, Knowledge Media Institute, Open University <kmi.open.ac.uk/projects/ceryle/>. Ceryle includes an

The lineage function (and its inverse, descendants) can be thought of as providing an analytical tool to excavate the *foundation* under an idea (or conversely, an indicator of its *impact*). From a navigational perspective, they can be thought of as offering *focused browsing tools*. In response to a *"Where am I?"* question, they give answers in terms of developmental context, positioning ideas in the literature in terms of their evolution.

To summarise, term-based information retrieval handles documents as isolated entities defined by the words in them. Citations in a document give no indication of authors' intentions in referring to other work; we cannot even tell if a paper is referenced because the authors support or are diametrically opposed to it. The examples of *Perspective Analysis* and *Lineage Analysis* demonstrate how the discourse ontology can make the connections between ideas in different documents explicit, enabling novel, powerful kinds of query.

9.7 Conclusion

We have identified a striking absence of tools for global research argumentation. As the tidal wave of online information builds, the ability to model and analyse expert debate and evidence on research problems will grow in importance. The Scholarly Ontologies project is envisioning how research publishing and discourse could evolve over the next decade, given current infrastructure developments. This is self-evidently a large scale project, but one which we hypothesise to be both socially and technically tractable. As a 'wicked problem' (Rittel and Webber, 1984; Buckingham Shum, Chapter 1; van Bruggen, Chapter 2), we have to build realistic tools to understand the problem space, and so are implementing the ClaiMaker system to mediate structured, distributed argumentation.

We have summarised the current status of this work in progress: a discourse ontology with a specific focus on scholarly argumentation moves, associated prototype analysis tools to assist in managing the complexity of a collaboratively built semantic graph of claims and counter-claims, and we have described the cognitive design issues that are arising in the creation of user interfaces for 'visual claim-making' with 'live' concepts and links that many other researchers may be using.

We are releasing versions for interested members of any research community to start modelling their literatures, for instance, to assist research, teaching or information analysis. The only way that a new infrastructure grows is when individuals recognise the value that it can add to their work. As significant examples grow, we aim to demonstrate the value of various information services for managing the complexity (e.g. visualization for teaching; structural querying; alerting services). We welcome approaches from colleagues who wish to be early adopters, and join us in mapping the new territory that is opening up.

---

enhancement of the *TouchGraph* graph visualization toolkit by Alex Shapiro <touchgraph.sourceforge.net>. TouchGraph delivers interactive, self-organizing maps over the web via a Java applet.

9.8 Acknowledgements

We gratefully acknowledge the support of the UK Engineering and Physical Sciences Research Council's Distributed Information Management Programme (GR/N35885/01), 2001-2004. Special thanks also to Ora Lassila for expert advice on *Ivanhoe* for lineage analysis, and to Murray Altheim for use of *Ceryle* for lineage visualizations.

9.9 References

Boland, R. J. J., & Tenkasi, R. V. (1995). Perspective making and perspective taking in communities of knowing. *Organization Science, 6*(4), 350-372.

Buckingham Shum, S., MacLean, A., Bellotti, V., & Hammond, N. (1997). Graphical argumentation and design cognition. *Human-Computer Interaction, 12*(3), 267-300.

Buckingham Shum, S., Motta, E., & Domingue, J. (2000). ScholOnto: An ontology-based digital library server for research documents and discourse. *International Journal on Digital Libraries, 3*(3), 237-248.

Buckingham Shum, S., Uren, V., Li, G., Domingue, J., Motta, E., & Mancini, C. (2002). Designing representational coherence into an infrastructure for collective Sensemaking. Invited contribution to: *National Science Foundation Workshop on Infrastructures for Distributed Communities of Practice*, San Diego, CA. Retrieved on August 1, 2002 from
http://kmi.open.ac.uk/projects/scholonto/docs/SBS_DCP2002.pdf

Chen, H., & Ho, T. K. (2000). Evaluation of decision forests on text categorization. *Proc. 7th SPIE Conference on Document Recognition and Retrieval*, 191-199.

Garfield, E. (1994, October 10). Research fronts. *Current Contents*. Retrieved on August 1, 2002 from http://www.isinet.com/isi/hot/essays/citationanalysis/11.html

Gruber, T. R. (1995). Toward principles for the design of ontologies used for knowledge sharing. *International Journal of Human-Computer Studies, 43*(5/6), 907-928.

Knott, A., & Mellish, C. (1996). A feature-based account of relations signalled by sentence and clause connectives. *Language and Speech, 39*(2-3), 143-183.

Knott, A., & Sanders, T. (1998). The classification of coherence relations and their linguistic markers: An exploration of two languages. *Journal of Pragmatics, 30*, 135-175.

Egghe, L., & Rousseau, R. (1990). *Introduction to informetrics: quantitative methods in library, documentation and information science*. Amsterdam: Elsevier.

Egghe, L., & Rousseau, R. (in press). Co-citation, bibliographic coupling and a characterization of lattice citation networks. *Scientometrics*.

Erdos, P. A. R. (1960). On the evolution of random graphs. *Publications of the Mathematical Institute of the Hungarian Academy of Sciences, 5*, 17-61.

Li, G., Uren, V., Motta, E., Buckingham Shum, S., & Domingue, J. (2002). ClaiMaker: weaving a semantic web of research papers. *1st International Semantic Web Conference*, (Sardinia, June 9-12th, 2002). Retrieved on August 1, 2002 from http://kmi.open.ac.uk/projects/scholonto/docs/ClaiMaker-ISWC2002.pdf

Mancini, C., & Buckingham Shum, S. (2001). Cognitive coherence relations and hypertext: From cinematic patterns to scholarly discourse. *Proc. ACM Hypertext 2001*, (Aug. 14-18, Århrus, Denmark), 165-174. New York:. ACM Press Retrieved from http://kmi.open.ac.uk/tr/papers/kmi-tr-110.pdf

Newman, S., & Marshall, C. (1991). *Pushing Toulmin too far: Learning from an argument representation scheme* (Technical Report SSL 92-45). Xerox Palo Alto Research Center.

Pajek (2002). *Program for Large Network Analysi*. Retrieved on August 1, 2002 from http://vlado.fmf.uni-lj.si/pub/networks/pajek/default.htm

Reader, W., & Hammond, N. (1994). Computer-Based Tools to Support Learning from Hypertext: Concept Mapping Tools and Beyond. *Computers in Education*, 22, 99-106.

Rittel, H. W. J. , & Webber, M. M. (1984). Planning Problems are Wicked Problems. In N. Cross (Ed.), *Developments in Design Methodology* (pp. 135-144). Chichester: John Wiley & Sons. (Published earlier as part of "Dilemmas in a general theory of planning", *Policy Sciences*, 4, 155-169, 1973).

Shipman, F. M., & Marshall, C. C. (1999). Formality Considered Harmful: Experiences, Emerging Themes, and Directions on the Use of Formal Representations in Interactive Systems. *Computer Supported Cooperative Work*, 8(4), 333-352.

Toulmin, S. (1958). *The Uses of Argument*. Cambridge: Cambridge University Press.

Trigg, R., & Weiser, M. (1983). TEXTNET: A Network-Based Approach to Text Handling. *ACM Transactions on Office Information Systems*, 4(1), (pp 97-100)

Watts, D. J. (1999). *Small Worlds: The Dynamics of Networks Between Order and Randomness*. Princeton, NJ: Princeton University Press.

Afterword

Douglas C. Engelbart

Bootstrap Institute, Fremont, CA

In a foreword I wrote for a book[1] about Topic Maps, edited by my friend and colleague Jack Park, I said that we need tools to integrate those conceptual maps with our vast repositories of documents and recorded dialog. My friend Simon Buckingham Shum, in this book, has described my quest for such tools, and I am now realizing that this book brings us to an awareness of the problems associated with our use of the symbols and structures of knowledge that I have long felt to be important. It is very rewarding to see the progress being made by the authors in this book.

I've been reflecting upon the concepts collected and presented in my Unfinished Revolution Colloquium[2], held at Stanford University early in 2000. They give special reinforcement to me in stating that the information presented in this book will be of great importance to those who would try to understand, to perform, as I am learning from reading here, *sensemaking* on all of our presentations.

For five decades I have been driven by an intuitive certainty that computer supported augmentation could increase humankind's collective problem-solving capabilities to a degree that was (is) greatly unappreciated, and that its explicit pursuit should become one of society's high-priority, "grand challenges".

And as pointed out in my 1962 report[3,4], using results from headway on this grand challenge could significantly facilitate progress on all the other grand challenges,[5] then

---

[1] Park, Jack, Editor, and Sam Hunting, Technical Editor, 2002. *XML Topic Maps: Creating and Using Topic Maps for the Web*. Boston, MA: Addison-Wesley.

[2] http://www.bootstrap.org/colloquium/index.jsp

[3] Engelbart, Douglas C. Augmenting Human Intellect: A Conceptual Framework, SRI roject No. 3578, Summary Report AFOSR-3233, Stanford Research Institute, October 1962,
<http://sloan.stanford.edu/mousesite/EngelbartPapers/B5_F18_ConceptFramew orkInd.html>

its pursuit could well deserve to be rated as top priority among the grand-challenge pursuits.

I have come to use the term "Collective IQ" to characterize the focus of this grand challenge. And, specially stimulated by this book, I rate CSAV to be a very important component within the much enhanced capability infrastructures necessary to support the significantly higher Collective IQs needed by our future organizations, institutions, countries – indeed, the whole world.

I have long felt that our collective IQ can be very significantly augmented, and that this will become centrally critical as our world begins to assess the really complex, urgent, and, yes, *wicked*[5] problems facing it now – and the ever more wicked problems emerging in a future characterized by a scale of change whose degree, rate, and world-wide pervasiveness far exceeds what any human society has ever survived.

I am quite convinced that the ideas, theories and technologies presented here are an important part of the Collective-IQ pursuit. And, vitally important will be the concurrent evolution of what we might call the "social changes" which must occur if schooling systems and widespread knowledge-development and -application processes are to be changed appropriately for effectively harnessing radically new concepts, vocabulary, technologies and skills such as described in these chapters.

Reading this manuscript has left me with some questions and comments. I would like to state them here, perhaps as a way to create stronger links between authors and readers of this book, and my ideas about *facilitated evolution of our improvement infrastructures*.

- Many of the chapters I read here talked about *facilitated* mapping. I feel that the greatest rewards will come when these processes can be applied effectively over the Web where time zones and participant scale will often make directly facilitated meetings impractical. How can these processes be used effectively in *asynchronous*, Web-based settings?
- I feel very strongly that we will need to apply these ideas to a large base of *legacy* documents. To support that, I have proposed a HyperScope[7] as a design

---

[4]   Engelbart, Douglas C. A Conceptual Framework for the Augmentation of Man's Intellect, In P. Howerton and Weeks (Ed), Vistas in Informaton Handling (pp. 1-29), London: Spartan Books; Washington, DC.

[5]   This book will orient you about truly big, wicked problems: 2002 State of the Future, by Jerome C. Glenn and Theodore J. Gordon; Paperback with CD-ROM. 100 pages print and about 2,000 pages CD-ROM; ISBN 0-9657362-9-6 Published: August 2002.

[6]   I am also happy to report that the jargon I am picking up by reading this manuscript is certainly inspiring!

[7]   Engelbart, Douglas C. Draft, OHS Project Plan.
     <http://www.bootstrap.org/augment/BI/2120.html>

concept for a tool set that would provide the ability to address objects in legacy documents, link them to other objects, very much like the ScholOnto project described here by Simon, and provide the ability to construct views, some of which portray discussions or arguments related to those objects. How closely can the ideas presented here relate to the HyperScope way of bringing legacy documents into the conversation?

Probably the most urgent questions I have relate to two very important issues, which are *scalability*, and *evolvability*. I am not even sure that I know how to ask such questions, but I feel that it is important to mention my concern that any theory or technology that aims to support large-scale, wicked problem solving must be able to scale up and evolve along with the global-scale communities that will need to be served.

And the very scale of change, involving many aspects of the way we work – of working vocabularies, of associated processes and skills, of organizational roles and practices, of the number of interdependent social factors involved, etc. – needs to be factored in with any rational approach to giving a world society the really significant improvements that will be ever-more essential to its survival.

I have come to believe that the answer is to pay special attention to the "improvement infrastructure"[8] which inevitably will be critically involved in large (very large) communities as they make very-large numbers of adjustments, within their operational infrastructures of capabilities, as they evolve their ways of adapting to the endless emergence of new technologies.

I also believe that no one is capable of predicting (much less designing) the details of how all of these changing elements should best evolve. I believe that the best we could do is foster the most effective improvement infrastructure that we can.

And I further believe that the key operational factor of this most-effective improvement infrastructure will be to effectively facilitate the concurrent evolution of a large number of ever more capable "social organisms," and to make visible for each of them the best possible view of the evolutionary pathways from which to choose their next "route" adjustments.

What has steered me into a special focus on improving Collective-IQ is the belief that any significant improvement in that collective capability would provide a highly valuable boost to the effectiveness of an appropriately structured improvement infrastructure. And further, that there would be special payoff for society if the earliest improvement communities put special focus on improving those capabilities which would best improve the effectiveness of improvement communities.

In my view of effective improvement communities, it would be critically important that a *Dynamic Knowledge Repository* (DKR) be built and maintained by the participants.

---

[8] Engelbart, Douglas C. Toward High-Performance Organizations: A Strategic Role For Groupware, 1992, Groupware Conference, San Jose, CA, June 19 92 <http://www.bootstrap.org/augment/AUGMENT/132811.html>

And I am sure that argumentation will be an essential part of that effort. I look forward to seeing that come about.

And another thing I look forward to is the effective utilization of these tools and processes in the collective pursuit of important new tools and processes which themselves significantly improve that collective pursuit. I have termed this "bootstrapping," and feel that this is a very important strategic practice in tackling the very wicked problem of large-scale augmentation of mankind's Collective IQ.

It is my hope that the next CSAV book will not only tell its readers how this is done, but will itself be an example product of the best CSAV tools and practices as used within this "improvement community" to develop the knowledge and produce an integrated exposition.

Index

Alphabetical Index[1]

Accountability, 32

ACT, 41

Action-learning teams, 152

Adoption, 117, 128, 130, 134, 139, 187, 195, 20

Aesthetics, 138, 154

Affordance, 37, 148

Allaire Forums, 54, 56, 57, 58

Answer reflex, 119

Aquanet, 18

Araucaria, 103

Argnoter, 14-15

Argumentation theory, 4

Argumentative design, 12, 18

Arpanet, 16

Artful questions, 121

Assumptions, 14-15, 29, 69, 78, 121, 153, 173

Asynchronous communication, 16, 17, 35, 36, 38, 54, 57-58, 126, 127, 130, 131, 132, 150

Athena, 103

Augmenting Human Intellect, 9

Author's Argumentation Assistant (AAA), 18

Belvédère, 39, 40, 42, 43, 44, 53, 54, 55, 57, 58, 60, 70, 71, 82, 91

Capturing discussions/decisions, 112, 124, 130, 133, 153, 162
    See also Design rationale

Chart Method, 4, 6

Claim, 8-9, 18, 165-76, 189, 191, 194

Closed questions, 121

Cognitive Coherence Relations theory, 188

Cognitive Load theory, 42-3

Cognitive overhead, 43, 44, 90, 91, 93, 119, 120, 192

Colab, 19

Collaborative learning, 4, 36, 55, 56, 69, 70, 71, 80, 91, 92, 93

Collaborative writing, 177

Collective intelligence, 137

Common information space, 126, 128

Communities of practice, 149, 185

Communities of purpose, 140

Compendium, 37, 93, 117, 122, 129, 135, 138-9, 153-5, 157-8, 162-3

Computer-mediated communication, 4, 16-18, 42, 52, 53, 54, 57, 68, 70

---

[1] This alphabetical index is followed by a categorised index which groups terms under broad categories that readers may find helpful.

Categorised Index

Out of print titles

Dan Diaper and Colston Sanger
CSCW in Practice
3-540-19784-2

Steve Easterbrook (Ed.)
CSCW: Cooperation or Conflict?
3-540-19755-9

John H. Connolly and Ernest A.
Edmonds (Eds)
CSCW and Artificial Intelligence
3-540-19816-4

Mike Sharples (Ed.)
Computer Supported Collaborative
Writing
3-540-19782-6

Duska Rosenberg and Chris Hutchison
(Eds)
Design Issues in CSCW
3-540-19810-5

Peter Thomas (Ed.)
CSCW Requirements and Evaluation
3-540-19963-2

John H. Connolly and Lyn Pemberton
(Eds)
Linguistic Concepts and Methods in
CSCW
3-540-19984-5

Alan Dix and Russell Beale (Eds)
Remote Cooperation
3-540-76035-0

Stefan Kirn and Gregory O'Hare (Eds)
Cooperative Knowledge Processing
3-540-19951-9

Peter Lloyd and Roger Whitehead (Eds)
Transforming Organisations Through
Groupware: Lotus Notes in Action
3-540-19961-6

Reza Hazemi, Stephen Hailes and Steve
Wilbur (Eds)
The Digital University: Reinventing the
Academy
1-85233-003-1

Celia T. Romm and Fay Sudweeks (Eds)
Doing Business Electronically
3-540-76159-4

Alan J. Munro, Kristina Höök and
David Benyon (Eds)
Social Navigation of Information Space
1-85233-090-2

Mary Lou Maher, Simeon J. Simoff and
Anna Cicognani
Understanding Virtual Design Studios
1-85233-154-2